CULTURE
SHOCK!

Greece

Clive L. Rawlins

Graphic Arts Center Publishing Company
Portland, Oregon

In the same series

Argentina	Egypt	Laos	Sri Lanka
Australia	France	Malaysia	Sweden
Bolivia	Germany	Mauritius	Switzerland
Borneo	Greece	Mexico	Syria
Britain	Hong Kong	Morocco	Taiwan
Burma	India	Nepal	Thailand
California	Indonesia	Netherlands	Turkey
Canada	Iran	Norway	UAE
Chile	Ireland	Pakistan	Ukraine
China	Israel	Philippines	USA
Cuba	Italy	Singapore	USA—The South
Czech Republic	Japan	South Africa	Venezuela
Denmark	Korea	Spain	Vietnam

Chicago At Your Door	A Globe-Trotter's Guide
Havana At Your Door	A Parent's Guide
Jakarta At Your Door	A Student's Guide
London At Your Door	A Traveller's Medical Guide
New York At Your Door	A Wife's Guide
Paris At Your Door	Living and Working Abroad
Rome At Your Door	Working Holidays Abroad

Illustrations by TRIGG
Photographs from Clive L. Rawlins,
Greek National Tourism Organization and Life File

© 1997 Clive L. Rawlins
Reprinted 1998, 1999, 2000

This book is published by special
arrangement with Times Media Private Limited
Times Centre, 1 New Industrial Road, Singapore 536196
International Standard Book Number 1-55868-359-3
Graphic Arts Center Publishing Company
P.O. Box 10306 • Portland, Oregon 97296-0306 • (503) 226-2402

Printed in Singapore

For Gillian, Stephen, Siobhan and Euan
Karen and Phillip
My favourite hellenophiles

CONTENTS

ACKNOWLEDGEMENTS

I must first single out certain friends who have made memorable my years in Greece and without whose friendship life would have been very much less pleasing: to them I offer my heartfelt thanks: Nikos and Maria Kaikas and Professor Van Canallakis and his wife, Eleni, must be preeminent; as must the friendships of Sophia Loudini, Pearl and Terry Mourgos, Pat and Ian Boss, Elizabeth Moraitis, Katerina Iliadou, Robert Ansell, Andreas of the Poros Sailing Club (who despaired of my knots), Jorunn Greve, Marlene Royle and Sasha Sokolov, Nicole Cohen, Katerina Dokopoulou, Thomas McGrath, Francois and the late Pamela Johnson, Sandra and Eric Marshall, Christos and Mia Papadopoulos, Wachter Gyorgy and his family, Richard Wolansky, Darry and Michael Heyers Lyford. I must not omit to thank the Staurianakis and Parlaloglou families – for mixed experiences; nor forget Sigmund Peterson, David Smythe, Benthe and Birgit Hjelbak. I thank Bishop Ambrose and his brother-monks at the Monastery of Cyprian and Justinian at Phule, Attica, for their hospitality.

A particular word of thanks must go to my family: Veronica Rawlins, whose help and encouragements are too numerous to list, made this book possible. Also my mother, Mary Rawlins; my sons Stephen and Philip and their respective wives, Gillian and Karen; and to Pat and Ken Jones.

It is a pleasure to record my gratitude to those who have offered their professional help: Consul Elizabeth Barnett of the American Embassy; Keith Baker, Director of the British Hellenic Chamber of Commerce; the library staffs of: the British School of Archeology, the National Library of Greece, the British Council Library, the EU Library in Edinburgh, and the Reference Library at Edinburgh; also to Gourdin and Jean-Paul Nadine, Midgely Fileri; and many friends and neighbours, too numerous to mention, with whom one has rubbed shoulders, quaffed ouzo, gnawed goat and octopus, philosophised, and reformed the Greek economy several times over. I must also thank two latter-day muses, Denise Collins and Lisa Roak, who appeared at my tourer somewhere near the Acropolis at Corinth, and dematerialised beyond Olympia. Much of my travelling and research was facilitated by Adriana Sofianopoulou of Arcturus Travel, Athens; and informed by the publications and help of the National Tourist Office of Greece; the Information Centres of the European Union (Athens and Edinburgh). I also wish to thank the staff of the World Wide Fund for Nature (Athens) and the Sea Turtle Society (Athens) for their particular inspirations.

I have used many books and periodicals in my researches, for which I offer my heartiest thanks, especially to Athens News, The Greek News (now sadly defunct), the Bulletin of the Athens News Agency, the EU's The Week in Europe, Eurostat, and its Background Reports. EBTA, the Hellenic Industrial Investment Bank SA, has supplied many statistical aspects, not least in its Annual report, as has the British-Hellenic Chamber of Commerce through their annual report Business, and their Business Directory.

For reasons of space, an extensive bibliography is not provided; reference to the authors and titles of the books I quote in the text will identify my main debts.

GREECE

INTRODUCTION

There is a particular and unique poignancy in the idea of living in Greece. It is a charged idea, redolent of history, the stories of the gods, of humanity's evolution through one of the earliest civilisations.

THE CRADLE OF WESTERN CIVILISATION

Greece has long been hailed as the cradle of Western civilisation, and that is partly true. It contributed massively to it, creating and initiating much of what we take for granted today in science, architecture, art, medicine, theatre and literature. For many, to come to Greece is to come home, to attain one's cultural roots, however distant or diluted. The country has not changed much over the millenia which separate it from its founding fathers; but in many ways it has changed out of all recognition: a typical Greek contradiction. Between those two, one encounters culture shock, for Greece is the changeless one who is ever changing; the ancient one who is ever renewing itself; both old and young. The paradox becomes it; it is part of Greece's essence.

ORIGIN OF LAW, LITERATURE AND MORE ...

Greece is no longer the world-power that it was, yet it continues to exert an enormous influence on the minds and actions of world leaders, in many areas of human interest and endeavour. Its widely dispersed peoples – the diaspora – attained positions of success and rank in almost every field of human endeavour. Its language is not spoken by many in terms of world-statistics (it is the least spoken language of any European Community country), yet its brilliance is enshrined in all modern Western languages and affects every one of us. Its literature is read less and less, yet its influence on Western literature – and on the theatre and cinema and television and the Press – is enormous. Its laws have honed the very idea of justice; many of our most cherished institutions – such as the jury – originate in it. The juxtapositions are endless; they are the hallmark of Greece; we respond to them, often unconsciously, gladly owning their riches and diversity, the freedoms they inspire.

The gateway to Olympia

CONTRADICTIONS ABOUND IN GREECE

Greeks thrive on opposites. They love contradictions, contrasts, inversions, antitheses. Law, for example, is deeply embodied in Greek society, yet it is the freest of any modern society; its freedoms often antagonise the more legalistic among us. As their phrase has it, *Ho nomos dev hermeneuetai kata gramma*: 'law should not be interpreted literally.' Opposing is as natural to a Greek as conformity is to a German, sophistication to a Frenchman, or *sangfroid* to an Englishman – to borrow some well known stereotypes. The Greek mind seethes with such possibilities; it is never happier than when involved in a convolution of thought and logic. Yet it can be rigorously logical. Logic is, after all, arguably one of Greece's greatest legacies – as lateral thinking is, too. There is a precise word for this aspect of Greece – *antisyzygy* – an amazing, useful word for describing Greece and the contradictions inherent there. It implies an arrangement of opposites, something at once real and unreal, complicated yet simple, confusing yet precise.

This juxtaposition of contradictions – old and the new, truth and falsehood, law and liberty, peace and conflict, reality and fantasy, loyalty and disloyalty, pagan and Christian – may appear to be a negative quality, yet it can be immensely positive, recognising that in opposites wholeness is found. It is a mindset that is inclusive and all-embracing – not exclusive or narrow. Eclecticism is native to the Greek mind; it borrows from whatever source it wills, even if apparently hostile to it logically. Greece is, for all its *macho* image, the lover of the feminine; more, it is the home of the hermaphrodite – the ultimate conjunction of male and female. The Greek male (hereafter *kyrios*) can weep effusively; the Greek female (*kyria*) can be as hard as nails; the sophisticated adult can be charmingly naive; the child can be astonishingly precocious. In Greece the human and the divine – often seen only in diametrical opposition – are reconciled.

Everything is subject to change, and it is not necessarily the old which is eclipsed. It is difficult to believe that Greece will ever lose

11

its historic and mythological powers, its sense of time and place. Yet they are seen daily in bitter conflict: in true culture shock. This needs to be recognised by all who would live here and needs to be understood and respected. Greece is changing, but it is changing from within itself, not in spite of itself. Echoes and shadows remain – for the discerning; for their enrichment and their inspiration. This past is always with them. It is for that reason that I make no apology for allowing it to obtrude into my account of Greece today; Greeks would be surprised even to hear me speak of apology in this context: there is nothing to apologise for.

THIS BOOK – AN INVITATION AND A WARNING

This book aims to help you understand and enjoy Greece, as many have done before you, as settlers or tourists. To some extent it rests on their experiences as well as my own, and the researches proper to it. It aims to inform you of Greece's history, language and mentality, of its *mores*, institutions and hope – though all of these items should be expressed in the plural, for Greece is a society of many peoples as well as an eclectic one.

This book is also an invitation to wonder, beauty, pleasure and truth; an invitation to enjoy this spectacular land and its lively, hopeful people. It is an invitation to enter into 'the spirit of place,' to use the writer, Lawrence Durrell's, pregnant phrase; to understand its culture and lifestyles; to help to make the best use of the potential; and to suggest how you may make your own contributions.

It is a warning too; a warning against culture shock! It is not easy to settle in a new country. Greeks are one of the most hospitable and welcoming of peoples, but it would be dishonest to omit that suspicion, even fear, exists; the fear of the *xenos*: the foreigner. Greece has had enough of such. It wants, it demands, to be itself. As it enters this, the fifth millennium of its history, it may even be true to say that fear is rampant. It would be wrong not to speak of its anxieties: the reductionism of their values through westernisation; of their failure to lead and the loss of their primary status; of the lessening of their strengths. Much of this is due to others' exports – of films and literature and television, as well as material goods; to foreign nationals and their wealth; even to returning immigrants who no longer respect the old ways. The ability to absorb has long been part of Greece's essence, but its peoples are not exempt from that pettiness, greed or savagery that mars other nations. Its literature and its history demonstrate that it is well aware of humanity's tendency to err. Indeed, it has enshrined that ability in a certain nobility, for honour (*philotimia*, comparable to the easterner's 'face') is a key concept in the Greek way of life, resting as it does on the individual's rights and social obligations – an aspect which is asserted in the Constitution and civil laws.

SHAPED BY HISTORY

Consider these dates from our own era: 330, 1204, 1687, 1823, 1826, 1832, 1912, 1916, 1940, 1941, 1943, 1967. Every one of these (and many more could be supplied) represents an historical defeat for the Greeks – whether by the Romans, the Crusaders, the Ottoman Turks, the Germans, or internal military *coups*. Some were engineered by the most callous acts of treachery and self-interest; some resulted from the indomitable course of events, of humanity, on the move. Few other nations have witnessed so many – and so many diverse forms of – national calamity as have the Greeks. They contributed spectacularly to the evolution of humanity; yet again and again they have been rewarded by subjugation and pillage and humiliation, by the most destructive unfairness, oppressions and barbarities – even within our own lifetime. Worse, the nations who have so dealt with them, pretending friendship, still refuse to make amends.

To speak of the Greek nation is to speak of a people with painful memories; victims of genocide and fratricide both. No one can travel through Greece without recognising that pain etched into countless faces; or listen to its songs or read its poetry without a sharp awareness of human anguish. I have watched some weep in the telling of it – of their parents' and siblings' sufferings, of losses in familial and personal possessions, of hardships, hunger, want – and of the degradations which lead to and derive from them. Some of the memories were literally unspeakable. At such points the conversation would stop, the talker arrested by grief, shame and fear. At other such points, heroisms and nobility surfaced, along with a fierce pride: 'we did it; and we did it our way.' Many writers have described such encounters. For instance, Nicholas Gage (Nikos Gatzoyiannis) did so in his book *Eleni,* as did George Psychoundakis in *The Cretan Runner.* We have enshrined their word for such suffering – *pathos* – into the English language; it carries the hallmark of reality, the stamp of hot tears and inconsolable grief.

The late Dilys Powell, who published her autobiography in 1959, referred to a quite different aspect when she remarked, 'In Greece the professional classes are no more than one step away from the villages' – by which she meant peasantry. Her remarks were penned in 1957, and very much has changed since then. But there is still truth in the comment, even in the Athens of the late 1990s, though there is also a high regard for the *anthropos kales anatrophes:* 'the well-bred person.' It is still possible to walk a lane with a rustic shepherd and his flock, a small-holder and his ass on their way to selling a bundle of hay or sticks, or sit next to a near-destitute person on bus or ferry – not that they would let on of their state. I am privileged to count among my friends those who were reared on the land, who witnessed their parents' and their siblings' slaving to coax greater productivity from the infertile soil and the uncooperative climate. They know how grim life has been; and they resent the insensitivity, and sometimes the scorn, of foreigners and newcomers who neither know nor care.

Other Greeks, of course, have made huge fortunes; they look down on the incomers and their little plots and little houses. Some have been brilliantly successful; others have been corrupt, selfish and mendacious; yet others have refused to use their talents for their

An old town walk

country, serving only their own interests, often enough abroad – to the great advantage of their adoptive countries. The importance of the individual, which underlies all truly Greek attitudes, has its roots in this need for survival, for self-assertion, come what may. But they are human, not uniquely Greek traits.

Charles Péguy once remarked that everything begins in mysticism and ends in politics. It is true of Greece as of any other society. Indeed it is especially true of Greece, the inventor of politics. Think of Delphi, Olympia, Dodona; think of Solon, Pericles, Plato; think of *The Iliad*, the *Greek Anthology*, the *Gospel according to Luke*; think of Pythagoras, Theophrastos, Hippocrates; think style – of Doric, Ionic, Corinthian; think of Aristophanes, Euripedes, Sophocles; think of the Parthenon, Knossos, Alexandria. To do so is to think Greek; to think big; to think of the ultimate.

The Greeks are proud of this history, as well they might be; but they are somewhat daunted by it. After all, there is nothing more difficult than living up to a brilliant ancestry, which is what many visitors expect of them when they come to Greece. 'Where are the Homers?' they cry, 'the Pheidiases, the Aristotles, the Alexanders today?' They are absurd questions, as absurd as asking where the Shakespeares, the Pascals, the Dantes or the Goethes are today in other societies. But many newcomers do ask such questions, if only subconsciously – and they expect to find them, which induces its own culture shock. Failing to obtain the satisfactions they expect, they respond negatively to Greek society, judge it by standards that are foreign to it, and draw a quiet veil over their own myopic nationalism.

THE ANCIENT CITY-STATE VS. TODAY

Misunderstanding, scorn even, is often levelled at Greek politics which is not so much the art of the possible as the art of getting things done – a more concrete reality. 'Politics;' the Greeks invented the word, as they invented democracy. But it was only an extension of the activities of the *polis* which was never more, nor less, than a city-state. Much in Greece even today revolves around this localised ideal. It may seem bizarre, in a book such as this, written for intending settlers and serious tourists, to refer to a book written a hundred years ago, but it is relevant and points up its salience. Commented G Lowes Dickinson, in *The Greek View of Life:*

> The present kingdom of Greece [it became a republic later] is among the smallest of European states; but to the Greeks it would have appeared too large to be a state at all ... the amalgamation of these under a single government was ... foreign to the Greek idea ... The limitation of size belonged to its very notion .... Their civilisation was one of 'city-states,' not of kingdoms and empires; and their whole political outlook was necessarily determined by this condition

That cannot stand so easily for Greece today, especially for those Westernised Greeks who have spent much of their time abroad and have taken on board continental and international aspirations. But it does enshrine a fact of irreducible importance, one carried over into Greek life and habits: their essential parochiality. It accounts, for example, for that inability to cohere as a nation for any length of time, as its multiple, ever splintering parties demonstrate, for the 'party-spirit' which underlies so much argumentation. Greece's glory lies in the individual, in the lists of individuals of genius it produced, not in the ability to domineer and subdue. 'Empires' of a sort it had – of the Minoans, the Athenians, of Alexander the Great, of the Byzantines, even the latter-day *megali idea* (Great Idea) – crushed before it was born. But think of the brilliance of these periods, not their longevity – and certainly not their inglorious ends; for they were but flashes in the night-sky of human history; mere stabs at ruling the world, when all Greece had to do was to be itself – and the world bowed in awe.

The modern state was built slowly, and not without a clash of ideologies that had their origin in the city-state mentality, which owed its vigour as much to geographical factors as to others, as we shall see. Greece now proudly took its place among the nations, with definite national hopes and goals, a redefined and refined 'spirit of place,' now facing both east and west. The experience of Greeks in their neo-nascent state (Rhodes and other islands of the Dodecanese were added to it as late as March 1948; their Constitution consummated as late as 1975) provided a crucial input, one acquainted once again with violence and hardship – ever their lot. What Greece's leaders have sought to do since the establishment of the state, apart from the very serious economic problems – and the hostilities and opportunisms they faced beyond and sometimes within their borders (under various guises) – was to define this nationhood; to weld this heterogeneous people into a single whole. It is this which urges us to discuss the thorny question, 'Who are the Greeks?'

It is partly the purpose of this book to analyse the people's qualities; to see how they work out in daily life and how they affect us personally among them, in our homes, work, social responsibilities and enjoyments. Their understanding is essential to your happy and useful life in Greece.

EXTRA HELP FOR THE NEWCOMER

You will find help offered from your own embassy and/or consulates, to which the Greeks offer their own contributions; but you may find both disappointing, especially in emergencies. Help is now at hand from another source for citizens of the EU. There is a splendid new service on offer: 'Citizens First.' Those with internet connections may go to: *http:/ /citizens.eu.int.* They will advise you in your own language, and on the basis of continuously updated material. Their advice covers all matters relating to work, living problems, study, training and research; it will soon be increased to cover consumer rights, health, safety-at-work and equal opportunities.

EBTA, the Hellenic Industrial Investment Bank SA, has provided many statistical aspects for this book; its *Annual report* is indispensable for the investor or businessman in Greece, with many attractive features, including resumés of new laws. Likewise the British-Hellenic Chamber of Commerce; its annual report, *Business*, offers the most useful essays and guides through the labyrinthine affairs of Anglo-Greek interests. It also produces a splendid *Business Directory*, listing members, classified trades and professions, and a host of miscellaneous information.

NOTE ON GREEK WORDS USED IN THIS BOOK

A word must be said about this before proceeding. 'It's all Greek to me' entails a problem which is several millenia old: the difficulties of the Greek language. Everything about it is different from the English speaker's point of view: its letters (they go back to it eastern roots in ancient Phoenicia); its syntax (though now much simplified); and its pronunciation (one's tongue needs the agility of an Aegean dolphin

to cope with it). Little wonder that the great St Augustine failed to master it – though I prefer to put alongside his view that of Samuel Johnson of Lichfield, 'Greek, Sir, is like lace. Every man gets as much of it as he can.'

How to transliterate it is my principal problem here. It is a much-debated subject, and one without a consensus view among scholars and writers. I cannot pretend to the nonchalance of T E Lawrence. My preference is to opt for the original spelling of Greek names and words whenever possible (e.g. Pontos, not the anglicised Pontus etc.), and to use as consistent a scheme of transliteration as possible. But there can be no rigid consistency. Some words and names are too deep in our memories. Plato is with us for ever; as is Aristotle; the island of Aigina is variously rendered by writers: Aegina, Aigina, Egina etc.; even the capital, Athens – *Athenai* – has its challengers: Athene, Athinai, etc. Consistency is not a notable Greek virtue. The index will help you through any difficulties.

Most of our difficulties revolve around the vowels. Greek has two 'e's, and two 'o's – long and short respectively, which I cannot differentiate in this book, thanks to modern computerisation. Traditionally, 'u' is represented by 'y'. I have not supplied accents and breathings, a capital sin among purists. The former serves pronunciation, the latter a letter change: the aspirate 'h'. Neither were original to the language. Such in other languages, e.g. French, are also omitted.

I have followed Divry's (revised) *Handy Dictionary*, not because it has a monopoly on accuracy, but because it is probably the most widely used one in Greece since 1944, when the government determined its policy based on the popular 'Demotic' language of the High Street. It is recommended for use in schools in Greece, as well as the independent Foreign Language Institutions. The fact that it is printed in the USA emphasises the huge influence that the USA and its agencies have made, and the tendency in Greece (as elsewhere) to opt for Americanised forms and accenting.

As to pronunciation, this is not within the range of this book. There are many specific works which offer such guidance, and I happily leave it to them. Suffice it to say that, generally speaking, each letter in Greek carries the same sound phonetically – unlike English; some exceptions do exist and are determined by specific rules. With two exceptions, *gamma* and *chi*, every Greek letter has an English equivalent; those two need to be heard in Greece, rather than approximated to in such a book as this. Diphthongs are much used in Greek and alter the letter-values; I merely transliterate both letters here. Of the letters that cause most problems, I show *beta* as v; *zeta* as z; *theta* as th; *kappa* as k, though c is well established, *xi* as x; *rho* as r; *phi* as ph (not f); *chi* as ch (not h); and *psi* as ps. No doubt some will sniff at this, but it involves no problem for those who know Greek, and further information is not helpful to those who do not at this early stage of their culture shock.

More important for the newcomer is to acquire a taste for the idioms and proverbs in the language, the metaphors that characterise them. It is these which set a language apart, which reveal the soul of its people. As has been well said, 'Language creates national character.' Accordingly, I have offered some here and there which I hope displays this ethnic 'flavouring' appropriately.

NOTE ON STATISTICS USED

There are three kinds of lies, Mark Twain observed, 'Lies, damned lies and statistics;' the hierarchy is apt. I have sought to be as up-to-date as possible in the figures I give, but I cannot guarantee all of them. The National Statistical Service of Greece in Athens is always helpful, but their statistics are not very prompt. The EU is very much better – but they rely on the NSSG for many of them. The newspapers are quickest, but not always reliable. Revisions of this book will rectify this, as well as the more substantive aspects such as changes in law and so on. Incidentally, the Greeks do not 'count heads,' as our saying goes; 'counting beans' suits them better, which is appropriate, for the bean has a long and distinguished history in Greece, even if Pythagoras, that arch-mathematician, did seek to prohibit them – as some would do statistics.

NECESSARY LIMITATIONS

In the following chapters I offer seventeen aspects of modern-day Greece which the incomer needs to acquaint himself with. This book could easily have been double the size, so fascinating is Greece, so kaleidoscopic its interests. Hellenism, unfortunately, is too vast a subject to be included here, having risen in the age of Alexander, attaining its chief centres on the west Anatolian/Turkish littoral. The order of the chapters is to my mind logical – how one encounters them, a chronology of culture shock one might almost say. But there is nothing crucial about this order; no Muse came to my aid in aligning them. Some may well wish to start at later chapters, others in the middle: it is for you to decide. Good luck, health, and happiness to you.

Chapter One

WHY GREECE?

TRIGG.

THE ATTRACTIONS OF GREECE

Why Greece? This is not a rhetorical question. There is a particular prestige about holidaying in Greece – even more of living there, despite its descent into easy tourism. Ten million tourists now find their way there each year, many of whom care not a baked fig about the Greece which formally entranced: its heroic past, the mystique and mystery of its mythologies, the music and poetry (they are inseparable entities) of Homer or Hesiod, Pindar or Sappho; the legacy of Plato or Aristotle; the political genius of Solon or

Themistocles; the artistry of vase or plate or cup; the beauties of Doric, Ionic or Corinthian architecture; the thrill of supreme tragedy and stunning wit; Minoan inventiveness or Macedonian conquest.

One can enjoy sea and sun, ouzo and souvlakis, retsina and *dolmades*, feta and olives, *kataiphi* and Greek coffee – and all the historical grandeur for which one could wish, to say nothing of some of the world's greatest literature. Sadly, the latter is all too often replaced by a piece of pulp fiction. I am not attacking such, still less the enormous financial benefits that accrues to Greece through these visitors, but it is dispiriting that the only reason for going there for so many is superficial. Many who do so quickly become bored, restless and unhappy; not infrequently they move on. Chief among their complaints is the Greek character; even the Greeks themselves. How often have I heard the view, 'This place would be heaven if it were not for the Greeks!' Several are still saying it years after their arrival. I have witnessed their slide from hopefulness and joy into a hurt sense of failure and angry notes of bitterness, which are sometimes overcome only by a return to their homeland, dreams shattered and purses emptied – or worse, a retreat into isolationism and anti-social behaviour. It behoves all who go to prepare themselves for change – for culture shock.

Greece *is* culturally different from the rest of Europe in fundamental ways. The greetings reserved for the casual tourist are quite different from that accorded to those who move there, lock, stock, and barrel onto the land long regarded as Greece, sacred to family memory and local incident; whose material wealth can be burdensome to those who have struggled all their lives with little or less. The Greeks are proud of these differences; they represent their individuality, their history, their culture. Visitors and incomers are no longer news – except when they make it for the wrong reasons.

Greece has far more to offer than the superficial enjoyments that occupy visitors, and it is far more serious about itself. It has a language of extraordinary depth and plasticity; a people of great inventiveness and tenacity, at once serious and fun-loving; a democracy which does not take its politics and freedoms for granted; a history second to none in expanding man's measure, the triumphs, not merely of mind over matter, but of mind and matter – in the arts, in science and technology, in mechanical and medical accomplishments; a history in political and legal and philosophical adventuring – and very much more, not least in that which links the new to the old worlds of the Middle and Far East through history, exploration and colonisation.

Greece holds all this *and* an uncommon sense of communal togetherness, of strong family values – in Greece, no less than other countries: 'blood is thicker than water' (*to aima nero dev ginetai*) – of openness to each other, of personal honour, courtesy and respect. Such is asserted by the body-language of its people – the gesture of hand or head, of arms or torso, some of which is precisely identical with that found further east. It is all exciting and meaningful; and it is enshrined in magnificent scenery, gifted with balmy weather, to which is added a glorious light, colourful vistas, fresh and clean-tasting food and excellent beverages. This is not the whole truth, but it is that aspect of it which seduces the would-be settler. The challenge is to make that good in new habits of lifestyle, language and culture.

All this – and we have but touched the surface – is mouth-watering stuff, a learning experience for several lifetimes not just one. But why Greece? Because it interests us? Arouses our feelings? Stimulates our intellect? Offers satisfaction to our needs? Provides beauty, warmth, food or drink? Or ... what? The question needs to be answered before one takes the great step of emigration – before the full weight of culture shock makes itself felt.

LIVING IN GREECE – THE REALITY

The cultural, linguistic, social and religious differences are too great to allow thoughts of an easy transfer to Greece – unless one is content to live at the surface of things, cut off from the real world, barred from entering into the lively experiences of neighbours, politics, art and

Walking through Athens; Mt. Lycabettus in the distance

social interests. Once there, once the initial magic has worn off, once you have been rubbed the wrong way by Greek bureaucracy, even misunderstood or insulted by your neighbours, or let down by the lack of water or electricity or fuel, you will need these deeper interests and aspirations to carry you through and beyond the rejections and disappointments. The best reason for going to Greece is Greece itself, its land and its people, but both need understanding, above all *philia*: friendship/love. It will be richly repaid.

25

Courage!

You should not expect to get much help from your embassy or consulates if you try – you are hardly likely to get their help even if you are a model citizen. You may not even get much from your fellow-expatriates. Emigration demands courage and resolution, which have to be based on genuine conviction and careful information: will-power reinforcing intellect. You may not even get the support of your family, let alone that of your friends, who may be jealous of your opportunities or resentful of your abandoning them. Do not be surprised on losing friends in your move, but the opportunity of gaining new friends will compensate for that – at the cost of climatic and cultural change – your change, which may be painful at times.

Some Words of Caution ...

Consider some aspects of the physical changes you will face on moving to Greece which, though often sensational, can be a cause of deep regret to some people (they will be dealt with at more appropriate length elsewhere): The sunlight is one of Greece's finest attributes, but in these ozone-depleted days its ability to precipitate cataracts is receiving a considerable amount of attention – to say nothing of skin-cancers and other carcinogenic disorders, sun-burn, heat-stroke and dehydration. Not all people do well in the heat of Greece, where tempers deteriorate (not least in the hills), and nervous breakdowns, crimes and accidents increase. Many people move to the countryside where few things are more uplifting than a panoramic view from a hill or mountain-side, and those lucky enough to have such are blessed indeed. But for older people, getting to it may be a problem; it will become increasingly so as age and infirmities increase. Those given to arthritic or rheumatic complaints may have their joys seriously undermined by being slowly cut off from their outings, or their lives made miserable by the sheer hell of joint-pain after every return home – but I have known some who have actually lost theirs; modern research has shown that exercise leads to bone-hardening and joint improvement. Those with heart complaints or circulation disorders have the same problem, in addition to the anxiety of being distant from emergency treatment.

... And of Encouragement!

Having said all that, Greece is a far fitter and healthier place for those who take it seriously: the food is usually fresh, the wine a delight, the walking brilliant, the warmth comforting, and the *ambience* – historical and social – exhilarating. It is cheaper, too, though much more expensive than hitherto. Greece is a sexier place, in every sense of that word, and that should not be taken lightly. Humanity is alive in Greece; appetites and body functions are taken seriously – not prudishly, save for some fuddy-duddy thinking in the Orthodox Church which you will have to learn to respect.

Athens – Pros and Cons

Some cities, Athens notably, do have particular health problems. They are almost all the result of carbon-fuel poisoning: the West's contribution to Greece, which is ruining its buildings and endangering its people – even though it is through typical Greek over-use, which has brooked no restriction, personal or industrial. The Big Issue is *nephos*, smog. For those with bronchitic or cardiac complaints, this is certainly not the place to be. But if you love city life or the arts, and cannot live without regular exposure to them – and Athens has some superb venues – then you have little choice but to reside there, even if only on a temporary basis.

Learn Greek Customs and Manners

This book is a strong recommendation of Greece and its *mores*. It is also a warning to those who would go there without the readiness to enlarge their viewpoint and take on new ones. 'Manners maketh man;' but Greek manners are not those of other nations. There is a two-way relationship in them which involves all aspects of social conduct. In moving to Greece, *you* will be expected to change; not them. To fail to observe their manners could unmake you: very many, young and old, have paid the price; as have their families.

One of the great benefits of reading the books of people such as Leigh Fermor, Peter Levi, Lawrence Durrell or Mary Renault is their studied care of Greek customs. Guest etiquette, for example, is of prime importance, if lessening somewhat in the city areas under the pressure of foreign films and television. But not so in rural areas, where tradition dies hard and customs are venerated. 'Spoon-sweets' are still given. Country expectations of the stranger speaking first is another example, though the Greeks are now so used to the 'bad manners' of newcomers in this respect that its ignoring will not raise their ire too quickly. But better not to err at all.

An Open Society

Greece is not like northern Europe or the UK; it is not even like itself in some parts! There are wide regional and local disparities which the traveller, the immigrant especially, needs to observe. Yet it is a splendidly open society. The freedom to be yourself is actually written as a right into the Greek Civil Code – its law of citizenship. You are expected to allow your neighbour to be himself, too. Unlike the UK or the USA, for example, Greece does not have the same prudish or hypocritical standards of, say, sexual behaviour. It is thus less restrained in the media, and there is a recognition of human need which allows, for example, 'adult movies' and the legalisation of prostitution. The latter is under strict rules: she must be over 18 years, work in a licensed brothel and be Greek; soliciting is a crime. Sadly, it is a measure of the economy that prostitution has risen by 75% since 1991; though 60% are said to be non-Greeks – despite the regulations. Contrariwise, nudity is almost everywhere illegal. Alongside this is a much lower crime rate, very little physical violence against the person, and a respect for women and children that is not far from the ideal. One walks at night, even around large cities, with pleasure – and without a thought of danger, though it is now becoming advisable to be careful. Nevertheless, I have never seen so many high fences, guard-dogs and padlocks as exist in Greece!

Know Your Own Limitations

In all this a consistent and very old message sounds down from the ancient shrine of Delphi: *gnothi seauton* – Know Yourself. Understand your needs, limitations and hopes. Discriminate between needs and expectations – they are not the same thing. To which should be added another factor of immense importance: know your partner's needs, for they are bound to be as challenged as yours will be. Consider your joint hopes carefully in the light of Greek attitudes, civilisation and society; do not expect them to change for you. This message of self-awareness sounds throughout Greek history. It is one of its most priceless gifts. It is the voice *par excellence* of Greece; its way to happiness and fulfilment there.

Chapter Two

A BIRD'S EYE VIEW

AN HISTORICAL CROSSROADS

Greece has stood at the cross-roads of history for several millenia and survived longer than any other nation in the western hemisphere, its language older and its *mores* more venerable. Frequently it was making that history, and then paving the way for the actual writing of it. Greece has stood at geographical, political, artistic and intellectual crossroads, and been a bridge between Asia, Africa, and Europe; a catalyst and a consumer of great historical movements and achievements. Its history is an immensely proud memory for the people, who live in a country as diverse as its distinguished contributions.

Greek society, indeed the Greeks themselves, cannot be understood apart from their physical landscape. The geography of Greece has created social divisions, as has its history, which are only now beginning to give way to a more unified state. Its peoples – the plural is emphasised – have been separated from each other by sea and mountain, as well as by normal ethnico-political factors in history. The mainland and some of the larger islands are corrugated by mountain-chains, valleys and ravines, seasonal rivers and forests (the latter two now diminishing gravely). With almost innumerable islands, the scenery is spectacular, but it has produced great independence in its peoples – one of Greece's most distinctive traits.

THE LAY OF THE LAND

Situated in the southeast of the Balkan peninsula, Greece borders on Albania, the Republic of Macedonia (still denying that state the right to the name), Bulgaria and Turkey. It lies at a latitude of 42–38°N and a longitude of 19–27°E. The mainland is bordered by the Mediterranean sea to the south, the Aegean sea to the east, and the Ionian sea to the west. More than 2000 islands belonging to Greece are scattered through these seas, with about 170 of them inhabited. The shape of Greece is that of a crescent, set at the northeastern tip of the even larger crescent known as the Levant. The mountains which dominate its territories are the westerly extension of the Himalayan range, which traverses Turkey and continues on into the Alps – via land and sea.

A Mountainous Landscape

Greece is an integral part of the Balkans (the latter is from a Turkish word meaning mountains) and around three-fourths of the mainland is covered by mountains. The mountains descend like exploring fingers southwards into the Greek mainland, in a northwest/southeast orientation. They have created and reinforced traditional differences, though these are now being reduced by better road and communication systems (radio and television not least). Within these ribboned areas are the lowlands, the plains and valley basins, not a few of which are further delineated by rivers and (dried-up) water-courses.

Around the whole lies a narrow coastal strip, completely populated and commercialised where habitable. Away from the cities and towns the population density falls away dramatically, though Greece's rural population is still high compared with other nations, as is its agricultural proportion (now at 25.3% of the working population). Its population density is actually 78.7 per sq. km according to the latest edition of *Eurostat*, the fifth lowest in the EU.

The two principal mountain chains are the Pindus and the Rhodope, both essentially limestone, the general sub-structure of the country. They are divided from each other by lesser chains such as the Pirin, north of Thessaloniki. To these must be added those of the Peloponnese, which also follow a northwest/southeast orientation; and those of Crete – which run horizontally, from east to west. In geological terms they are all of recent date and technically still active. This accounts for the seismic shocks which disturb and shatter the country from time to time. Happily, most of their epicentres are at sea, so damage is usually minimal. Some extra statistics throw an interesting light on the land: it is 70% hilly, 40% of which is 'highland' (i.e. over 500 m), in which there are innumerable peaks of about 2000 m; only 34% of the land is below 200 m. Mt. Olympus, of well-known repute, is the highest peak in Greece and reaches 2917 m.

Rivers

The rivers of Greece play their part in delineating the landscape. Large ones are noticeable by their absence, and those that exist are not notable for length or power. There are no inland waterways of commercial usage in Greece but the proximity of its towns to the sea compensates for that. On the mainland the most important rivers are:

A cottage view from Mt Ares

the Mesta (Nestos), northeast of Thessaloniki; the Vardar and the Struma; the Aliakmon (Vistrista) west of Katerina; the Pinios, west of Larissa; the Arakthos and the Thiamis, near Ioannina; the Sperkhios, near Lamia; and the Mornos in Phoki. The Peloponnese has the Ladhon, northwest of Argos; the Alfios, near Olympia; and the Evrotas, near Sparta. Others exist; some of which are subject to flash-flooding which should never be under-estimated. Some of these are proving dangerous to road and housing schemes, particularly in Athens.

Fresh water is one of Greece's major problems. Behind this lies Greece's erratic rainfall, which is highly localised, and the country's increasing population, agriculture, industrialisation and tourism. The low levels of rainfall make the rivers useless for navigation, and cause immense problems for the water-supply authority. The situation is not helped by the porous quality of the underlying limestone.

A Land Surrounded by Sea

The sea and coastal plain characterise much of the rest of Greece. The sea comprises no less than 80% of Greek territory. The Greek coastline is 15,000 km in length, of which some 11,000 km belong to the islands. Its marine dominance may also be judged by the fact that no inland point is further than 50 miles from the sea. Crete, to the south, is the largest island, but since the cutting of the Corinth Canal in 1896, the Peloponnese has been effectively a land-bridged island (reflected in its ancient name: meaning 'Pelops' Island'). This land area occupies about 21,440 sq. km, against the mainland total of 130,000 sq. kms. The islands themselves come to a little less than 20% of the mainland area, i.e. about 25,200 sq. km. They are represented by seven distinct groups:

- *The Ionian islands:* These lie to the west between Greece and Italy. In Greek they are known as *Eftanisa* which indicates seven in number. They include Corfu, Ithaca, Kephallonia, Kythera, Levkas, Paxos and Zakynthos.

- *The Sporades:* These four islands are in the northwest of the Aegean Sea. They are: Alonnisos, Skiathos, Skopelos and Skyros. (Evia, Greece's second largest island, is often numbered with them, but incorrectly).

- *Limnos and neighbours:* In the northeast of the Aegean are seven islands, not favoured with a corporate name; they centre on Limnos plus: Chios, Ikaria, Lesvos, Samos, Samothraki and Thassos.

- *Saronic islands:* Five islands lie to the southwest of Athens, in or near the Saronic Gulf—Aegina, Hydra, Poros, Salamis and Spetses.

- *Cyclades islands:* These lie southeast of the Saronic islands, forming a rough circle, hence their name. They are centred on Delos and number twenty in all: Amorgos, Anafi, Andros, Folegandros, Ios, Kea, Kimolos, Kythnos, Milos, Mykonos, Naxos, Paros, Antiparos, Santorini, Serifos, Sifnos, Syros and Tinos.

- *Dodecanese islands:* From the word, 'twelve' these islands are situated to the southeast, but actually number fifteen – Astypalaia, Halki, Kalymnos, Karpathos, Kassos, Kastellorizo, Kos, Pserimos, Leros, Lipsi, Nissyros, Patmos, Rhodes, Symi and Tilos.
- *Crete:* This is the largest island. It and its satellites are almost equidistant between the Greek mainland and North Africa, proud of their independence and cultural ambiguity.

The People and Their Landscape

Merely to describe the physical attributes of Greece is to raise its demographic and economic problems – part of that culture shock which affects all settlers. Its cultivable land comprises just under four million hectares, of which only about 8,500 technically constitute lowlands. It may be the land 'chosen by the gods,' as the tourist brochures claim, but it was not over-blessed by them in agricultural, mineral and other resources. This land, and the inward investment of its ever-adventuring people, supports just over ten million people, 40% of which are located in the Greater Athens area. It is a curious fact that disproportion characterises the country which sets most store by the ethic of proportion: *medan agan*: nothing in excess.

The rugged terrain that occupies much of the land area lies at the heart of Greek economic problems. It has been described as a country 'disjointed, fragmented, and altogether broken in pieces' by its geography. This has, however, been a great bulwark against invasions – the Romans thought twice about entering Greece for this reason. More recently, during the Second World War, the Greeks, though hopelessly outnumbered, brilliantly beat off the Italian forces. But the landscape has at the same time created insuperable barriers, and the resulting independent, even insular, spirit in its peoples has affected its life and progress.

The Balkan peninsula is, however, very different from the Iberian (Spanish) or Italian ones, in that the latter two have high mountains at their borders, the Pyrenees and the Alps, which separate and

Going to market

protect them from their neighbours. Greece does not, at least to the same degree, and its coastline is open – hence the long and repeated defeats at the hands of invading and immigrating peoples. The difficult terrain and the constant attacks to which it has been subjected has contributed in no small way to the Greek mentality, in part that of a mountain-people characterised by toughness, intelligence, inventiveness and an unyielding spirit. To this, must be added the more ethereal aspects of the numinous and the superstitious – plus a poetic and musical imagination of which their language is a fine expression.

CLIMATE

Greece enjoys a temperate climate, like other Mediterranean countries. This climate is characterised by short winters and long summers – a great advantage. Local variations occur, particularly in the northeast beyond Thessaloniki; in the south; in the Cycladic and Dodecanese islands; and in Crete. It is usual to speak of two main seasons, summer and winter (spring and autumn being much shorter than in northern Europe). Winter, which commences the agricultural year, is traditionally from St Demetrios' Day (October 6), to St George's Day (April 23). Spring should not be over-looked, however, for at its commencement (between late February and the middle of March, depending on your location), nature bursts into a glorious profusion of texture and colour with an astonishing dynamism. As E R Dodds neatly asserted, spring is 'the right time for holy drunkenness.'

Greece's weather pattern is produced by a low pressure system which originates in the west, initiating the winter season; it is characterised by warm, moist winds. The warm air rises, drawing in cold air from the northeast (known in antiquity as the Borean winds) and a general depression results. The northern summer winds are known as the Etesian or Meltemi winds. The summers are uniformly hot, especially in the southwest. Rainfall is limited to 400 mm in Attica, the Saronic Gulf and the Cyclades; 600 mm in the southeast; between 800-1000 mm in the Ionian islands; and 400-800 mm in Thessaly, Macedonia and western Thrace. This lack of moisture in the air produces Greece's famous light-effects and its blue skies.

FLORA AND FAUNA

The flora and fauna have evolved with this climate, though their natural evolution has been much changed by the people and their needs. The chief victim has been forests, followed by the loss of top soil. The latter has gone for ever; evidence of the former may be seen in the incredible fossilised trees on Lesvos. Most of what we regard as characteristically Greek are actually old imports – e.g., grapes, oranges and tomatoes. Not a few of these imports are the result of the country's marine and merchant adventuring, of which it has a brilliant and long history – one of the longest, in fact. It continues yet, for Greece now leads the world in shipping tonnage. (Not so in fishing, where it is seventh from last in EU, plus the Russian Federation and Poland, with less than 150,000 tonnes; in catch terms it is third from last, with approximately 300,000 tonnes, according to FAO figures, April 1997.)

DEFORESTATION

Greece was once blessed with huge forests, replete with wildlife. These have now all but gone, the victims of man's intemperate use of his resources; sometimes of his deliberate vandalism, ignorance and greed. Fire has often been the agent; and still continues to be one. The area of forests being lost has more than doubled in the last twenty years – in contrast to most European nations which have been making real progress in forest protection.

Deforestation commenced in classical times, when shipping and marine power became important. But the greatest damage occurred in the last two hundred or so years, particularly since Independence in 1827. The Turks are often blamed, but it is an unfair accusation: their system of dominance was essentially idle; they had very little to do with the land, content to leave it in the largely uncaring hands of overseers and tax-farmers. The growth in population since independence, land-hunger and the great need for timber for building, furniture and fuel (charcoal-makers may still be found hard at work wherever there are trees) made tree-felling unavoidable. Short-term profit-taking led to the planting of softwoods, pine in particular. Where pines have not been planted, barren land or a useless scrub known as *maquis*, alleviated only by holm-oak or Aleppo pine, fill the vacuum – to no one's advantage.

Goats Wreaking Havoc

What man failed to preserve, or wantonly destroyed (usually for buildings), has been further degraded by the goat population. This is particularly so in hilly areas, where goats alone thrive. These goats are an important part of the livelihood of impoverished hill-people who depend on them for food and clothing. Over the centuries many a family kept a slender hold on life thanks to goat's milk, meat, skin and bone, and its excrement, which makes an excellent fertiliser. Goats, however, are terrific eaters and stop at nothing to satisfy their

Goats eat their way through the sparse greenery

appetites: I have seen goats climb trees in their search for food! In their paths new growth, especially young saplings, stands no chance: the evidence lies before every viewer of Greece's barren hills; another part of its culture shock. But everything in Greece is connected; the word for tragedy simply means 'goat-song.' What would the world have been without Greek goats and Greek theatre?

Other Environmental Damage

With the loss in forests, of course, went some of Greece's traditional fauna: boars, bears, deer, etc., and birds and snakes – to say nothing of rare and important plants. The effect of this tree loss on topsoil wastage and water management, as well as on the scenery and aesthetics, has also been incalculable. Every winter hundreds of tons of topsoil are washed away by the rain, or blown away by the wind. It has been estimated that 90% has been lost since classical times, an essential resource which took millenia to create. Given the lack of tree and shrub-life that now exists there is very little chance of the topsoil being replaced. Furthermore, the trees that are planted are usually not broad-leaf trees which would produce mulch, a fundamental requisite of good soil. Today, new forestry covers only 16% of the land, very little of which represents the original forested areas; two-thirds of this is state-owned.

AGRICULTURE

Given all these negative factors, and with a mere 30% of its land (5.78 million hectares) available for agrarian use, or 43% if hillside endeavour is included, agriculture represents about 12% of the GDP (which contrasts badly with the work-force figure of 21% engaged in it). Only 6% of this is derived from land-holdings of more than one hundred *stremma* (a *stremma* is equal to 1000 sq. m). The actual use of this land is as follows: 2.92 million hectares are arable; 1.07 million are devoted to permanent crops, 1.79 million are grassland, and 5.75 million are woodland.

In the last twenty or so years, the population has grown by some one and a half million (from approximately 8.7 million to 10.2 million); arable land, by contrast, has been *decreasing* steadily. Over that same period crops on arable land (including vines) have decreased, save for vegetables and tree-crops; the latter have increased by almost 50%, offering quick profits but having a dramatically negative effect on the water-supply.

FISHING

At sea Greece now has 3750 vessels under its flag, representing no less than 15% of the world total – the largest maritime nation. Greece's fishing fleet has more than quadrupled of late, as mentioned above, though the actual amount of fish caught has not even doubled. (About 11,000 tonnes were from inland lakes in 1995; the rest from the Mediterranean.) The lowering of fish-stocks is a major calamity which will have a major impact on every aspect of life – economic, cultural and health. Greece has become a major importer of fish, not least for its tourist market, but the quality is down.

INDUSTRY AND OTHER SECTORS

Greece, in some areas, is still struggling out of the conditions that more northern neighbours threw off after the industrial revolution. It is still a nation of small businesses. Manufacturing industry is split between minor and major units, the defining point being ten workers. When ten or more are involved, the unit are designated major.

Manufacturing Units

Greece has 144,717 manufacturing units all told – an apocalyptic number! Its agricultural units outnumber them by nearly 10:1. It is surprising to see that footwear heads this list, transport equipment comes second, followed by food, metal products, wood and cork products, then furniture and fittings. Next comes electrical machinery and appliances, non-metallic minerals, non-electrical machinery, textiles, leather and fur, printing and publishing. Leather and plastic limp along behind these with just over 3000 units; beverages follow them. Were it to be placed on this range it is interesting to see that tourism would come tenth, with 6991 units – there being 4858 hotels: 3632 (75%) are at C standard or below, the rest are apartments blocks (1025), boarding houses (162), motels (35), and guest room premises (717); there are over one hundred hotels offering conference facilities, of up to 2200 delegates.

I set out the regional distribution of industrial units, and place alongside them the comparative figures for agricultural units:

Region	Indust. Units.	Agri. Units
Greater Athens	47,332	17,544
Central Gr & Evia	11,549[a]	154,896
Peloponnese	11,246[b]	172,880
Ionic Islands	2,332	33,712
Epiros	3,246[c]	54,328
Thessaly	8,150	109,612
Macedonia	29,629[d]	235,232
Thrace	3,503	56,796
Aegean Islands	5,244	64,448
Crete	6,757[e]	99,428

(a) Mainly Attica (b) Mainly Achaia (c) Mainly Ioannina (d)Mainly Thessaloniki (e) Mainly Iraklion

During the last twenty years, the mining industry, crafts, electricity, gas and water supply, construction and public works, transport and public communications have all seen their productivity levels remain virtually static, i.e. within a percentage point of each other; industry and crafts increased by 2.4%. The 1994 *Eurostat* figures show that 23% of the work-force was in industry; a little below this was in agriculture; 55% in services. In commerce, restaurants and hotels the figures increased by 5.8%, taking their share of the GDP to 17%; while banking and insurance figures rose by 2.2%, to 6.6% of GDP; 'other services' increased by 8.1%, to 18.9%. The EU employment average for agriculture is about 6% of the working population; for industry it is 31%; and that for the services is 62%; the EEA statistics are almost identical with these.

The average GDP per head on the basis of PPS (i.e. purchasing power, not monetary equivalence) is 9500, the lowest in the EU (whose fifteen-nation average was 16,800; that of the EEA was 18,100); when compared with the 1983 figures it was second lowest, just above Portugal whose average is now 13,000. This compares very adversely with a report in the *Athens News* which claimed that Greeks work longer hours than any other EU nation. It is a trenchant critique of their productivity, of their failure to make or process things.

TELECOMMUNICATIONS

In telecommunications the Greeks show that love for novelty which has ever characterised them. OTE (the national telephone network) is pursuing a programme of total regeneration, belatedly rescuing itself from near chaos. Some have waited many years for installation. Now, however, there has been a revolution in OTE's status and efficiency. Firstly, it is now by far the largest and most profitable corporation in the Balkans, having a monopoly on terrestrial services. Secondly, it has been privatised. Thirdly, its customer services are now close to normal Western standards, e.g. telephone installation is within 10-30 days of the order being placed.

Street life is now subjected to the use of mobile telephones and associated traffic hazards. Faxes and modems are also abundant, contradicting Aristotle's dictum that the perfect size of a city is one which requires but a single herald, whose voice can be heard from one end to the other.

ADMINISTRATIVE DIVISIONS

The country is divided geographically into 18 regions, broken into 10 *periphereia* (administrative districts); 51 *nomarchia* (prefectures); 147 *eparchia* (provinces); 272 *demoi* (municipalities; the singular is *demos*, which has given us 'democracy'); and 5766 *koinotetes* (communities); plus a large number of *oikismoi* (localities). The administrative districts centre on: Ioannina, Thessaloniki, Alexandroupolis, Larissa, Patras, Athens, Mytilene, Syros, Heraklion. In addition, there are two Metropolitan areas: Athens and Thessaloniki (aka Salonika), the first among their cities and the key centres of the western and eastern areas of the county respectively. Patras is the third largest city, situated in the north-west of the Peloponnese. Thessaloniki and Patras are port-cities; Piraeus serves the interests of Athens, with minor ports (such as Palaia Phaleron and Lavria) supplementing it. Another important port is that of Volos, which serves the interests of the north-central mainland.

View over Athens (without the smog!)

—*Chapter Three*—

GREEKS AND GREEKNESS

'Let Greeks be Greek.'
—Anne Bradstreet, American poet

The average English person warms to 1066; French to 1789, Americans to 1776. Greeks warm to a different time-scale – strictly speaking, a non-time-scale; for their time-scale is beyond history, in prehistory and myth, poetry and song, in timeless absolutes.

ROOTED IN HISTORY AND MYTHOLOGY

A few years ago Nicholas Gage (aka Gatzoyiannis) wrote the story of his mother, who was murdered in the civil war which shook Greece to its foundations at the end of World War II. *Eleni*, the resultant book, became a best-seller and a successful film. It is a minor classic of modern Greek literature, the sort of book that defines and exemplifies Greek experience for the modern world.

Early in the book Gage, who was separated from his mother at the age of nine when transported to the USA, never to see her again, speaks of the mental jump – the metamorphosis of understanding – that he was forced to make when writing it. It centred on the need to distinguish the memory of his mother he cherished as a child from the adult he never knew. He did so in language that is both characteristic and suggestive of the essence of Greekness which foreigners encounter all the time: the *pervasive* sense of literature and history in the Greek psyche and of their oneness with their nationhood. Here are the extraordinary words Gage uses to analyse his aims:

> Before my search was over I had to find my mother, to see her with the eyes of an adult, and to uncover the secret feelings about the world that caged her .... I had to communicate with her across the chasm of death to discover if, as she climbed that ravine to her execution, she was Antigone, meeting death with resignation because she had purposely defied a human command to honour a higher law of the heart, or if she was Hecuba, crying out for vengeance.

Several aspects of Greekness appear here – predominant feelings, *post-mortem* communication, the higher law of the heart etc.; we shall meet them elsewhere. It is the historico-mythical sense, the easy and natural references to Antigone and Hecuba, that now detains us. Gage is speaking of an uneducated peasant woman, bereft of her children, disowned by her father, treacherously treated by her neighbours and friends, tortured and brutally murdered by sadists. The only thought-forms adequate to the task are those of his literature, the Greek classics. They alone approximate to this horror. Of all the human emotions which coursed through him, of all the verbal resources at his disposal – Gage was a distinguished journalist – it was only the language of the ancient poets, Euripedes and Homer that could adequately project his feelings and encapsulate them for his readers. He assumed they knew the referents. It is not possible to live intelligently in Greece not understanding this trait.

But Gage was not taught these classics at school, as children everywhere are taught their nations' history and their roots. His roots had been disrupted; he was moved to, and educated, in the USA. Nevertheless he thought like a Greek and needed to convey his story in Greek mode. Its components – the literature, the experiences presented by it, the language in which it is cast, the history and the geography, the 'spirit of place' – were native to him; in his blood. His long nation's history is his-story; whether myth or not, its truth is substantive. Aristotle may have said that history is less important than

The Museum at Corinth

poetry, but every Greek knows that it is truth nevertheless. That is the reason why Alexander the Great, Aristotle's pupil, travelled with a copy of Homer's *Iliad* next to his dagger under his pillow: the first for self-authentication, the latter for self-protection. The *Iliad's* message resonates through the very being of Greeks, it energises their imaginations, surrounds their hopes. They do not need to explain it; they live it.

The Past is Ever-present

It is so with all Greeks. George Seferis, the Nobel (and noble) prize-winner is another example, as his stunning poetry demonstrates even in translation. The Greeks' interior world is peopled with the past, those feelings and those actions; today's language reflects and embodies those times, the images and metaphors that were then moulded: the past is ever- present. They do not need the archaeological sites or the great monuments to remind them; their experience is all around them, within them. They name their children after the historic and mythic heroes and savants. Their heroes names are encountered in the names of their cities, their streets, even their pets. Their greatest post-war figure was *Constantin* Karamanlis; the present Prime Minister shares that name; his predecessor was *Andreas* Papandreo; the leader of the opposition is *Miltiades* Evert; names that go from grandfather to grandson, from gia-gia (grandmother) to grand-daughter, without break, down through history.

The Greek Orthodox Church

Even the Greek Orthodox Church demonstrates this preoccupation with the old order. Many of its rituals are the re-worked activities of the shrines and temples of the past: the use of incense, holy days, holy places and so on. Many of its 'saints' are simply the half-disguised re-embodiment of pagan heroes and deities. For example, St Demetra, an uncanonical saint whose following is still strong in certain places such as Elefsina (Eleusis). In her, the old corn-goddess, Demeter, has a revered, if transmogrified, place in the hearts and lives of members of the post-pagan, 'Christianised' world. Or take the title 'Mother of God': *Theotokos*. This concept, strictly speaking, is a contradiction that Jews and early Christians would have died to deny. If self-generation is indicative of deity, divine motherhood is logically impossible. It has no place whatsoever in the *New Testament*, and is specifically and repeatedly rejected in the *Old Testament*. But through the Greek Earth- or Mother-Goddess cults, the idea was so firmly embedded in Hellenised minds and practices, that room was eventually made for it in the new religion.

Yet other examples may be found on many hill-tops of Greece, dedicated to St Elias (the prophet Elisha). St Elias? Since when did the eclectic people *par excellence*, the Greeks, have any regard for this destroyer of syncretism? Everyone who is biblically literate knows that it has nothing to do with the prophet Elisha save for a slight proximity of sound. It is not 'Elias' who is intended, but *Helios*. The aspirate h, represented in Greek by a simple breathing mark (') , often falls silent, making easy the connection. Veneration for the holy prophet thus becomes that for the sun-god, whose cult was perpetuated on the mountain tops of old Greece as he rose to spread his rejuvenating warmth across the globe.

Whatever the broader reaches of such things, one cannot have a truly intelligent conversation of any length with Greeks without being made aware of this crucial dimension to their mindset; nor can one understand Greeks without seeing its importance in their present-day *mores* and morals. The more one gets to know them, the more they trust one, the more this element becomes apparent – an unexpurgated and unexpungeable part of their lives and of their brilliant past.

WHO ARE THE GREEKS?

The question was raised in its historical form over sixty-five years ago by Sir John Myres (*Who were the Greeks?*). It was not a new question then, and it is still being asked today. Before Myres' day the hellenophile, G Lowes Dickinson, had offered this warning, 'There is nothing so misleading as generalisation, specially on the subject of the Greeks.' We would do well to heed it. Myres' answer to the question, a generation later, observed the essential continuity of the people. 'They were,' he said, 'ever in process of becoming.'

Greeks, Hellenes or Romaioi?

Even the name is open to question, having been foisted upon the Greeks by their Roman oppressors, who called the colonists of Cumae – the name of a small district of Boeotia in western Greece – *Graii* . This name developed into *Graeci*, then *Graecea*, thence Greece. It came from Latin into the Old English form before 1150, and stuck. The Greeks' self-designation was *Hellenes*, which is derived from the name of their country, *Hellas* (the original name of a tribe which settled in Thessaly in the north-east). Today they prefer the names *Ellen* or *Ellas* and their language *Ellenika*; the adjective describing Greekness is *ellenikos*. (It will be noted that in all these the aspirate has been omitted). Sometimes, especially among themselves, they call themselves *Romaioi*.

A People of Mixed Race

The arguments concerning the purity of the Greek race need not too long detain us. Today it is little more than an academic diversion, of limited anthropological, sociological and national importance. Questions about it continue to be asked; they will not go away. Some want to deny, others to assert, that pure racial types exist – that true Greeks exist, Athenians not least. What is abundantly clear is that a very large measure of cross-racialisation has taken place throughout Greek history; that many peoples invaded Greece, and many were taken from it by force; others left of their own choice, in search of a better life. Many returned, Odysseus-like, full of stories, sometimes poor, sometimes rich. It was difficult – impossible – to forget the *patrida*, the homeland; as those who stay away cannot.

Invaders Absorbed

We know that in the past, from the time of the Assyrians at least, it was the practice of conquerors and invaders to deport when they did not massacre. They transferred out the top echelons of society – an action that was designed to weaken and disrupt the invaded country while relieving it of its treasures; but allowing its economy to continue and attaching tax revenues to pay for their troubles, always ensuring that the ability to retaliate was reduced to zero. The remaining population, the peasants and lower stratas, were left to care for the land, to keep the economic machinery turning – and to remit the resultant wealth to their new overlords. The likelihood of the *crème de la crème* of society being preserved was remote, save in exile. In their place the invaders often deposited 'trustees,' old soldiers (a Roman habit, by which their colonies were maintained) or other segments of their own people who quickly made themselves at home – at the top. This new stratum was therefore of foreign extraction, but it fulfilled their interests to fuse with their new ethos as completely as possible. (Only Jews and Muslims had qualms about this, on the grounds of religious purity.) Most incomers became thoroughly, even energetically, *graecised*; since the Classical era (c. 500 BC onwards) Greek civilisation was the best; its ability to absorb whatever was good in others' ensured its success. But for over three hundred years before that date Greeks had been establishing themselves overseas and colonising them, though often returning with their new families to the old country, as they have continued to do ever since.

Many believe that an answer to the question, 'Who are the Greeks?' cannot be supplied on the basis of race. For example, Lawrence Durrell, that arch-hellenophile, did not believe that it was possible, or relevant, 'Greece ... cannot have a single [i.e. racially pure] Greek left ... the present racial stocks are the fruit of countless invasions,' undoubtedly an overstatement, but one to which any number of corroborative quotations from Greeks and non-Greeks can be added. As Nicholas Hammond averred, 'the genius of the Greeks ... was perhaps to be able to absorb peoples of different stocks and origins and languages and to integrate them into their own civilisation and communities.' Their own language reflected this, in such words as *mixellene* or *helenoskyth* (the latter an improbable mixture of Greek and Scythian).

Yet Pride of Purity

The new and old stock alike took the question of their national (Greek) purity very seriously; by the third generation their origins were all but forgotten. A friend in Athens once remarked that, when a young man, he was informed that his grandmother was Albanian. He had been brought up to believe in his racial purity and was very proud of it. This news – especially the despised Albanian aspect – so shocked him that for two days he was almost catatonic. His awareness of his roots and his confidence in his social well-being were traumatised. His proud boast and his strong self-confidence – like all Athenians who have echoed throughout history the boast of their pure-breeding – was destroyed in one brief sentence. Other Greeks take a different view, for sure; Greece would not be Greece without its teeming opposites. Those who came from Asia Minor in the population exchanges of 1922–3, for example, argue fiercely that it is they who represent the purest Greek stock and point to their name-structures for proof. It is an argument likely to be resolved only when the DNA map of humanity is completed – if then.

Physical Features

Nicholas Gage described Greeks as being 'short, squat and dark' – an unflattering and unfair description, never more than half-true. This is not the place to enter into the discussion concerning physical anthropology. Suffice it to say that the Greek's appearance is as varied as most Near Eastern or European societies, if not more so, and certainly as varied as the exceptionally varied 'Jewish type.' The 'Mediterranean' appearance predominates, but not exclusively so: i.e. of short cranium and stature, dark hair, olive complexion, etc. All such descriptions risk the criticism of stereotyping.

Here is another comparison, one of some acuity by Professor Forest: 'If Plato is the best introduction to the way Greeks talk, Greek pots are the best introduction to the way they look.' Any illustrated book on Greek pottery will confirm this. Sit on a bus or stand in a queue anywhere in Greece and you will see these same faces everywhere: it is one of the few joys of travelling on the metro in the rush hour; some even manage to scowl geometrically.

The linguist/traveller, Leigh Fermor offered a different suggestion:

> The most striking thing about Greek faces – especially peasant faces – is the eyes. The whole of Greek history seems to be coiled up behind them ... a mixture of experience, a rather sad wisdom and innocence ... melancholy and deep-gazing, alert and ready for anger or for kindling with amusement, collusion or laughter; above all they are filled with a wise, phenomenal, uncircumspect candour.

A People United by Culture

Thus Greekness is much more than mere physicality. It is a state of mind, of soul, above all of language; and – historically at least – of membership in the Greek Orthodox Church. The historian, William St Clair went as far as to call the latter the Greeks' 'main unifying institution' (presently becoming less and less true through secularism). Is it this heterogeneous quality, this eclecticism, which makes so many different people feel at home on arriving in Greece?

Professor Hammond's emphasis is in line with that of Isocrates nearly 2500 years ago, in his *Panegyricus*: that being Greek was not a matter of genetics or tribal membership, but of culture. C M Woodhouse, a historian, tartly remarked that 'the only practical definition of a Greek is that he is somebody who thinks he is a Greek' – to which he added that the individual must have solid grounds for so thinking, grounds which include 'language, consciousness of history, almost inevitably religion, but not necessarily place of birth.'

Passing from the physical to the psychological arena is much more interesting, though a dangerous step; dangerous because of the fallacy of stereotypes. It is in his speaking that the Greek manifests himself; the word for 'word' (*logos*) means also 'reason' or 'mind': his words reveal himself. It is a great mistake to interpret only their speech verbally. When a Greek speaks, his whole personality is involved: body, soul and spirit. In him, often in spite of him, the spirit of Greece is heard. He does not speak mere words, but things, realities. These realities compose history, philosophy, religion, song, literature, warfare, want: the whole spectrum of humanity *à la Grecque*.

Body-language

A broad, vibrant humanity surges through the Greek's use of language. Not for him the quiet composure, the frigidity, of north Europeans. Body-language is his language; it offers precise, intellectually conceived and emotionally charged enunciations. Humour, gaiety, *jeux d'esprit* abound in Greek speech; but it is serious humour, reasoned gaiety, and intelligent word-play. One sees his words and observes his emotions, declared through his vigorous mannerisms – of eyes and lips, brow and mouth, of head and torso, hand and arm, foot and leg. All are employed, and all are meaningful.

Love of a Good Argument

With this it is appropriate to introduce another aspect: the argumentative nature of Greeks. They are as quarrelsome as sparrows, and practise this national art (it is that) argumentatively. Gregory of Nyssa, a theologian living in the 4th century, can be quoted here:

> The whole city is full of it, the squares, the market-places, the cross-roads, the alleyways; old clothesmen, money-changers, food-sellers; they are all busy arguing. If you ask someone to give you change, he philosophises ...; if you enquire about the price of a loaf, he theologises; if you ask, 'Is my bath ready?' he disputes doctrine with you ....

Politics has now taken the place of philosophy and theology; history, too. But the change of subject has not reduced the argumentativeness. Greeks are great discriminators, whether talking of social values or politics, sport or religion, water or wine; they use their language with care; they resent the imprecise and the clumsy in language, not least in sound and modulation. (It was this which produced that totally Greek word *bar-bar-oi* for barbarians, from the rough sounds they heard from the lips of foreigners which sounded like so many sheep.) They have an extraordinary feel for words which express the essence of things; they refuse to be content with mediocrity of expression, with generalisations. It can be embarrassing to listen to visitors talking to a Greek, full of their own self-conceits, unaware of the scorn that their ignorance (and often enough their impoliteness) evoke. Culture shock works in both directions. Clarity is fundamental to Greeks. It is that which produced their great thinkers and scientists. The ability to distinguish, to classify, to see the *differentia* of things is native to them; a clarity which, perforce, encompasses wholeness.

Greeks can be partial in argument, more concerned with winning than truth, a tendency facilitated by their flexibility of mind and language, in which mere competitiveness urges them on. Their language is more precise, more flexible, than English; less given to opacity when used correctly. Nevertheless George Seferis (Sepheriadis, sometimes Seferides), the Nobel prize-winner, a former ambassador to the Court of St James, never tired of calling attention to its misuse in modern times. He called it anarchy. To read or listen to his use of it, even in translation, is to see and hear poetry and music and philosophy in flight, a divine experience. In contrast, many misuse the language. But the Greeks' misuse of it is nothing compared to the misuse of English today – as in the UK, to say nothing of its bastardisation in the United States. That, alas, is the nature of language; for that is the nature of man.

Worry Beads

Said the writer, Lawrence Durrell, 'No Greek can sit still without fidgeting, tapping his foot, jerking a knee, or making popping noises with his tongue.' Who else would have invented 'worry beads' (*kombologion*) for the simple reason of having something for their fingers to play with? (I ignore the almost certain origins of the 'rosary' practice of Muslims, mediated through the Turks.) James Pettifer identified this aspect of their physicality very differently when he spoke of 'the devastating ruthlessness and driving energy that characterised Onassis's *modus operandi*.' In many ways that poor-boy-cum-billionaire is very typical of many Greeks: another contradiction, for they are proverbially laid-back.

A Ferocious Energy

The Greeks do have a ferocious energy, one that originates in their environment. It is this which enabled them to progress so phenomenally in every art and science and human endeavour, mental and physical. It was this which created of them a great colonising nation, a great merchant class, great mariners, and a formidable soldiery. Only a quarter of the population of the Ottoman Empire was Greek, but the Greeks all but ran it for their masters who were but its idle figure-heads. The Greek State may have been drained to its dregs by the end-1940s, but no one can doubt the enormous energies which were spent leading up to that time, against terrific odds; or of the industrious activities taking place today. In the re-birth of the Greek State we see a modern-day miracle in the making.

Alongside this we must place the Greek people's ability to sit and ponder – on great things and of nothing. In another book I referred to the difference between Jew and Greek thus, 'The Jew sits under his fig-tree, and thinks; the Greek sits under his, and sits.' One is always surprised to see how easily Greeks can sleep in public, in all sorts of positions and conditions, despite discomfort, careless of others' opinions.

A Strong Economic Sense

Another aspect of Greekness is their economic sense: the very word is Greek. Experience has taught them, like the Scots and other nations, that resources matter, that waste cannot be tolerated. (Sadly it is not so regarding their fly-tipping.) Scant resources breed parsimony – and bargaining skills; that competitive element again, which runs so deeply in their nature. They abhor anyone getting the better of them in argument or negotiation; if this takes place unfairly they never forget. As with other easterners, they have a high sense of 'face,' of *philotimia*: 'love of honour,' i.e. personal and social positioning. To lose face for them is to be savaged internally, to *be* – not just to feel – insulted. This sensitivity can be traumatic, for all parties concerned; a great danger for the unwary newcomer.

Yet they have a large capacity for self-criticism and self-mockery. They are not averse to denigrating their own or their nation's achievements. As the artist Niko Ghika once commented, so unfairly, 'They never do anything else.' So many conflicting elements – the hallmark of Greekness.

Individualism ... and Chaos

The possibility of losing face gives rise to distrust and unconcern; it heightens that individualism which has always characterised Greeks, an outcome of the geographical make-up of the country. The traveller, Leigh Fermor characterised it as 'a world of chronic anarchy' (he was speaking specifically of his experiences in the Mani), which it often appears to be. Greeks are never happier than when balking official-dom or of talking of their victories over it, even when those victories have been secured at the cost of truth or justice. Hoodwinking taxation or customs officers is but one aspect of this. Their history is littered with defeat borne of self-interest, with the shameful displays of politicians and power-wielders who refused to give way even when played out. Durrell once asked some fisherman on Rhodes about the practice of every man deciding differently in Greece: 'That is indi-vidualism,' they replied. 'But it leads to chaos,' Durrell objected. 'We like chaos' came their nonchalant *riposte*. And they do, as over 80 administrations in 170 years of their recent history demonstrates: monarchical, republican, socialist, communist, centre and right-wing – to say nothing of countless *volte-faces* by those who clung to power regardless of principle. C M Woodhouse states that there has been no coherent ideology among Greeks for the last 1600 years, i.e. since the fall of Byzantium.

How They View Themselves

Contradictions, paradox and ambiguity are as natural to Greeks as roast beef and Yorkshire pudding are to the English, or candy-floss to the American. But their apparent contradictions do not diminish their intellectual power, or their resolve when once set on a course of action. At such times resolve can turn into downright, unyielding stubbornness, an ever present reality in the Balkans. The Greek, in fact, is two men – the biggest culture shock. When asked by a stranger, he will say proudly, 'I am a Hellene.' When asked by a fellow Greek the word changes; the proud title of *hellenos* becomes *romaios* .

It is not a word used when foreigners are present. Understanding this dual nature is of critical importance to those who would understand Greeks. Nicholas Gage, the writer, limits the difference between *hellenos* and *romaios* to three simplistic epithets each: *hellenos*, applying to their noble, courageous and creative aspects; *romaios* to their devious, obstinate and selfish qualities. Not to be aware of this dichotomy is to fail to understand the ambiguity which pervades all Greekness.

A Curious Nature

The Greeks' boundlessly curiosity is a more appealing trait, even if unsettling to the less open newcomer. 'How much do you earn?' is not an unusual question posed after initial introductions. He wants to know everything about you. He has his secrets, his private affairs – and nothing will wring them from him if he is unwilling to do so. But on the whole he is much more outgoing than his northern neighbour, much more communal in his lifestyle, much less concerned at preserving social and superficial differences. Perhaps it was this that caused the High Priest of Thebes, centuries ago, to comment, 'You Greeks are mere children.' It is a symptom of inverted ethics to believe that innocence is a childish trait. Greeks have great street-wisdom; they are worldly-wise. Yet they project this sense of openness, of innocence, which is endearing.

This inquisitiveness lies at the base of all science, art and technology. It was shaped by the freedoms Greece won and the geniuses it spawned. But there is more than mere curiosity in the Greek mind: there is wonder. 'It is through ... wonder that men began to philosophise' commented the great Aristotle in *Metaphysics*. The word for wonder is *deinos*, which can mean great or terrible or clever – i.e. that which propels us beyond ourselves, which sloughs off our conceits. Knowledge is sacred to the true Greek – a sacred task, demanding effort and integrity; a sacred deposit, demanding maintenance and loyalty.

Social Cohesion

Their sense of *parea* – that circle of friends that continues throughout life, resumed spontaneously even if in disrepair – is largely foreign to the West. It is a means of great social cohesion – like the family itself – though it is also responsible for producing an element of cronyism in the social fabric.

Sexuality and Nudity

Sexuality is refreshingly open and natural in Greece. It does not have the immaturity of smuttiness that blights Britain and the USA, though it can be coy or coquettish. It is enjoyed, not excused; spontaneous, not craven. The Greeks do not suffer from hypocrisy or prudery, as Americans or British do; nonsense about the birds and the bees leaves them sardonic: why not have real fables? They are very serious and very light-hearted about sex, as becomes people at ease with themselves. They can be prudish about nudity under certain conditions – a mannerism foisted upon them by the Orthodox Church. I have even seen Greeks showering in their underpants; be-sporting themselves provocatively is a rarer thing. The law forbids nudity, generally speaking, but attitudes are relaxing on this. The Orthodox Church prohibits women wearing in church so-called 'men's clothing' – i.e. slacks, or clothing considered to be irreverent (non-sleeved items, short skirts, plunging necklines etc.). It is often forgotten that the trigger of the Colonels' *coup* in 1967, which ostensibly backed the Church, was a reaction to mini-skirts on women (and beards and long hair on men). The Church has no such concerns over infant-baptisms, however, which take place in public and the child completely nude.

Prostitution is taken for granted, controlled by law – to the benefit of society as a whole, for men and women. Hard-core films, adult magazines and sex-shows are also accepted, though they are not permitted to be flaunted. Child pornography is illegal. In antiquity the Games were conducted in the nude, women were excluded, yet they were essentially a religious event. The gods had made the body and they too celebrated its joys – as did the goddess Demeter in eating, Dionysios in drinking, Artemis in hunting, and Aphrodite in sex.

Women are respected in Greece. But foreign women have forfeited this by their behaviour, which is considered loose. It is not merely the *Shirley Valentine* syndrome, but more general aspects of talk, demeanour and dress. In this regard the activities of the 'harpoons' (*kamaki*) is notable: they are usually unmarried men who stalk women for deliberate sexual advantages. The dress and demeanour of some foreign women encourage them. The harpoons are tolerated, and not a few women suffer from them. Greeks are terrific starers, the men particularly. 'Eyeing women up' suggestively exists on a broad scale. Greek female friends have also spoken of this. Eye contact, which acts as a 'come-on,' should be avoided.

Being Greek – Legally

Technically, there are six methods by which Greek nationality is legally obtained: birth from a Greek father or mother; legitimisation before the age of thirty; adoption before the age of thirty; naturalisation by the Ministry of the Interior; by joining the armed forces (which is only open to those already designated 'ethnic Greeks,' a process within the process); and through special procedures arranged by the courts (also available only to 'ethnic Greeks').

MEN IN GREEK SOCIETY

Let us, finally, take a closer look at the sexes, impolitely starting with men, for this is a male-dominated society.

Dress

The *kyrios* is almost always well-dressed and coiffured, if somewhat unorthodox from the staid European's point of view. His clothing will be clean and well pressed, shoes well polished. The jacket may not match (to our way of thinking) the trousers, still less the shirt or shoes (socks may not be worn at all); but he is asserting his individuality, his Greekness: 'I am different, therefore I am.'

By and large he will have short hair and be clean shaven. Moustaches and beards exist, but are not over-common. Our male may not shave every day (especially if he is a manual worker), and may prefer to do so in the evenings so as to be at his best when it counts, i.e. socially. Greeks have a questionable attitude towards the early morning. They are night people – it is not for nothing that the owl is the symbol of Athens! To ride in the metro between 7-9 a.m. is an eye-opener in more ways than one. Many, however, are at work by 8 a.m. – and earlier.

Individuality is asserted in a multitude of ways: in posture, style, opinions etc. He is not worried about opposition or inconsistencies; he can live with both and delights to do so; he worries still less about time-keeping, food and drink habits, his sexuality – whatever. An eccentricity still practised by some is the deliberate growth of the 'pinkie' finger-nail: an old device (from the east) to demonstrate intellectual preoccupation, a disdain for manual labour. Other acts of foppishness are found in the cities.

Out-of-town dwellers are robust in their love of nature, the soil and its related work. Today they are a diminishing breed; technology is taking over. Neighbourhoods have been impoverished by a flight to the towns for education and work; the result is a somewhat wizened society left behind – the rearguard action of old Greece. They pack the smoke-filled *taverna* or *kapheneion*, playing backgammon, cards or chess, the television set at high volume, everyone contributing to news broadcasts or the even more popular sports programmes.

Posture

Posture is important; essentially a matter of inwardness: how one feels about oneself. No matter how small, the Greek stands tall with his neighbour. They are taught thus at school – the males have the great advantage of conscription to straighten their backbones and increase their sense of national pride – to say nothing of the care lavished upon them by doting parents. The royal practice of standing or walking with one's hands behind one's back is considered arrogant and impious, in church particularly. (It is curious that the Greek-born Duke of Edinburgh favoured this style; perhaps arrogance becomes royalty.) The raising of the hand palm extended outwards is a gross gesture of commination.

Individuality and Assertiveness

His individuality matters and is assertive. He thinks things out, is argumentative in stating and defending his views. Vociferous and public are his comments, yet he will display great flexibility once cornered; if losing the argument he will subtly shift the goal posts – his definitions, the subject. He will not easily give way. He is a rule-bender by instinct, a trait we shall encounter frequently. History is present in all his thinking; he lives it. He has any number of role-models, though Odysseus the Wily is perhaps most influential – aka 'Odysseus of the nimble wits,' whose story was described as 'the poem of the Compleat [i.e. Greek] Man.' In many ways this hero of Homer's epitomises Greek masculinity: its daring, courage, flight from danger, intelligence, tenacity, thrusting self-interest, wanderlust, love of home and country, sense of right, and calm espousal of untruth and deceit: opposites multiplying!

Love of Debate

'In the beginning was the word' could only have come from the mind of a Greek. He knows the power of words, whether farmer or lawyer. He loves to talk, and rarely stops doing so – whether sitting, standing or walking, even in church, where a certain murmuring is continuous despite the priest's pious ardour. He is stronger on answers than on questions; hair-splitting is civilised debate. His logic can be formidable or capricious, moved by emotional impulse or strict reasoning, but certainly not after the manner of the ancient scholars, the 'Schoolmen.' His thinking is logical, albeit lateral or 'left-handed' thinking.

Whiling the time away at a kapheneion

Opinionated

It is because of this self-confidence in his insights, this *philotimia*, that arguments tend to become highly personalised; to oppose his opinions is to challenge his *amour-propre*. He will go to any lengths to win his case, including insults and denigration. The long running war between Papandreou and Mitsotakis, former Prime Ministers both, is a well documented and public illustration of many such verbal conflicts throughout Greece. Our Greek will not easily recognise defeat; that form of sportsmanship – of magnanimity – are not his natural style. It was this quality which caused the Danish Foreign Minister, in 1994, at a moment of frustration, to call Greece 'the spoilt child of Europe;' an unpolitical indulgence which cost many of us our bacon, cheese and butter supplies for months! (Their importation was banned in reaction to the comment, a curious reaction for adults.)

He is highly opinionated, and he will offer advice willy-nilly, in private or in public, whether he knows you or not. He will be offended if ignored, but more likely he will shrug his shoulders and press on.

But don't be surprised if he snubs you next time. Verbal violence is common, but the Greek is not a violent man.

He can be exquisitely polite, and flagrantly rude; his tact can be great, though he may not choose to use it – and if he does it may not convey his real feelings. But feelings are often more noticeable than intellect. It is an attractive feature of Greek society, this openness, this warmth and affection: kisses and hugs, arm-linking and hand-holding, mutual tears and laughter: physically expressed concern, noisy encounters and sad partings. Anger may be displayed as much as affection or grief, but you know where you are, though a smile or laugh may be merely a face-saving grimace. As Nicholas Gage warns, a smiling Greek can be a very angry Greek; even worse is the impenetrable stare.

Self Control

Greeks often act unfazed, even in provoking circumstances, despite their emotionalism. It is part of their culture to do so. Self-control and moderation hark back to remote antiquity and are the classical marks of the well-formed man. Lucian, quoting Epicharmus, added a touch of cynicism, 'Keep sober, and remember to disbelieve.' In my experience Greeks are often better behaved and more polite than the average north European, an aspect which is reflected in the crime figures. The opposite of this can be seen in the daily confrontation between motorists and the police when the former, asserting their individuality (read lawlessness) and the latter, asserting their importance, are reduced to bad-tempered displays of arm-waving and whistle-blowing – and worse. It can be very diverting.

Sense of Honour

One of the advantages of Greece's freedom from Roman Catholicism and puritanism is its relative absence of guilt. Short-comings and faults are handled less judgmentally than in the West, which uses guilt-feelings (not least in religion) to demean the individual. Shame is a potent, if sub-Christian, weapon. Perhaps this is one of the reasons for the individual's self-assurance in Greece. At any rate, even when caught and convicted, he can walk tall; even if reduced to being a half-measure of all things, he is still a man. In one area, however, the sense of unworthiness is never lower than when his self-respect, his honour (*philotimia*) is impugned. This honour is even written into the Greek legal code – though not always applied for foreigners; it has a distinct social application. In this regard loyalty, first to one's family (broadly defined), and thence to one's friends and fellow-nationals, is paramount: you don't 'grass' on them; you may even lie or perjure yourself for them. It is the Greeks' defence against a history of international disrespect, and much worse.

WOMEN IN GREEK SOCIETY

Greek women share the foregoing qualities, as appropriate. They are slowly emerging from the grip in which male dominance held them. That said, they have ever been key figures at home, and the position of the mother-in-law (with whom the son and his wife stay traditionally, a practice now breaking down) was vital. A good case can be made out for the females being the backstay of the nation, through her home-making, child-rearing and religious proclivities, as well as her contributions to the family income in field or garden, now more and more in part-time or full-time employment. Not a few men are intimidated by their womenfolk, hence the saying *tov agei kai tov pherei he yuvaika tou:* 'his wife leads him by the nose.' If loyalty be a Greek virtue, then the Greek *kyria* has it in abundance; she will defend her man, her children (especially her sons), her family, to the nth degree.

Natural Beauty and Style

The *kyria* has natural beauty and vitality, along with a high dress-consciousness that often distinguishes her from her north European sisters. It is courting criticism to say it, but it as at least as high as that of Paris or Rome or New York. The Greek clothing industry is vastly under-rated. Behind the better dressed males usually resides a caring mother or wife, whose nimble fingers have added the final touches. Her beauty is historic. Greeks love the beautiful, whether it be a woman, a landscape or a pot – but especially a woman. They love their beauty particularly, and are quick to say so: a strong factor in the courtship rituals. She loves to dress in good clothing, adorned by her jewellery (a matter with which her mate may well compete), using plenty of make-up and perfume.

Smart but Diplomatic

She is passionate and lives zealously. She is both modest and exhibitionist, coy and daring, like her male counterpart; contrasts recurring. She is at ease with her sexuality, without that self-conscious

Photo courtesy of Life File

The mother-in-law is a key figure in the extended family

silliness with which some western women cloak their nature. She may not be far behind her mate educationally or professionally; indeed, she may be in front of him. But if so, she will be a skilled diplomatist. The male must still rule – an unwritten law – even if he does not equal her. She will not defy his *philotimia*.

At Home

Greek women are natural and first-rate home-makers, good cooks, and very industrious, not least in household chores. This does not extend much beyond the fence or balcony wall: a matter worth remembering when walking underneath. I have seen more than one person covered in dust or debris. When not found caring for the home or family, out shopping or looking after an aged parent, a woman may well be found in the garden with hoe or spade or secateurs in hand.

One must also mention the *gia-gia*, or grandmother. She is an institution in her own right, a formidable centre of stability traditionally for the Greek family; after whom the first female child is usually named.

Greeks make excellent hostesses and can be depended on to make a party go with a swing. Before that long hours will have been spent in the markets and the kitchen preparing. Those who are attracted to the simple life and a modest table should be ready to see the very opposite at even low-grade parties. Abundance is the watchword, with many plates – rather than courses, for in Greece everything tends to come together – of everything: fish, meat, vegetables, main and side dishes, salads, bread, cheeses and fruit; to say nothing of wine and spirits – which her husband will handle, though arranged by her.

More Religious

Women are traditionally more religious than men; at least more openly religious, more given to the tending of ritual and the following of superstition; Greek women not least. The ancient past and its customs superimpose themselves on current practices, so an odd fusion of paganism and Orthodoxy is manifest. The Church seems little concerned with this paradox, presumably because, being male dominated, it takes a patronising and chauvinistic view of women.

A PHYSICALLY DEMONSTRATIVE SOCIETY

Children and youth share the foregoing qualities – the vitality, charm, sullenness, intelligence, loyalty and so on. Their relationships appear closer than in north European families. Mothers kiss adoringly their teenage sons, who respond with deep affection, even fondling them in public which would evoke tart comment further north and west. The children offer each other a like affection – as do soldiers, airmen and naval personnel; it is not an unusual sight to see men walking hand-in-hand along a street, unashamed and unprovoked. If one were to select one facet of Greek life which most surprises – culture shock – it is this physical affection. Within a highly competitive framework, one which is not unused to lively friction and aggressive argument, Greek society offers genuine safeguards, especially towards its own. It is evident even among the young who are often more socially responsible and more polite than those of north Europe. Thankfully its crass yuppieness has not yet affected Greece.

GREEK YOUTH

Sasha Sokolov, the Russian novelist, a former neighbour of mine on Poros, once remarked that he found a striking difference between Russian youth and Greek. In Russia, he argued, children are all but ignored until they achieve adulthood, when they become the darlings of their parents. In Greece, he found exactly the opposite: they are loved and cossetted to distraction throughout childhood, but once adulthood is reached they lose that special treatment and show evidence of trauma in so doing. That, Sasha believed, accounts for their 'wounded faces.' All generalisations are dangerous, this one not excepted, but I find more than a grain of truth in it, though I do not know whether it stems from parental coolness (which I doubt) or the effect of finding oneself plunged into a world whose promises are

Photo courtesy of Greek National Tourism Organization

Children quickly gain maturity and learn about the family sense of honour

always more generous than its fulfillings. Given the exposure to northern European and American affluence seen on television and in the films, Greek youth has a growing problem in coming to terms with the sheer unfairness and the injustices of the modern world.

Greek parents are not ungenerous towards their children; quite the opposite. They are often immersed in their affection and goodwill, given everything the parents can afford – and more. They grow up in a secure society, internally at least, with strong family ties. The Greek family is not the 'nuclear family' of 2.4 children of elsewhere; but the 'extended family' which includes grandparents, aunts and uncles, cousins – and even remoter members, though this is now breaking down somewhat. Moreover, young Greeks care for the younger members. Child abuse does take place, but on a greatly reduced level compared with some countries. Families and society are well bonded. According to *Eurostat* there are about 700 one-person households in Greece out of a total of 3600.

If there are signs that the children are somewhat spoilt, it must also be urged that they are more independent and mature than many of their international neighbours. Many work harder, too: at school and in their parents' businesses. School hours are long, made so by a tradition of extra-schooling paid for by ambitious parents. It is not unusual to see quite young children in shops or kiosks (the *periptera*), or even on the actual streets, selling whatever they may. It is usual to get polite and efficient service from them. The lack of vandalism and other forms of anti-social behaviour speaks highly for the cohesion of their society – a reverse form of culture shock. There are signs of it developing, but it is little compared with the anarchy and destruction known in some places such as parts of Britain. Criticism may be levelled at the 'noise pollutants,' an aspect shared with all young people who have access to canned music and ghetto-blasters, but they usually respond to others' wishes politely.

The children are great talkers, which derives from the broader range of interests encountered at school, and those found in the home and on the street; they manifest a cheerfulness not always found in their elders. Foreign languages appear to be more readily handled by them than by British and American young people. They are equal to them in being abreast of fads and fashions, music and dancing, and very keen on sports and physical development. Computerisation is endemic in Greece, and they share in its advantages in work and play. The speed of the computer boom means that Greece may leap-frog other countries that were once ahead of it.

The denim era passed long ago in Greece; it is now more a worker's overall than an accepted item of dress. Greek tastes are influenced by film and television, and that of the stars, with the ever-present insistence on 'doing their own thing.' A veritable anarchy of style exists for young females, who are not slow in following their choices. Good sense and a quiet modesty is perhaps the best generalisation, the wilder forms being left to the few, mainly city-centred, young people.

MINORITIES IN GREECE

All governments are concerned not to inflame problems by drawing attention to them, which makes the job of the social historian or commentator more difficult. Despite the near fifty pages given to population analysis in the *Statistical Yearbook of Greece (SYBG),* which measures the population and its activities in every conceivable form and location, there is not a word concerning minorities, race, colour or creed, though it does mention twice, albeit in footnotes, the Lausanne Treaty of 1923 (without explanation). Successive Greek ministers have stressed that there is no racism, colour or related problem in Greece; not everyone agrees. This is not only because the *parea* system tends to nepotism, cronyism and an extended patriotism, but because Greeks manifest an in-built sense of superiority which harks back to their history and the 'barbarians.' But what is quietly voiced within polite circles breaks out into a roar of public outrage from time to time over ethnic minorities and their alleged malpractices and ambitions.

Albanians

There are over 300,000 ethnic Albanians in northern Greece (as there are thousands of ethnic Greeks in Albania); many have come south over the past few years. They call themselves Shqiptars. They are not always treated fairly, to put it mildly. At one time one could see bus-loads of them being escorted back to the border by the police. Frequently they were simply dumped back over it, only to return a few days or weeks later via different routes, desperate for lodgings, work and food. That said, it would be a grave injustice to say that all are so treated. Many are given food, shelter and jobs by Greeks – legally and otherwise. The same can be said for the Pontic Greeks (from the southern Black Sea coast) who have returned to Greece since the collapse of the communist east, though they are much better placed. They are all but welcomed on to various programmes to enable them to fit into Greek life.

The Vlachs

The Vlachs have a distinctive language, akin to Romanian, and Latin in origin; plus some curious habits and superstitions. They are found in the northwest of Greece, and its north-central regions, also in the southern Peloponnese (in the Mani all outsiders are called Vlachs), and beyond Greece's borders – in Albania, the Former Yugoslav Republic of Macedonia, and Bulgaria. For a long time they practised a policy and lifestyle of seasonal migration, but it is rare today.

Sarakatsans

Similar to the Vlachs are the Sarakatsans (known among their neighbours outside Greece as the Karakatchans), also nomadic pastoralists, who have a more pronounced awareness of their linguistic and cultural past, and preserve it more energetically. Some of it is distinctively pre-Christian. If Greeks enjoy independence, the Sarakatsans are the professionals at it – a point which worked in Greece's favour during the War of Independence, in which they served with distinction. They are loth to have settled dwellings, refuse to intermarry, and have a huge, arcane vocabulary. They are more widespread than the Vlachs, though not found in the southern Peloponnese or some of the islands. The past is represented in their love of music and song, though they play no musical instrument save the flute. They are usually taller and fairer than the Vlachs.

Gypsies

No account of minorities in Greece can omit the gypsies, perhaps its most intractable social problem. They proliferate throughout the country but are chiefly found around Athens and Thessaloniki, always gravitating to the outer edges of society, always refusing its overtures to integrate with it. In one sense they perform a useful service, for they mop up much waste, especially scrap metal – though some of it before it becomes scrap. One writer called them the professional thieves of Greece. The damage made by them to some aspects of the social fabric is far more than their positive attributes. Over the two summers of 1995–6 I watched a pretty sea-front park in Old Phaleron, admittedly neglected, become completely ruined by their contrivances – the dumping of waste, the destruction of shrubs and trees, the breakdown of paths and fences, etc. Police raids were made, but were paltry and ineffective; the gypsies returned within days, more determined than ever – and the police looked the other way.

Their lifestyle is in the open, though far from being open socially, and not without recourse to gang or family rivalry which at times almost borders on tribal war. In health and education matters they fall far below the national average, not least in literacy. They have their own language, though they also usually have passable Greek. Their families are large and ever self-dividing (necessarily, as they live in vans and lorries). There appears to be a curious absence of older folk among them. Everyone works – on the streets, at whatever comes to hand, be it in selling boxes of matches, paper handkerchiefs, plastic garden-ware, fruit and vegetables, washing windscreens at road junctions, or simply collecting junk. Many of them beg, persistently, their faces contorted with need, the young mothers and their babies particularly. (They are organised by their male counterparts, being delivered by van in the mornings to the most profitable corners, and collected from thence at the end of the day.) They used to have great music traditions, playing a variety of instruments – clarinets, drums, guitars, lutes, violins, zithers, etc. but this is giving way to canned music and the television.

Unsurprisingly the gypsies provoke much hostility. I asked one Bishop who was known for his community's social involvement with them. His answer was brusque, 'They refuse our offers of help. They won't participate in civilised lifestyles. They insist on independence. They only have themselves to blame.' Matter closed; the priest walks, again, on the other side of the road.

Jewish People

No account of the minorities of Greece can omit the Jewish people. The obscene racialism that characterised the Third Reich resulted in the virtual elimination of Jewish communities which, even today, have not regained anything like their former strength.

Historically, the Jews have been in touch with the 'Greeks' (if one may use so elastic a term) since the Iron Age, and there is good historical evidence of their being settled in the area since 1200 BC. By the first century AD there were Jewish communities from Neopolis to Corinth and well beyond, in all directions, all of them at strategic trading points; all of them becoming centres of the new religious growth which flowered into Christianity. Jewish experience in Greece was subject to the ups and downs that its people have suffered from throughout history, often picked out for exemplary treatment – and often enough through envy rather than pure racialism. For example, in the War of Independence, on 5 October 1821, more than 200 were murdered for their 'connivance' over Turkish rule. Prior to this Jewish people had enjoyed great freedoms under the Byzantines; were rewarded, in fact, by them for their intelligence and industry. Under the Turks they enjoyed a large measure of toleration, even patronage, Islam being more open to Jewry than Christianity – not least for the former's determined monotheism. As a result, under the Ottoman Empire a very large number of Jews made their way into Greece, into Thessaloniki in particular.

By the earlier twentieth century they were numbered in the tens of thousands. By 1942 they were virtually extinct – over 50,000 of their number were deported to the concentration camps from Thessaloniki alone. Since the war their community has slowly been rebuilt, but the establishment of the State of Israel in 1948 has naturally favoured their hopes and limited the growth of Greek Jewry. Today they number around 7000. Anti-semitism is rare.

Turks

Away to the northeast a fairly difficult problem simmers: 'Turkey in Europe.' This refers to the 100,000 or so ethnic Turks who stayed behind after the population exchanges of 1923. They have never given up their Turkish ways, especially their Islamic faith, and look to Istanbul as the gravitational centre of their citizenship. Their five times a day prayer-ritual, as well as regular mosque attendance for the men, is a powerful way of keeping their hopes alive. They are separated from Greeks not only by their religion but by language, culture and fierce nationalistic ambition.

Turkey borders their world in every respect, geographically not least, a fact which lays great stress on Greece's defence budget. A little further north Bulgaria acts as a magnet to such nationalism, frequently fanning it despite the treatises and pacts made between the two countries. Turkey itself never loses an opportunity to harass Greece, whether by claiming oil or mineral or other rights (such as shipping lane sovereignty in the Dardanelles), or even coastal or land rights on the smaller north Aegean islands. In this Greece has a natural partner with Cyprus, bifurcated since 1974 by Turkish aggression and aggrandisement.

The Region of Macedonia

This brings us to the problem of Macedonia, which actually brought down the government of Mitsotakis in 1992, neatly returning Papandreou to power. Foreigners fail to understand Greek sensitivity on this issue, often citing the ancient rivalry between Athens and her allies and the Macedonian kings, whose greatest scion was Alexander the Great. The recent fracas was not simply a question of names and flags, as many believed. Were the region of Macedonia to secede from Greece, or be taken over by another state, Greece would lose a very major portion of its territory and wealth – the latter particularly, in both its agricultural and industrial-commercial aspects. It has been calculated that something like a quarter of Greece's agricultural holdings would disappear, plus half its cattle, a sixth of its sheep, a fifth of its goats, a quarter of its pigs, a fifth of its poultry, a quarter each of its wholesale and retail strengths, a quarter of its manufacturing capacity and nearly half its electricity production – a nightmare scenario.

It is not just a 'little local difficulty' as someone famously commented. In speaking of the menace to his country, the late Andreas Papandreou spoke of 'the forces outside the Balkans' that were covertly threatening Greece. Nor had he forgotten that Georgievski, the Vice-President of FYROM (Former Yugoslav Republic of Macedonia), had tentatively given shape to a Macedonian State drawn of the peoples of FYROM, Bulgaria and Greece. The claim has never been withdrawn. The Greek Prime Minister's fears were aggravated by the speed at which Bulgaria, Russia and Turkey rushed to back such moves by elements within former Yugoslavia. Meanwhile Europe and the United States prevaricated; it has never been any different. The Balkans are the Balkans, the anvil on which many a promising career has been broken; Greece is an active part of them. In this regard it is the majority without which is as much to be feared as the minority within.

—Chapter Four—

PILLARS OF SOCIETY

There are seven pillars of society. The Church, however, requires a chapter to itself:

- The Constitution
- The Presidency
- Parliament
- The Judiciary
- The Armed Forces
- Local Government
- The Church

THE CONSTITUTION

The history of the constitution reflects the history of Greek democracy as much as the instability of the young nation since independence from the Turks. It also represents the fruition of Greek political thought from classical times to the end of the Byzantine era. The Independence struggle of 1821–7 unfolded a process which was to continue for nearly one hundred and fifty years. It was only in 1975 that the constitution reached its modern form; even then it was subject to a major revision in 1985. It defined Greece as a republic, organised as a 'presidential parliamentary democracy.' Its path has not been an easy one.

A Revolutionary Assembly created a National Constitution at Epidauros in 1821, based on the French model and fashioned after the *Declaration of the Rights of Man*. It saw repeated amendments – at Astros in 1823, when parliamentary government was introduced; at Troizen in 1827, when the presidency was given executive powers and offered to John Capodistrias. It was suspended in 1832 following his assassination. A Protectorate was then instituted by the great powers: Russia, France and Britain, which put the Bavarian prince Otto on the throne as King Otho I. His refusal to allow constitutional change led to many rebellions. In 1843 a bicameral parliament was introduced, the king retaining certain powers of veto. He was not a success, and was overthrown in 1862. A new constitution was formulated two years later which established Greece as a 'crowned democracy.' This provided a measure of guidance through the mainly economic misfortunes, until 1911 when it was amended to allow for major reforms especially land ownership.

The tumults of the Balkan Wars in 1912–13 and of World War I, and the exchange of peoples that followed it, led to the rise of an aggressive republicanism in Greece. A plebiscite demanded this in 1924; another new constitution came into effect in 1927. Its biggest change was the abolition of the monarchy. Greek politics weathered badly in the Depression and the monarchy was restored, in 1935,

79

along with the constitution of 1911. The dictator, George Metaxas, a former colonel, abandoned it a year later. He held power from 1936 until 1941 when the occupation of Greece by Germany ended its short independence, a cathartic event which shook the nation to the core. It ended, not with the expulsion of the Germans in 1944, but in a complex civil war: republicanism vs. monarchy, communism vs. capitalism, and left vs. right – opposites multiplying; a wrecking period of some four years. Following its cessation, and the dubious legality which allowed the reintroduction of the monarchy, a revision of the 1911 constitution was made in 1952 which, though breached from time to time, lasted until its effective death at the hands of the *coup* by the 'Colonels' in 1967.

With the restoration of power in 1974 to Constantine Karamanlis, parliamentary democracy was reintroduced with an executive styled presidency; the monarchy was written off – the sixth vote Greeks had made on the subject since Independence – and many other reforms engendered, not least moves on admission to the EEC (as it was then called). The new constitution came into force in 1975, and remains in force save for the amendments of 1985 (concerning the powers of the President, which were substantially reduced).

THE PRESIDENCY

Thus Greece's constitutional position became a presidential parliamentary democratic republic, based on a multi-party system. The President is the Head of State, a largely decorative function. He is elected by parliament on the say-so of the Prime Minister, and holds an essentially non-executive office. He has the power to refer bills back to parliament, to call for a referendum on matters of national importance, and to advise the government through the Prime Minister. Presidential Decrees have the full force of law once they are promulgated and published in the Government *Gazette*; they are usually issued with the agreement of parliament, and on its terms.

Parliamentary guard

PARLIAMENT

The sovereignty of the nation resides in the people itself, as embodied in the *Voule*, the national parliament, which is situated at Syntagma ('Constitution') Square, Athens. Universal suffrage of all nationals over the age of 18, who are not mentally defective, is basic; the people must vote. Women were enfranchised as late as May 1952, as long as they were aged twenty-one and above; they can enter parliament if over twenty-five. In a new move, even prison inmates are allowed to vote. Parliament is constituted from a multi-party system, which competes in free elections for the will of the people on a regular four-year basis. All matters of State derive their direction from, and are mandated by, the parliament.

Proportional Representation

The country is divided into 300 constituencies, each sending their own elected representative to parliament, known as the National Assembly. Its mandate is cancelled when the government falls or resigns. It does not follow the 'first past the post' election system, i.e. of a simple majority, but of proportional representation (PR) – a highly complex system first introduced in 1926, which has evolved through 'modified,' thence 'revised' forms.

Members of Parliament

The members of parliament (deputies) are not well paid. Out of the eight leading European nations they are seventh, just above Spain and below those the United Kingdom. They earn about one-third of Italian members' stipends (the highest in the EU), and about a quarter of that of members in the USA (the highest in the world).

Prime Minister

Parties choose their own leaders; the leader of the winning party automatically becomes Prime Minister. He has great power. His first duty is to select his cabinet from among the elected representatives, then he and his Ministers are inducted into office by the President, with the blessing of the most senior religious figure: the Patriarch of Athens. Oaths are sworn on the Bible; for Muslim members the Qur'an. The party short-lists and backs the candidates; on selection the deputies, based on their performance at the polls, are listed and chosen according to the party's preferences. Insofar as proportional representation thus disallows the constituencies from choosing directly their own representative, the system can be said to weaken the democratic ideal native to Greece.

The party leader wields great power at every level: he influences his party's lists; if Prime Minister, he selects his ministers; and he selects the new President once the old term of office is completed. This requires a minimum of 180 votes out of 300.

Bills

Much parliamentary business can be done outwith the Assembly itself. A kitchen-cabinet will steer the main policies through. Ministers place their bills before the PM, thence parliament, prior to their enactment as law. Debates are lessened by this means, as is full parliamentary control. (The word *voule* for parliament is cognate with *koivovoulion*, from the root 'to will'; thus the Greek parliament might be said to be a 'willing' forum – the PM's will being predominant – rather than a 'speaking' forum, as is suggested by the French-related '*parly*-ment'.) A frequent criticism is that more debating takes place on television than in parliament. It is claimed that Greece is more a patriarchal society than other European states, a point borne out by the ratio of female to male deputies: the lowest in Europe.

Ministers

The number of Ministers varies according to the Prime Minister's resources and policies. The 1995 government had 52 Ministers, who are responsible for the twenty or so Ministries of State – a variable and disproportionate number: compare, for example, Greek's 52 Ministers to 10.2 million people, with Britain's 31 Ministers to 56 million people. A better proportion obtains with EU representation, which is controlled by EU law. Over-manning, so evident in commerce and other forms of Greek society, is apparent in parliament. Their numbers are controlled by law, but it is a generous law allowing for one Minister per Ministry, plus Deputy Ministers and Ministers without Portfolio, and even Vice-Ministers. It is a mute point whether Greece is better governed for this, though it cannot be said that Greece has been over-governed, i.e. over-regularised; its involvement with the EU is changing that and is a cause for local concern.

In appointing his Ministers the PM tends to discharge various political debts, as all PMs do. He may also discharge the ministers, on nomination to the President. The level of such patronage, an endemic element in Greek society, is high, and goes beyond the exercise of

83

parliamentary procedure. In addition to appointing his Ministers, the PM can also appoint new leaders in the offices of state, in military as well as civil posts. At such times heads roll as if on Bastille Day, as vendettas are pursued and old scores settled. A General Election can be the precursor to general turmoil. This diminishes effective government.

Cabinet Committees

The business of government is publicised in the *Gazette*; new laws must be publicised in it before coming into force. Four statutorily regulated Cabinet Committees are responsible for ensuring that the Cabinet's decisions are implemented:

- **The Government Council** is a five-member body chaired by the PM. It has the overall responsibilities of implementation and co-ordination.

- **The Government Council on Foreign Policy and National Defence** is a nine-member body, chaired by the PM, which oversees public order, intelligence, defence and foreign policy matters. It also appoints the leaders of the armed forces.

- **The High Council for Economic Policy**, a five-member body is also chaired by the PM and is responsible for the co-ordination and implementation of the government's economic plan and agenda. Its decisions are made within the parameters set by the Government Council (above).

- **The Prices and Incomes Committee**, a six-member body, chaired by the Minister of National Economy, adopts and oversees the economic decisions of government, particularly those of Committees one and three above (regarding prices and incomes).

Locally

At the grass-roots level, the implementation of the government's policies are in the hands of the *Nomarchoi*, the heads of the prefectures, who are also government appointees. Their role is dealt with below, as it is an aspect of local government. All elections, General and Local, are held on the same day, successful candidates being mandated for four years.

THE JUDICIARY

Judicial independence is axiomatic to Greece, the courts operating in theory – and usually in practice – wholly independently of ministerial or governmental influence. They are defenders of the Constitution, specifically enjoined not to apply laws whose provisions are contrary to it. They enforce the laws enacted by parliament within the rules of competence which govern their status.

Greek law is divided into seven categories: Constitutional and Administrative, Civil, Commercial, Admiralty and Private Maritime, Labour and Social Insurance, Tax and Investment, Criminal. Moreover, there is a vast area of international law which supplements – and sometimes conflicts with – Greek law and procedure. The most notable aspect of this is EU law. A brief over-view of civil law is given in Chapter 6. But it cannot be too strongly emphasised that the only correct way of attaining your rights and protections in law in Greece is to seek the services of a (recommended) Greek lawyer.

The Constitution enumerates three main types of court: Administrative, Civil and Criminal. Above them is the Council of State, which is an administrative court (introduced in 1928, and based on a French model). It has an advisory role and acts as the Supreme Court of Appeal, though it can also hear important cases of the First Instance. Additionally, the Supreme Special Court, a recent innovation, has the power to nullify Acts of Parliament; it also oversees elections and referenda, along with constitutionality and the interpretation of law in the supreme courts and in international laws (e.g. of the EU).

Administrative Courts

Administrative Courts, with the foregoing exceptions, are either of the First or Second Instance, the latter chiefly for appeals against the decisions of the former. They hear unlawful, unconstitutional and administrative cases, including those concerning statutory instruments, but not Acts of Parliament.

Civil Courts

Civil courts cover all cases of disputes between individuals, bodies corporate, and cases relating to 'non-contentious proceedings' (i.e. personal status or rights). There are three types of court in the Districts, of which there are about 300: those under a Magistrate or Justice of the Peace; One-member; and Three-member courts. The JPs handle agricultural and minor financial proceedings; the others handle the rest, centred on sixty-three prefectures – one of each type to each prefecture. Appeals from the District Courts go to the twelve Courts of Appeal based in the key cities except for appeals from JPs courts, which are heard in Three-member courts. Courts of Appeal are entitled to review aspects of the law as well as the actual findings of the lower courts. Above them is the Supreme Civil Court, based in Athens, usually a five-judge panel or a 'full bench' of up to fifty judges, eleven being its quorum. Its duty is to review aspects of the law, but not findings in particular cases.

Criminal Courts

Criminal courts are sevenfold: Mixed Courts are responsible for the majority of felonies, composed of judges and jurors; Three- and Five-member Courts of Appeal, the former trying the more complex felonies, the latter being a court of Second Instance; Misdemeanor Courts, of One- and Three-members, their competence being distributed according to the gravity of the offences; Petty Violations' Court; and the Juvenile Court. The Supreme Court may be appealed to regarding errors of law from most of these courts.

One last point – even if sentenced to jail, such sentences can be 'redeemed' through a payment scheme calculated on a daily basis. The present rate is for more or less 1500 drachmas per day; sometimes sentences are amalgamated so that one payment may do for both sentences. Such concessions are in the hands of the courts, and cover the less violent crimes.

Greeks and Regulations

'Athenians were fond of litigation and regarded it as a pleasant pastime' commented Athanassios Yiannopoulos in K D Kerameus' and P J Kozyris' excellent *Introduction to Greek Law*. They are so today, along with a very large number of fellow-Greeks. It is another form of their love of opposites: a hatred of over-regulation (for themselves); a demand for its rigorous implementation (for everyone else). The phrase *kata ton nomon!:* 'against the law!' is regularly heard.

Lawyers

The result is one of the largest lawyer-to-population ratios in Europe. In 1994 no less than 17,660 of them registered for tax liability. Their average declared annual earnings were 2.1 million drachmas, which shows that law and justice are not equatable terms. This figure is about 50% of the income declared by medical doctors; even pensioners declared 2.2 million – hence the government's stiff response to tax evaders. Their response was to go on strike!

Lawyers come in three types: attorneys, notaries and marshalls. The former two are fully trained lawyers, graduates from one of the three law schools in Greece (Athens, Thessaloniki or Komotini). They are aided by a specialised staff of law secretaries, who have their own training schools. Marshalls are not fully trained in the law; they act as document-servers and procedure-enforcers, though it is the police who are the chief law enforcers.

There is no discrimination between attorneys in Greece such as there is, for example, in England (i.e. between solicitors and barristers); all attorneys must pass their bar examinations, which follow at least eighteen months of pupillage in a law firm, which entitles them to practice. They tend to be jacks-of-all-trades, specialisation being scarce in Greece – a point intending clients do well to consider *very* carefully. Lawyers working in the higher courts are promoted to them on the basis of experience.

THE ARMED FORCES

Greece's history has created a special need for the most vigilant and careful defence measures – by land, air and sea. As a Balkan state, on the edge of the Muslim world; indeed, with part of its territory actually in that world, it is subject to the movements for which these societies are notorious: instability, political competitiveness, ambition, geographical aggrandisement, and so on. Not least is it subject to the machinations of the great powers – of America, Russia and Europe; and of the independent states of the eastern bloc, Turkey and parts of the Islamic world and their institutions. Its past is littered with political intrigue within and without.

Its defence pillar has to be a strong one, and somewhat secretive – more so than in other states. This is reflected in the budget, in which, in 1991, Defence had the fourth largest spending, below that of Finance; Health, Welfare and Social Insurance; and the Prefectures' Ministries. Its budget is also one of the fastest growing due to the increased instability of the area caused by the collapse of totalitarian socialism, the Gulf War and Turkish aggression. In the five years between 1986 and 1991 its budget almost doubled, from 230.4 billion drachmas to 449.1 billion. These figures exclude the expenditure relating to NATO and SYKEA, and Public Order expenditure – which has more than doubled in the same five year period, from 58.4 to 147.3 billion. A further 17 billion was spent by the Justice Ministry in 1986; 36 billion in 1991.

The armed forces are divided into two parts: internal and external. External defences are secured by the Army, Navy and the Air Force. Conscription still stands in Greece, for all young men (the women's lobby has not yet had its way); this has recently been reduced from 24 to 18 months' service. While not exactly popular, it is accepted by most Greeks who see it as a useful social agent for social discipline and unemployment (presently standing at 28% for young people). I once lived near an inception and basic-training centre, and can only commend the officers and recruits for their excellent behaviour. I never once saw anything approaching the foolishness that is sometimes seen elsewhere (i.e. drunken, loutish behaviour, etc.) and was very impressed at the familial solidarity shown on its Open Days. Indeed, the only incident I saw in five or so years was the arrest of a Japanese tourist who was caught photographing the area, which was forbidden. I got him off by pointing out that he could not read the prohibition signs which were in Greek and English, French and German, but not Japanese. The courtesy with which my intervention was received was in itself a notable aspect, and totally without that officiousness that characterises other institutions. Greeks' ability at 'square-bashing' is not commensurate with good behaviour; perhaps there is a message there.

The Police

The police (*astynomia*) are usually armed in Greece, which is one of the reasons for their following the above section. They do not see their role as a socio-advisory one. With the exception of the Tourist Police, who do advise, they are primarily a law *enforcement* agency – that is the operative word. Theirs is the practice of power in the interests of the state, not the individual; they uphold the law, and brook no discussion as to their activities or manners. They can be rough and tough, and do not seem to have marked interest in preventive action or detection. Said one of their number, when informed of a burglary that cost a friend of mine a large sum of money, on being given the details, 'What do you expect me to do?' When he was told that finding the villain might be useful, he developed aggressive tendencies. They prefer to turn their backs on casual law-breaking, e.g. motoring offences – but woe to the man caught having committed one which has cost life or injured property or persons: a point all the sharper in that Greece has the worst record in Europe on the roads. In the words

89

of a notable *koine* Greek writer of the first century, 'they do not wield the sword in vain.' It is illegal to photograph a police officer. They can also be charming though. I was once given a pillion ride into town by one, who realised that I was going to be late for the Post Office. But it only happened once in six years!

The Tourist Police are a different type of police. It is their job to help and defend tourists (in respect of travel, residence and related matters), oversee hotel classification and the charges set by government, and protect property or persons from wrong-doing, over-exuberance or whatever. If they cannot help, contact the Greek branch of the European Network of Legal Information and Assistance for Tourists (known as EKRIZO; in Athens 330 4444). Next to the Tourist Police, you are likely to meet the Customs Officers and the Port and Traffic Police, whose functions fit their descriptions. At the larger markets you will find Market Police (*agoranomia*) from time to time, usually in pairs, and working with a small table and a set of scales. They are there for customer protection; you can have your purchases weighed and checked by them. Military Police are confined to the personnel of the armed forces. The main policeman (or woman) is a sort of *gendarme*, found at all local police stations, and handling a wide range of duties and affairs. There are also more elusive police officers who handle the major aspects of crime detection, national security, etc. Additionally, there is a body of men who are in charge of boundary and border matters, ensuring that apparently disregarded land is not purloined or misused.

LOCAL GOVERNMENT

Greece is rightly proud of its contributions to the democratic process. Citizenship – its rights and its duties – was at the heart of this, as it is today, though much has changed which reflects historical and social advances.

We discussed briefly government at a national level; it is the lower level of everyday activities that interests most of us though: education and health, sewage and street lighting, even if we take most of these services for granted. One ton of waste per day is produced for every 3.5 million people in Greece, so 3 tons for all – over 300 tons a year. The problem is one of bulk as much as health. The island of Karpathos even has a Festival of Rubbish and Junk; audacious, if not exactly tourist oriented. Local government is bi-focal in Greece: regionally, via the *nomoi* or prefectures (essentially an arm of national government); and at the City or Town Councils, its local expressions. The representatives of the latter are elected at the time of the General Elections, for a four-year term.

As we saw earlier, the Supreme Special Court handles electoral problems at the national level; local problems are handled by the local courts, who have the power of dismissal of anyone found guilty. Any elected official found guilty of a criminal offence is automatically ejected from office.

Nomoi *(Prefectures)*

There are fifty-three *nomoi* in all; they are political entities in their own right. Each is headed by a *nomarchos*: Prefect or Governor, a direct appointee of the government. He is backed by the *Nomos* Council, a group of officials drawn from central and local government officers. The *nomarchos* has enormous power within his area, subject only to the Prime Minister and the courts. In two *nomoi* the government has reserved to itself this power and rules directly – in the Aegean and in northern Greece, both of which are internationally sensitive. Because of its enormous size Athens (which contains 40% of the country's population) is divided into five nomoi; Thessaloniki has two.

Demoi *(Town) and* Koinotetes *(Village Level)*

The Town or Municipal Councils (*demoi*) and the smaller (Village) Communities (*koinotetes*) are the next layer of democracy. The difference between them is one of pure size: demoi are either areas of 10,000 or more people or capitals of *nomoi* or spa-towns; the *koinotetes*

91

have fewer people. The latter can opt for municipality status as long as they can achieve a vote of 75% of the electorate, and underwrite the necessary income. The *demoi* are governed by Councils of about forty-one (but not less than eleven) elected representatives under the direction of the *Demos* committee, a sort of cabinet made up by the Mayor and six councillors; some areas have Deputy Mayors. Their powers should not be under-estimated. I once lived in a *demos* where the mayor sacked the entire police force for 'judicial' murder, doubtless with the say-so of central government but awesome nonetheless.

Demoi enjoy a large independence of operation, though always within the policy-decisions of the government and its *nomarchos*; not least within their budgetary provisions. The *nomarchos* audits all local budgets, and may add expenditure to them. Appeals against his decisions have to go before the Council of State – unless the Minister of the Interior or the Finance Minister intervene and over-rule him. The *demoi* can introduce by-laws within parameters laid down by the government.

Koinotetes have seven to ten members acting under a Chairman, with reduced powers of operation compared to the *demoi*.

—Chapter Five—

THE GREEK ORTHODOX CHURCH

huper pisteos kai patridos: 'for faith and fatherland.'

A PILLAR OF SOCIETY

The Greek Church is one of the great pillars of Greek society. Unlike the others, the Church is not governed by parliament, theoretically at least. Indeed, it is not subject to any democratic processes as we know them. It is above all that, claiming to be directed by God, having its own very distinct ethos, structures and rules; to an extent even its own language.

93

A State Within a State

Its history is somewhat different from that of the nation, for it preserved some of the territory of old Greece – and fought hard to reintroduce it at independence under the term *megali idea*: the Great Idea. Some of its interests remain supra-statal. It is more of a state within a state. Indeed, the peninsula on which Mount Athos, 'the Holy Mountain,' is situated, demonstrates that notably, for it is a republic within the republic. However, 'republic' here is a misnomer. The community of Mount Athos is technically a theocracy; its powers are not derived from the people but from God. Its people are not normal people, but God's. And thanks to the *Avaton* of AD 1060 only half of humanity – the male half – is allowed on its sacred soil. Women are excluded from their borders; even female animals are excluded. It is presently opposing an EU directive concerning the opening up of border controls, anxious to defend its 1000+ year history of absolute control; not least as women are *not* allowed on the peninsula. It could develop into one of those huge, friction-filled episodes that characterise Orthodoxy.

Religion in Daily Life

Is Greek society secular? There are many who think it is; others who would wish it even more religious. To walk only a few paces in Greece is to be confronted by an unmistakable religious awareness: a priest in a 'stove-pipe' hat; a wayside shrine; an ornate, square church; the drift of candle smoke; the odour of incense; the chanting of the service over a loud-speaker; icons of all shapes and sizes – whether suspended from taxi-drivers' mirrors, the entrances to houses or shops, or an entire iconostasis; a monastery perched precariously on a mountainside, and so on. Even the Tourist Board projects this religious aspect: 'Greece, chosen by the Gods' – no matter that the plural is unacceptable to most Greeks, Muslims included. The country is replete with religious activity and religious symbolism. Everyone who reads that captivating book by Sofia Constantinidiou-Partheniadou, *A Travelogue in Greece and a Folklore Calendar* will find it resonant with such, though her biblical citations are often quite incorrect – Greeks are not strong on biblical matters, not even the priests I have talked to. Unlike Jews and Protestants, they are not a people of the Book.

This religious tone in the country is immensely ancient, very simple, and profoundly thought-provoking. It permeates Greek life at every level: in the home, at work, at leisure, in its morality, its politics, its art and literature, the theatre, and so on. It confronts people from birth to death; it very largely dictates their lifestyle – 'from crib to coffin' – and beyond. No other institution does this. Not so many years ago it was even more dominant; one friend was only allowed to have his son baptised by agreeing to the priest's name for his child. Had he refused, all sorts of social – and even economic – problems would have arisen.

A UNIQUE HISTORY

Greeks have a right to be proud of their Church. The apostles walked its ports and towns; saints sanctified its streets; theologians and preachers graced its language; thousands of priestly activities impressed themselves on its customs; millions have followed in loving obedience. Long before 'the pale Galilean' conquered, Greeks had been in thrall to deities and their minions of every type. These deities have left their mark not only in its art and literature, its sculptures and theatre, but in the countryside itself, in the feel of places – the spirit of places, the names of towns, the rhythms of their civic life, and the national festivals. Yet this multiplicity of pagan divinities gave way to a single – and Jewish – God, whom they made their own.

No Guilt

There are two facts basic to the Greek Church's position: One, that it was founded by the apostles and their disciples. Luke, who seems to have played a major part in the nascent church at Philippi and contributed two books to the New Testament, the gospel which bears his name and *Acts*, may have been a Macedonian; he could write beautiful Greek as every theological student knows. Two, that the Greek Church developed out of its own distinct ethos, not out of the Western or Roman traditions as the majority of Churches have. This has led to quite different emphases, e.g. the comparative lack of guilt. Western churches made spiritual capital out of shaming people; Greeks were reluctant to do so; respect for the individual was an essential ethic. Further, the Church has been largely by-passed by the Renaissance, the Reformation, the Counter-Reformation and even the Industrial Revolution.

The New Testament – A Greek Document

When we read its basic document, the New Testament, we read it in the language – Greek – that its early writers themselves spoke and wrote, albeit as a second language. Paul's mother-tongue was 'Hebrew' (i.e. Aramaic); as was that of Jesus himself. The text of parts of the New Testament suggest that they originated with, or are translations from, Aramaic documents. But the New Testament is essentially a Greek document; the gift of the Greek Church. Even today readings from it are in the *koine* Greek of the apostles: we hear their authentic voices through it.

When we examine the Greek Church – its leaders, ordinances, documents and rituals – we feel that we are in touch with the quick of historical Christianity. Of course, its history is idiosyncratic; it has developed its understandings from what the original leaders and documents said and did. Greek eclecticism is identifiable, as we have seen. But we should note that it claims that such developments are integral to them, not extraneous. We should also note that the language and many of the thought-forms of this once new religion were Greek (though Hebraisms abound); that it was a revolutionary outgrowth of the old religion of the Jewish people, whose parallel writings – such as those of Philo of Alexandria, of Josephus, and especially the translation of the 'the Old Testament' (called the

Septuagint) were themselves in Greek, and reliant on those same Hellenistic thought-forms. Nothing is more Greek than the Logos doctrine of John.

The developments in the Orthodox Church are thus to the root what trunk and branches are to the tree: inseparable parts, necessary for its full fruition. That is the strength of the Greek Orthodox Church, a Church which soon found itself dispersed around the world; the spiritual counterpart of the Greek diaspora. This latter concept must not be taken too lightly. 'The people of the diaspora are another Greece,' claimed Vyron Polydorus in the 1996 election, further claiming that its number was equal to that of Greece itself, i.e. ten million, though EBTA claims but 5.3 million.

INCORPORATION OF PAGAN BELIEFS

There is more to the Greek Church than religious awareness. As a proud bearer of the best in Hellenistic culture it has claimed the right to preserve and fashion that inheritance according to its own lights. Claims were frequently made to include unbelieving philosophers as harbingers of and contributors to its theology; for example, the philosophical absolute was often equated by its thinkers with the Christian God – a very different thing from Paul's 'God and father of our Lord Jesus Christ.' The Church has incorporated pagan belief and superstition that are diametrically opposed to its tenets into the Church's practices. Lawson's book, *Modern Greek Folk-lore and Ancient Greek Religion*, detailed much of this over eighty years ago; many have amplified it at both popular and academic levels since.

Take another example: the status and veneration of Mary the mother of Jesus, an outstanding example of how the Mother-Goddess motif of the old pagan world has been incorporated into theology. The very term 'Mother of God' is a self-contradiction if self-existence – an absolute concept of monotheism, based on Exodus 3:6 – has any meaning. Further, it undermines the Oneness of God – as Jewish and Islamic theologians are quick to point out. Early leaders waived these

Apollo's temple at Sounion

objections, fearing the immense power of the Mother-image in the minds of their people around the Fertile Crescent, and admitted it into their creeds despite opposition.

A host of less important borrowings exist at lower levels. For example, the place of Artemis (an important goddess), has been accorded to 'St Artemidos' – changing her gender in the process! Lady Kalo, a minor goddess, became St Kali. The same process transmogrified male deities into saints. Sometimes pagan rites – even animal sacrifices – became part of the Church's functioning, though this latter aspect usually took place in the remoter parts of Greece.

UNDER THE TURKS

Under Turkish subjugation (mid-1400s to the 19th century) the Greek language was banned. During this time the Church was the institution – the pillar, to use our metaphor – which kept the people's hopes alive. It maintained the worship and the teaching of the one true

God against Islamic persecution; it also kept alive other things which it 'moulded' to its own preferences. The language is an example of this, the Church kept alive *koine* Greek, and deliberately opposed attempts to translate the New Testament into the popular 'demotic' Greek. Curiously though, it collaborated in the effort to have it turned into the pseudo-Greek known as *katherevousa*.

The Church was the sole source of education under the Turks; its monks and priests risked much in safeguarding the nation's historical and literary documents. Many churches and monasteries kept clandestine schoolrooms which were in reality revolutionary centres.

Leading the Independence Movement

The Greek Church kept communities together, and played an important role in unifying Greeks at home and abroad. Both were necessary. Until the formation of the *Etairia Philike* (Friendly Brotherhood), a patriotic conspiracy in 1814, there was no co-ordinating mechanism for Greek nationhood. Even its role at first was with the expatriates and from thence with the growing band of hellenophiles who sought to aid the independence movement in Greece. The Church, therefore, from 1453 on, was virtually alone in a task it thought sacred: the liberation of its people. Enormous gains were made by it through its links with other Orthodox Churches, particularly the Russian. It was a fifth-column movement at the heart of the empire. It even promoted some abortive revolutions, such as that of the Orlov brothers in the late eighteenth century.

It was at the Church's monastic base at Kalyvryta, in the Peloponnese, that the actual overthrow of the Ottoman Empire began, when Bishop Germanos raised the Greek flag and led his people, through much bloodshed – not a little of it, priests' blood – to their long awaited victory. Independence was thus won to no small extent by the Church, the saviour of Greece. It is a burden it has happily shouldered in many other matters. It is not a responsibility it will give up lightly.

THE CHURCH AND THE STATE

Despite the close relationship between the political and the religious spheres, Orthodoxy does not adhere to the concept of a State Church. The Greek Church is not 'established,' as are the Anglican or Scottish Presbyterian churches. Public officials are not required to be members, though the President takes an oath affirming trinitarian belief (which is designedly anti-Islamic, of course). There is a distinct separation of powers in Greek society: the kingdom of heaven and the kingdom of men. 'God and Caesar,' to use the biblical language, are served separately. Thus State law is recognised and its obedience is enjoined. The Church cannot interfere with its processes, though it has – and exercises – the right to influence public opinion concerning it. It has been very successful with this in the past; less so today.

Similarly, the State cannot interfere with the laws of the Church – the Canons. This necessarily involves a measure of contradiction, for the laws of the Church regarding the family sometimes contrast sharply with the radical thinking of the modern State. It is hard set against civic marriages, for example. Couples and individuals are often left to sort out this clash of ideologies between themselves. It has a particular effect on mixed marriages, which can be upsetting for newcomers to Greece. Evangelism, understood as proselytism, is forbidden by law in Greece.

The State does play some part in the affairs of the Church, e.g. it pays for its secondary and tertiary levels of education in the schools and colleges. There were twenty-five ecclesiastical schools in Greece with a student population of 1788 and a teaching staff of 147 in 1989/90, when 699 graduated. Only 126 of these belonged to private schools, of whom 53 graduated. The State can also intervene in senior appointments, even dismiss bishops. Great controversy was stirred up recently by this very thing happening to the Bishops of Attica, Larissa and Thessaly who had been instituted during the infamous 'Colonels' regime of 1967-1974. They were subsequently dismissed by Archbishop Serapheim of Athens – to be reinstated by the Council of

State on appeal. The government objected, and commenced legal processes to have them ousted from office, a procedure requiring a Presidential Decree. It led to street brawls and acrimonious slanging matches. More sadly, it divided the Church whose Synod is composed of eighty bishops, about fifty of whom supported their Archbishop while at least fifteen actively worked against him.

SELF-GOVERNMENT

There is only One, True, Holy, Apostolic Church. But there are several Orthodox Churches, all of which are Eastern Churches. They have no difficulty in this multiplicity, nor do they have problems over the alleged need for administrative unity; uniformity is not of its essence. Its proper role is that of the faithful bearer and guardian of the faith – the right, or orthodox faith, which supplies its name. There are four historic, self-governing churches; they are centred on former regional capitals: Constantinople, Alexandria, Antioch and Jerusalem, all headed by Patriarchs. The Patriarch of Constantinople is called the Ecumenical or Universal Patriarch; he has primacy. There are another eleven self-governing churches of more recent date: Russian, Romanian, Greek, Serbian, Bulgarian, Georgian, Polish, Cypriot, Albanian, Czechoslovakian, and Sinaitic (in Egypt). Younger Orthodox Churches also exist – in China, Japan and Finland, but they have not yet received self-governing status. There are also branches in Europe, North and South Africa, and Australia. These are known as 'ecclesiastical provinces'; they hope to acquire self-governing status, but are said to be kept waiting due to alleged unorthodox elements.

STRUCTURE OF THE CHURCH

It is a federalist institution, the executive power being shared by the bishops. But the Patriarchs, Metropolitans and Archbishops (the latter two are more or less regional variations of the former) are pre-eminent. It is the bishop who mediates apostolic succession. In a sense he is the Church; for he is seen as the living embodiment of its

A priest of the Orthodox Church

principles, the manifestation of its life and purposes. He governs the Church, keeps it faithful to the apostolic doctrines, and celebrates its sacraments. Some of these duties he delegates to priests and deacons; by whom he extends his apostolic role. But it is by his authority, and in his name, that they perform their duties.

The Orthodox Church recognises an hierarchical order of sanctity which appears to be linked to function rather than states of grace: laity and priesthood; monks and priests; bishops, patriarchs and martyrs: a pyramidal structure. Monks are 'white martyrs,' as opposed to 'red' ones who have forfeited their lives. The former nevertheless forfeit their natural instincts and ambitions, devoting themselves to God instead. Unlike the monks of Roman Catholicism, they do not indulge in secular activities, but spend their time in prayer and worship, not least in the very long services and prayer routines of the Orthodox Church; a practise that may be starting to change as social awareness deepens.

DOCTRINE

Only bishops may teach authoritatively. They are responsible for the doctrine of the Church and give formal utterance to its precepts. But they are not infallible. Purity of doctrine is propounded and maintained by the Councils of the Church, over which rule the Patriarchs or Metropolitans. Beyond these Councils are the Great Ecumenical Councils of history: two at Nicea, three at Constantinople, and one each at Ephesus and Chalcedon. It is they who defined Orthodoxy. Behind them lies 'the Tradition' – that corpus of living belief that has existed since the time of the apostles and the Councils. 'Right Doctrine' for the Orthodox is not merely the Bible, as with Protestants (interpreted in particular ways, if only they would admit it!); nor the Bible, the Councils and the Thirty-nine Articles, as with the Anglican Churches; and certainly not the Bible, the Councils, and the Encyclicals of the Popes, as with Roman Catholicism. As Bishop Kallistos (aka Timothy Ware) explains in his brilliant book, *The Orthodox Church*, 'It means the books of the Bible; it means the Creed; it means the decrees of the Ecumenical Councils and the writings of the Fathers; it means the Canons, the Service Books, the Holy Icons – in fact, the whole system of doctrine, Church government, worship and art which Orthodoxy has articulated over the ages.' Somewhere J B Priestly speaks of 'tradition, the great hocus-pocus of the British.' Long before the British concocted their hocus-pocus, Greeks had led the way, the Orthodox Church being foremost in its ability to look backwards.

ICONS

It is not an exaggeration to say that some churches are crowded with icons, a key aspect of Orthodoxy; they are of every description – not all of them obviously religious. They are found on walls, windows, doors, pillars, ceilings, and especially on the iconostasis (a partition or screen separating the sanctuary from the nave). Three things need to be emphasised:

- Orthodoxy's rejection of idolatry – the worship of images; it rejects the idea that icons promote or condone it; to venerate is not to idolatrise.

- Icons are drawn and painted to particular stereotypes, a strictly regulated art-form. The reason for this is not artistic but religious: icons are pointers to realities beyond themselves; they are symbols, not the things themselves. Their function is to focus thought on the fact, idea, or person they represent; on the Beyond, not the Here-and-Now; on the numinous, not the phenomenal. Like parables, they teach in pictures.

- Icons derive their justification from the Christian doctrine of the Incarnation which states that God assumed a human nature in the form of Jesus Christ. Because of this astounding event, the rules changed and since then, the divine has become resident in the earthly, the human; matter has been made holy, a vehicle of the divine. It is this, say the Orthodox, which allows the use of images: human (or anthropomorphic) images which *pictorialise* the divine: 'the Word was *made* flesh; the Word *was* God.' Just as words 'paint' a picture of the reality of God and his dealings with men – in the Bible or the creeds – so icons portray those realities by means of their stereotyped imagery. In this the Orthodox do not go as far as Catholics with their statues, which the former believe contravene the Second Commandment against images and their worship and are thus strictly forbidden. Their one-dimensional stereotypes are not equatable with the Catholics multi-dimensional, sculpted figures.

THE SACRAMENTS

Even non-religious Greeks defend their Church. They are proud of its role and happy to see it continued – but not too far. It thus has no official power to challenge the government except by calling for public attention to its actions, and no priest sits in parliament. But in the personal sphere it exerts great pressures, in the home, at school, and at work.

Baptism and Confirmation

The Church's influence starts very early, with the baptism of the child at six months. It is a service of both baptism and confirmation ('chrismation'). The former takes place in the nude, with the infant being immersed in a mixture of oil and water – water sanctified by oil – three times; by a bishop or priest, or in emergency circumstances by a lay person. The chrismation of the child 'seals' the child under the sign of the Cross – on forehead, eyes, mouth, nose, ears, hands, feet and chest. By this the entire child – his intellect, senses, affections and actions are all dedicated and blessed. Thereafter his life is circumscribed by five other sacraments: Eucharist (Communion), Confession, Ordination, Marriage, and the Anointing of the Sick.

Communion

The child's first Communion takes place immediately after its baptism. There are four types of Communion Services: St John Chrysostrom's (the regular one), St Basil the Great's (shorter; ten times per year), St James' (on his Feast-day), and that of the Presanctified [Elements] (a shortened version of the first, in Lent and Holy Week). The usual service is long and intricate, parts of which are private – by priest and deacon; and parts public – the whole church. The central point is an act of transubstantiation, when the bread and wine 'truly, really and substantially' become the body and blood of Christ; a divine mystery. That last aspect is essential, but Orthodox are not enthusiastic to explain the mechanisms of the rite. It is a thing given, to be accepted and believed, not intellectually analysed in its intricacy. It is typical of the Church's attitude towards mystery and the ineffable.

Confession

Confession – the fourth sacrament – is also essential, and takes place in private with the priest, under the seal of the confessional. It is usual for it to take place before communion, though not necessarily at every communion. Repentance is seen as it should be seen, as *metanoia*: a change of *mind*; not an emotional display by which the person is shamed or shames himself. (He may well be ashamed; that is a different matter, for which priestly help is offered).

Ordination

Ordination is not for everyone; it is a divine calling. The number of men presenting themselves for it has been dropping over the years, as also with other denominations. It is effected exclusively by a bishop, with one or more bishops in attendance; it is essential for doing the work of priest or deacon. The training of priests takes place in universities, thence in seminaries. The minor functions of sub-deacon and reader also require ordination. Once ordained, marriage is forbidden, but intending priests can marry; their marriages are fully recognised by the Church. They have to decide early whether to become priests or monks, the latter dedicate themselves to a life of celibacy thereafter. Should a priest's wife die, he may not remarry. No bishop may marry, though some widowed priests have been raised to the office of bishop.

Marriage

Marriage is the sixth sacrament of the Church, which sanctifies and validates the couple's union. The service is in three parts: vowing and the exchange of rings; the betrothal itself; the crowning (which celebrates their state of grace and their joy). Marriage is for life, theoretically indissoluble; its breach implies sin. This is one reason for the low divorce rate in Greece (another is the great strength of the family). But many couples live apart and are left out of the statistics; many wives have been abandoned, often left in great hardship – especially non-Greeks. The law provides safeguards for this, but in practice matters are far from easy. Divorce is possible, a recent innovation, chiefly based on adultery. As is remarriage; a reluctant concession to human weakness. Remarriage at church demands a church-sponsored divorce, subject to its ethical judgments. The service is shorter than the normal one, with penitential prayers being included and the element of joy – so splendid a feature normally – deliberately weakened. Third re-marriages are allowed, but not fourth ones.

Birth-control is not permitted officially. But the Church deliberately refrains from making a public point of it, and most couples practice it. The Church is particularly against mechanical and chemical means. It simply turns its back on a sincere discussion of such matters, leaving couples to formulate their own decisions though there are many spiritual counsellors.

Final Sacraments

The final sacrament is the equivalent of Extreme Unction in the Roman Church but there are important differences. Principally it is a life-avowing act, not one preparatory to death. It is used for the terminally ill as well as the sick. It follows confession as a symbol of forgiveness. In death it is not always possible to hear the voice of triumphant Christianity: the faith of the resurrection is drowned out by the tolling bell, its mournful, hypnotic note carrying far and wide. Fear of death is widespread; an avoided subject.

FUNERALS

Professional mourners are still used in some parts; the spirit of the occasion is a one of consummate grief. After a dolorous service in Church the procession makes its way to the cemetery, led by the priest, the pavements lined with old friends and neighbours in the smaller communities – even amid the howl of incessant traffic. There is no cremation in Greece; it is forbidden by the Orthodox Church despite its presence in Greek literature and history. The body is still regarded as the person, and so its decease is tragic and painful. The internment can be marked by acts of physical violence against themselves by the mourners. But this is diminishing.

It is a mark of familial piety to attend the grave on stated occasions, even to take food there, another throw-back to ancient customs. Some believe that the dead reappear on Maundy Thursday, returning on Ascension Day. After three years the bones of the deceased are dug up – only the rich can afford permanent graves – washed with wine and attended by the prayers of the *papas*, then placed in a container in the charnel house. The reason for this is mainly economic: land is scarce, the cemeteries are always nearly full.

THE CHURCH AND DAILY LIFE

Most of the foregoing activities take place at 'crisis points' in the life of the individual – at the rites of passage. They should not obscure the all-year-round activities of the Church's calendar. Private prayer is inculcated by the Church, but it prefers to keep itself at the centre of the individual's life. One of its manuals actually states, 'Personal prayer is possible only in the context of the community.' All major decisions and functions are geared to the Church: marriage and birth, naming and caring, education, blessing the home and the work-place,

A wayside shrine overlooking the Saronic Bay

new buildings and projects, sickness, guilt and forgiveness, death and disposal. Around town the Greek will cross himself as he passes churches and shrines, as he embarks on a journey or an important project, at the scene of accidents, etc. He is encouraged to do good works. He rarely reads the Bible; that function is taken up by the long services, in which scriptural portions form an important part.

ORTHODOXY VS. ROMAN CATHOLICISM

Beyond the borders of Greece, some of the most important issues concerning the Church are in regards to the unrest that has taken over eastern Europe since the collapse of communism and the recognition of religious freedoms that accompanied it. The Church's relations with Roman Catholicism have faltered since the death of Pope Paul VI. (In fact, less than a dozen meetings took place between the Ecumenical Patriarch and the Pope since 1054.) Pope John Paul II soon lost their confidence, mainly because of his travelling and influence which was seen as proselytising. The much publicised 'Dialogue of Truth' movement of 1980 (towards mutual understanding between the Orthodox Church and Roman Catholic Church) failed to germinate, amid growing concern as to the Pope's motives, his personalised authoritarianism, and his expansionism. He was even denied visiting Patmos on its 2000th anniversary.

THE CHURCH AND WESTERN ORTHODOXY

Another issue is that of 'Western Orthodoxy' – as opposed to normative Orthodoxy; i.e. the westernisation of Orthodoxy under outside influence. Many adherents of the former are converts who see value in their former habits and beliefs and wish to merge them with those of their new commitment. Resistance to change is instinctive with many Orthodox. This debate is bound to continue, as Western Orthodoxy gains in strength. Contrariwise, the spread of Orthodox spirituality has been achieved through purely secular channels, such as publishing.

A SPIRITUAL SANCTUARY

The hospitality of the monasteries is famous, and many offer such to the person seriously in search of a deeper religious awareness. There is no better way of acclimatising oneself to Orthodoxy than through time thoughtfully spent at one of them. Obedience, prayer, meditation, praise, humility, self-denial and service characterise their lives: they are the latter-day spiritual Spartans, who are less afraid of society or its developments but seek to keep spiritual values at the primary level.

Chapter Six

YOU AND THE LAW

Auto antikkeitai pros ton nomon: 'This is contrary to the law.'

AFTER THE TURKS

Newly independent from the Turkish regime in 1832, the Greek nation had to create itself *de nouveau* in nearly every respect, not least in its legislation. It did this by a return to the old regime of the Byzantines, rewording and reclassifying its laws to suit modern conditions, but also making use of French and other models, a process still incomplete at the time of John Capodistrias' assassination in 1831, its chief architect. Following him King Otto had four codes drafted, which rested on French and Bavarian types. (He hailed from Bavaria, had Bavarian advisors, and was guarded by Bavarians.) The

Code dealing with Civil law and procedure stayed in force until 1968; that dealing with the Organisation of Justice continues yet, though thoroughly amended; the Penal Code and the Code of Criminal Procedure lasted until 1951, when they were replaced.

LAWYERS

Recourse to civic and commercial law is initiated by the plaintiff via a lawyer, in common with most countries. It should be said that Greek lawyers, having taken their client's instructions, tend to act without much contact with their clients and even less explanation. They do not see their role as law-counsellors, instructing clients in its labyrinthine ways and guiding them through the processes, but as paid activists who simply get on with it – if the price is right – and in their own time. The most regular comment made to me concerns this feeling of 'being left in the dark.' One senior embassy official told me it cost a good deal of their time in clearing up the resultant anxiety and confusion. The lessons are clear:

- Select your lawyer from the accredited lists of the embassies at home or Athens. They will not accept any responsibility should matters go wrong.

- Ensure that the one you choose offers expertise in your particular problem-area. They will be reluctant to say no to a customer, and even more reluctant to confess to professional inadequacy, but you must secure confirmation of this. Personal recommendation is the safest method – so long as the lawyer in question is not related to the one recommending!

- Small-town or island lawyers are often inhibited through lack of specialised knowledge, and reliance on a network of relationships and friendships (*parea*). In the latest list of lawyers from the British Embassy in Athens only city practitioners offer particular skills – i.e. civic, criminal, maritime, commercial, etc.

- Beware of costs. Be careful not to get involved in matters yielding barren results. The old saw, 'Only fools sue beggars' holds here.

- Instruct your lawyer personally. Ensure that he confirms his understanding of your claim to your satisfaction.

- Follow it up in writing to him, and mail it by recorded delivery.

- Insist that all pertinent statements and documentation are translated professionally if your Greek is not perfect. Keep in touch with the arguments to your best ability, or get a knowledgeable friend to do it for you.

- Keep him at it. Lawyers' diaries are dictated by urgent matters and wealthy clients. Beware of your case being buried by others' interests.

- Insist on receipts for all payments, and keep them.

- Do not expect much help from others once embarked on a lawsuit. Lawyers do not lightly risk interfering in a fellow-professional's case, nor will courts or embassies handle matters outside their prescribed routines.

IF INVOLVED IN CRIMINAL PROCEEDINGS

Should you become involved in criminal law processes – they may be initiated by the police or by 'a civil claimant,' and civil proceedings may be commenced against you at the same time – notice will be served on you by a police officer, who may or may not arrest you. Detention is required only for the most serious offences (felonies), or if the investigating officer fails to complete his work quickly! There is a limit of eighteen months' detention for felonies, nine months for misdemeanours. You may have limiting restrictions placed on you: of movement, place of residence etc.; it is normal for passports to be held during such times. Should you hear that charges are about to be brought against you but not yet laid, it is recommended that you voluntarily present yourself to court with your lawyer, which demonstrates 'gentlemanly bearing.' That will stand you in good stead with the authorities, I am told.

Pre-trial Procedure

There are two stages in a criminal process: pre-trial procedure and the trial itself. Their aim is to discover the truth of the action(s) involved. No public hearing takes place in the former stage; it is a strictly investigative procedure based on two principles: secrecy and written documentation. It commences with a summary investigation, chaired by the investigating officer (a magistrate, or a policeman under the guidance of the Public Prosecutor). The charges are outlined, usually by the PP; witnesses will be examined, expert opinion taken, searches undertaken – of house, boat, car, etc.; submissions made; and records scrupulously kept. In serious cases a judge may chair the proceedings. It is the PP's duty to refer the matter to trial, to ordinary investigation, or to a 'judicial counsel' (in which judges act in secrecy) – or recommend to acquit without trial. Blatant cases may be sent directly to trial, so long as the offence is not serious and the issues are clear.

The Trial

If the motion to move to trial is made, the accused will be informed by the Public Prosecutor of this along with the written documentation. If a civil action is involved, this is advised and a list of witnesses given. This may not be complete from the accused's point of view; no disclosure is required if others are added to it. The accused's presence is essential, except for very minor offences, in which case the accused can be represented by his lawyer. Greek law allows trials in the absence of the accused or 'against persons unknown' (*in rem*). If the accused fails to appear for a misdemeanour he will be tried in his absence; if he fails to appear for a felony, a deferred trial results, almost certainly after his arrest. Following the identification of the parties, the charges are read and a general statement made by the defendant. The witnesses are next examined, then the experts' reports. The formal defence statement follows, then the examination by the Public Prosecutor and/or the judges. The verdict follows. If found guilty the penalty is announced, followed in turn by any civil claim.

Appeals may be made *de novo* – i.e. from First-Instance courts to the Second, which follow the same procedure. Appeals to the Supreme Court are required if an error of law is apparent.

COURTS

Magistrates' Courts are found all over Greece; every town and most communities of any size have them. Courts of First Instance are also broadly distributed. Courts of Appeal are found in the following twelve centres: Athens, Aego, Dodecanese, Thessaloniki, Thrace, Ioannina, Corfu, Crete, Larissa, Nafplio, Patras, Piraeus.

The Minister of Justice is responsible for the efficiency of the legal system, under the PM's and the President's watchful eyes. Criminal and civil aspects are included in his responsibility, as is the organisation and management of all the courts. The Council of State represents the ultimate supervisory body. It is responsible only to parliament, and is outside the jurisdiction of the Minister who can be summoned by it. Beyond this, appeals may be made to the Court of Human Rights at Strasburg.

CONVICTION STATISTICS

Conviction statistics tell us a great deal about Greek society, with the well known lack of crimes that preponderate in Europe and North America. I detail the recent figures of the criminal courts: against the person, 10%; against honour (*philotimia*), 2.4%; against property (a useful but not exclusive index on vandalism), 4.4%; against the community, 10.3%; against other Penal Code law, 1.2%; against market law, 13.6%; against labour protection laws, 6.2%; against motor vehicle laws, 25.1%; against military law, 1.2%; against all other transgressions, 25.6%.

The number of offences in Magistrates' Courts have increased in the last five years by 23.3%; in the Courts of First Instance they have decreased by 17.1%; they have decreased in the Appeals' Courts by 3.3%. Offences in the Administrative Courts have increased by 11.3%, but their appeals have decreased by 4.7%.

THE CIVIL CODE

The Civil Code is a document of the greatest importance to anyone living in Greece and it is well worth obtaining a copy. (Not that self-help in law matters is a wise thing if practised without professional expertise.) It gives an additional insight into the Greek mind and society, as well as your own responsibilities and rights under the law – e.g., of inheritance, property procedures and taxation. It could save you making expensive mistakes. Some EU laws now offer broader rights; e.g. the *EU Citizens' Charter* is very important. Other nations must seek advice from their own Consulates/Embassies as to individual Treaty concessions, which are innumerable.

Unhappily, the Greek Code is only available in English in a translation of considerable laxity and verbal datedness: that of Constantine Taliadoros of 1982: *Greek Civil Code*, a volume of 334 pages, plus a *Supplement.* The Table of Contents appears at the back of the book, in the French manner. Sadly, the index is poorly done, omitting important subjects – such as real estate or property; it requires a fairly detailed knowledge of the Code before it surrenders its secrets! Taliadoros has not bothered to enclose a contents page or an index for the Supplement, whose structure is confusing. An over-view of the Code is given in chapters 4-7 of Kerameus' and Kozyris' excellent *Introduction to Greek Law*, 1988, which I highly commend.

Property Rights

Book Three of the *Civil Code* (Sections 947-1345) deals with 'real rights,' i.e. property rights. The 398 articles of this law (19.6% of the entire code) are the basis of your security as it pertains to property-law in Greece. The EU has recently warned Greece that its failure to bring its property laws into alignment with its own may result in a hefty fine. This needs to be watched, not least if you sell property. There are many laws which cross-reference with each other. Articles of law can never be taken in isolation from the ethos, the whole corpus, within which they are found; nor without reference to their interpretations in the courts. It is advisable to have some knowledge of it but, if caught in a problem, you must see a lawyer and take proper legal advice from him.

The range of the Articles demonstrates the seriousness with which Greeks take property ownership, which is not surprising since this country has the highest level of owner-occupiers in the world, to say nothing of high levels of second-property ownership. (In a survey of 1987/8 it was found that owner-occupiers amounted to 76.8% of the population; only 23.2% lived in rented accommodation. The average number of persons per home was found to be 3.08 – as opposed to the 2.4 'nuclear family').

THE ROLE OF EU LAW

Present changes to the laws of Greece constitute a major revolution in its social history, as does new legislation which pours out of the EU from year to year. This aims to clarify and equalise the rights and

duties of members of the EU, but they sometimes collide with the laws of independent States. Such collisions are neutralised by specific legislation.

We should be in no uncertainty as to the reality of EU law, even if its effects are delayed, legally or otherwise. It imposes responsibilities; but it also offers strong protections. It binds equally its citizens and its Member States; and it takes precedence over the laws of individual nations. Thus the European Court of Justice judgment (in *Costa v Enel*, 1964):

> By contrast with ordinary international treatises, the EEC Treaty has created its own legal system which, on entry into force of the Treaty, became an integral part of the legal systems of the Member States and which the courts are bound to apply.

This wider aspect has been built into the revised Greek Constitution of 1975 in a twofold way: to allow the use of its powers by the EU (Article 28.II), and to restrict the exercise of national sovereignty (Article 28.III).

Moreover, this new legal system has created a new democratic body: a People's Europe. That same court enunciated:

> ... the Community constitutes a new legal order of international law for the benefit of which the States have limited their sovereign rights, albeit within limited fields, and the subjects of which comprise not only Member States, but also their nationals. Independently of the Member States, Community law therefore not only imposes obligations on individuals but is also intended to confer upon them rights that became part of their legal heritage. (Quoted from European Court of Justice, *Van Gend and Loos*, 1963.)

This is very important indeed, one which many returned Greeks, who gave up their Greek citizenship for American, rue. It enhances the rights of EU citizens, which were already high thanks to Greece's noble recognition – built into its Constitution – of the value of the individual (as in, 'the value of the human being, including equality, free development of personality, respect for life and corporal integrity, free movement, legal rights, sanctuary of the home' and so on). This is not to say that the implementation of EU law is immediate, still less that individual officials – such as civil servants in government departments – are not unable to 'reinterpret' it to block its enforcement. They are, and they do. In such cases recourse to the law (or the Press) is sometimes the only way out. The embassies of wronged individuals promise to look into it, but it is not a function that they enjoy: they usually have larger interests which undermine their sense of equality, honour and justice.

Certain member states have sought to speed up the process of Europeanisation by private treaty. For example, in 1985, Germany, France, Holland, Belgium and Luxembourg signed the *Schengen Agreement*, which was designed to remove the frontiers between those countries; a remarkable piece of thinking given the recent conflicts between them. In 1990/1 other nations committed themselves to it: Italy, then Spain and Portugal (Great Britain has so far set its face against this splendid step forward.) In 1992 Greece followed their lead (it was implemented in January 1997), thus providing for 'the free movement of goods and peoples' – key aspects of the Treaty – from the southern Aegean to the English Channel. Non-European nations are observing (and encouraging) this process and, once settled, will move to amend appropriately their own Treaties with Greece. The actual implementation of this Treaty was delayed due to technical requirements, especially the completion of SIS – the Schengen Information System – a computerised network which would make available to member States criminal data, especially that concerning drug-trafficking and illegal immigration.

Beyond the EU safeguards are extra protections: the *European Convention for the Protection of Human Rights and Fundamental Freedoms*, of 1950. Greece formally ratified this before the Colonels'

119

coup; and it ratified the more recent Protocols (numbers 2, 3 ,5 and 7) once it had got rid of the illegal regime, in 1974. It also signed, but has yet to ratify, numbers 6 and 8; 4 is still pending. All these have become part of Greece's own laws, as has the *European Social Charter*, which it ratified in 1961; and the *International Covenant on Economic, Social and Cultural Rights*. The UN's *Covenant on Civil and Political Rights* of 1966 remains unsigned.

Chapter Seven

MOVING AND SETTLING IN

Getting to Greece creates few problems; it is a matter of careful preparation, the choice of good carriers and costings, attention to detail at every point, and a willingness to proceed at the pace dictated by the authorities, a matter now much speeded up by EU regulation.

FOREIGNERS IN GREECE

According to the Ministry of Public Order, there were 225,624 foreigners with residence permits in Greece in 1989, which fell considerably by 1994 due to concerns engendered by the Gulf War, the break-up of Yugoslavia and the declining economy. It excludes the 'returned immigrants' (i.e. Greeks) who refuse to surrender their foreign nationalities; they are mainly Greek-American. British citizens top the list of expatriates (14,812), followed by Germans (9908), Italians (5473) and French (5364). Many people do not apply for residence permits, which is illegal, so these figures are not a true statement.

CHOOSING WHERE TO LIVE

'Where in Greece?' is an even more difficult question than 'Why Greece?' It is advisable to get to know the country well before moving there. It is highly variegated with different locations offering quite different experiences. Why not spend a couple of months simply touring it before making the big decision? Of course, if you are going there for business purposes they will control to a large measure your location. In talking to people recently become resident I have been surprised at their precipitation, as well as their willingness to be (mis)guided by others: a friend's or relative's nonchalant suggestion, a chance encounter. One couple even chanced a pin in the map.

Greece is a very beautiful country, with very different terrains and climates and marked regional differences. It is not simply north or south, sea or mountain, city or countryside. Many of the publications on Greece will help, especially those issued by its Tourist Board. Even better are the experience-centred books of Leigh Fermor and Peter Levi. But nothing can replace personal investigation. By all means choose the region from the literature, but on no account choose your location without having stayed in it for at least a fortnight – and out of season. During this stay you can survey the area from all points of view: climate, land- and sea-scapes, housing types, travel facilities, health-care, neighbours, amusements, education perhaps, and so on. Think to the future as well as the present.

Tales of Woe ...

Every expatriate can recount horror stories. I used to watch an expatriate elderly couple, both stricken with rheumatoid arthritis, struggling up the steep slopes to their home – the result of leaving their choice in the hands of their inconsiderate son-in-law. I watched an obese lady reduced to tears over the sheer hell of climbing vertiginous paths in the summer heat to get to her pretty hillside house. I listened to the interminable moans of another couple who thought they were enterprising in buying several acres of mountainside, only to find that their days were plagued by constant toil and worry over its upkeep and lack of water. I knew a senior bank clerk who all his life had looked forward to retiring to his paradise in Greece. 'I'll live like a king' he boasted. When he got it, he could not handle it – it was too far from town, too lonely, too many planning difficulties, his building supplies failed to turn up, then turned up wrong, there was too little rain, the soil was too thin, the weeds were too rampant; and he loathed snakes. He had spent a small fortune building his castle-in-the-air, only to find that he could not live without the city-life in which he had been nurtured.

Others have complained of getting back to their home country, having first a full days' journey to get to Athens! For those living outside the cities, there was a lack of telephone connections, neighbours who moved their borders, destroyed their trees, stole their produce, who built unauthorised walls – even a house which ruined the view, and so on. Almost everyone has tales of neighbours who are too close, too noisy, too friendly, too presuming, too overbearing, too Greek!

... But Also Joy

Against these there are, of course, many stories of delight: realised ambitions of mini-paradises, climate and health joys, lyrical happiness. They are usually the ones who planned, and re-planned; who twice measured their cloth. One lost the rheumatism that had plagued him for years; others found a new career, new friends and pastimes, were made to feel at home from the start. Perhaps the secret is to preserve a 'pioneering' spirit; not expect too much – nor give too little.

Plan a New Home Carefully

In Greece you do not always get what you pay for. Sometimes you get much more, sometimes much less – which can ruin a well earned retirement. In choosing your place, think winter as well as summer. Can you handle five months of relentless heat? Or two months or more of rain and biting winds? Or being hemmed in on an island by rough seas or unreliable transport? Some places that are full of people between June and October are empty for the rest of the year. I once visited a bay with thirty empty houses – and not a soul living there. Can you enjoy such solitude? Will you be safe in it? If you are person- or culture-oriented, will there be enough pastimes: theatres, cinemas, cafes, museums, libraries and contact-groups to match your needs?

Do take advice from the local people, expatriates as well as Greeks. Be careful of the enthusiasts; sometimes their enthusiasms are intended to cover *their* regrets; your presence may be regarded as essential for their continued well being: subjective advice. You are looking for 'felt value;' what J K Wright called geo-piety – a good feeling for the land and the locality, an attachment to its people. It calls for knowledge of a wide range of traits that must be satisfying to both you and your partner. Can you, for example, live without trees? You may have to if you do not choose your place carefully. You may choose a home with a fabulous sea-view, but can you look on its relentless movements for ever, without wishing for fields or bushes or animals or people? In winter even the ubiquitous goat can disappear, to say nothing of warmth-loving neighbours who all but hibernate after the end of November. The glorious blue of the Aegean is often enough 'the wine-dark sea' of Homeric epithet in winter. 'Just like oil' a Greek friend used to comment ruefully as we sat shivering on the sea wall, the beaches barren of people, the *taverna* closed. Not all Greeks are at their best in winter – and some go curiously haywire in the fierce days of summer. Beware of too facile a 'location pull.' There is more to life than scenery and a temperate climate, wonderful as they can be.

RIGHTS OF EU CITIZENS IN GREECE

Greece is anxious to assert itself as a full member of the EU. This means that many changes now taking place there are geared to its laws and citizenry. Non-EU citizens are still welcomed, especially from the USA and the Pacific basin, but it is advisable that you contact your own embassy for particular details, or your company if you are being transferred to Greece by it – in which case special arrangements may well have been made.

There are two principal rights for EU citizens: the first relates to working in Greece, by job-transfer, finding employment or by setting up your own business; the second relates to residing there, which includes receiving the full range of EU services covered by the treaties. These are dealt with later. It is worthwhile acquainting yourself with these guarantees before you go, especially as the EU Information Centre in Athens keeps few materials in English; rather more in French and German. No one speaks English there: if your Greek is negligible, brush up your French or German.

These treatises offer you the same rights and benefits in Greece as has a Greek citizen, though they may not be so interpreted. Having once left your country you will no longer have recourse to your Member of Parliament or your EU representative, and you will not find your Embassy over-helpful. Courtesy and endless patience are key qualifications for dealing with the bureaucracy; perhaps a good lawyer ultimately. It is only fair to say that some Greeks are very concerned at this injustice, but they are not usually the ones in a position to influence the right people.

These rights cover remuneration and workshop conditions, vocational training, trades' union membership, social security, and health care. Further, you will have the resources of the Greek Employment Agency at your disposal, which is part of the Manpower Organisation (OAED). Greece has obtained certain temporary exemptions from the full implementation of these rights. For example, employment in the civil service is presently restricted to Greeks. Not a few employers interpret the regulations nationalistically, so do not envisage an easy situation; only lower paid jobs are usually available. Work permits are obtained from the Greek Embassy and must be cleared by the Labour Counsellors' Office at the embassy. Failing that you must contact the OAED on arrival.

OBTAINING A RESIDENCE PERMIT

To obtain residence rights you must possess a full passport, valid for at least six months. British, EU or EFTA (European Free Trade Association) passports allow you three months' stay in Greece without further ado; longer stays there require a residence – and possibly an employment – permit. They may be refused if you have a criminal record. Should your passport run out while you are in Greece your embassy will arrange for its renewal, but you may have difficulty in having it counter-signed, and it takes time.

To obtain a residence permit you are required to have a permanent address in Greece, proof of which (e.g., a rental agreement, documents of property purchase or taxation etc.) may be demanded. If you have a special passport or hold diplomatic status you must advise the Greek Embassy in your country before your departure. A medical certificate is also required technically, certifying that you are free of any infectious diseases. The authorities prefer those which have been issued by their own people – a doctor or clinic. (I have yet to meet anyone who fulfilled this requirement, or was asked for it.) If you are taking a relative who is mentally defective or has some other incapacity, you should check their residence rights with the authorities. Legally they are not allowed into Greece, but official certificates and assurances as to their actual capabilities may prove acceptable.

You may be asked to prove adequate means of support – e.g., from employment, pension or investments. The present Greek salary (in mid-1995; the latest figures available) averaged at 120,000 drachmas a month – say £350; yours should not be less than that. Do remember, if you are on an indexed pension that it is indexed to your country's inflation, not Greece's. The latter has now fallen to 5.7% per annum (June 1997 figure), an amazing turn-round since the bad days of less than five years ago; but even that, over a five year period, can wreak havoc with your lifestyle if you are coming from a country with a much lower inflation, such as the 2.5% rate in the UK.

A Greek bank account is essential, and easy to open. There are many to choose from, including several overseas banks; the manager will be glad to advise you. Or you will find the National Bank of Greece in every town of any size, and only too glad to help. It is still essential to keep paperwork involving cash transfers, despite EU authorities claiming otherwise. They are known as 'pink slips,' and are your guarantee of your income and ability to support yourself; they will also support your taxation papers (of which more anon).

Residence permits must be applied for – if you don't acquire them at your home country's Greek Embassy – at the local police station within eight days of arrival, or at the Aliens' Office if you are staying in Athens (see below). Do not be too surprised if you are sent from office to office, or to Piraeus if you live on one of the islands. A philosophical response is best, and a good book to while away queuing time. You will need at least one passport-size photograph of yourself. It is a good idea to get your local photographer to run off several. A fee is charged for the permit, and a receipt given. Be careful to follow the rules; beware of the job's-worth man (or woman). If you are already living in Greece there should be no problem getting the residence permit – so long as your stay was not longer than two years. The permit will be dated from the time of your arrival, not of your application.

THE CUSTOMS AUTHORITIES

The residence permit is essential if you are to obtain a waiver against import duty for your goods and chattels. The Customs Authorities may ask for proof of EU residency over the last five years in addition to this permit (sometimes called a *Certificate of Transfer*), plus the following:

- Your passport(s) covering the past four years, plus those of your spouse and dependants.

- The vehicle registration documents of your car, mobile home, boat or motor-cycle (over 250 cc). These must show that you have been the owner of these vehicles for six months prior to entry into Greece. It is advisable to keep the receipts for them, which are required for VAT confirmation – otherwise you may have to pay it again. The road tax must also be paid.

- Your full driver's licence, covering the last six months.

- Your Inland Revenue Assessments, or their equivalent of the last three years, and your latest equivalent for the self-employed.

- Your last General Rates invoice, with receipt of payment.

- If you are importing a boat its documentation must be up to date. If it is new or over 7.5 m in length it must be reported to Customs; its VAT rating is payable.

Personal goods and chattels, furniture, appropriate appliances, tools and fittings may be imported. Have the invoices and receipts for any new ones, and VAT receipted. It is recommended that you list every item of value £25 or over and have them in chest- or box-numbered order. Careful listing facilitates insurance matters, as well as Customs. Have one copy for yourself (in plastic wallet, with their receipts etc.) and one or two copies for the officials. Ask for them back once they have passed you through; there is no point in advertising your possessions unduly. If you have photographs of the more expensive items, so much the better.

Some items – motor vehicles, electrical goods, silverware or plants can attract particular attention. Ensure that you are not contravening any regulations; your removals' firm should have the latest. If in doubt, ask at the embassies. Plants must be covered by phyto-sanitary certificates affirming that they are free from disease. Animals must have full inoculation and be certified by the MAFF.

Your vet will give you details, but confirm it with the Greek Embassy before leaving.

A lot of bother and delay can be avoided if you arrive with your effects, but this is not possible if using an international carrier. Accompanying you they will probably be waived through; arriving separately they will go through Customs' Clearing House and thence into the removal's distribution centre. Clearance will take time – and possibly more money.

Moving Your Belongings

Ensure that your contract terms are crystal clear. The contract will be covered by the law in your home country and its customer-protection safeguards. Insist on a door-to-door arrangement, with one company being responsible for the entire journey. Involvement with agents, if separately contracted, can be hazardous. You may still be asked for extra payment on receipt, but this you can recover from your company (unless it covers Greek VAT). Always ask for official receipts. It is a good idea to have a portable rubber stamp with you. Greeks love official-looking stamps!

If you only get provision for port-to-port removal real difficulties may arise, with extra payments being added, plus delays. £100 extra is not unusual. You may be required to bargain a bit to get your effects released, but do it in good grace otherwise you may find yourself being given the run-around. An acquaintance foolishly opted for a door-to-port contract, as a Greek friend had promised to hire a lorry and an unloading mate to transfer his goods from the port to his new home. The lorry did not turn up on time; when it came it was too small; having failed to get to the port before closing time the three of them had to take hotel rooms for the night – plus extra for food. Then he was surcharged by the port authorities for one day's extra time to which he foolishly objected; this occasioned more delays and a second night. He still had to pay the extra charges, during which haggle they found some VAT payments were necessary (he had not kept his purchase

House-moving, Greek style

invoices). The unloader then left him, having other matters to attend to; another was eventually found – and paid for. His 'cheap' arrangements proved very expensive. On arrival he found some of his furniture damaged; no one took responsibility, blaming the other parties. I used Bennetts of UK/Athens; in less than seven weeks it was all over, without a single quibble or hitch.

If your premises are not ready to receive your effects, contact the removals' company and ask for their storage costs. Some companies are very helpful in this regard, others less so. It is a problem which should be foreseen at contracting stage. Try not to accept local storage in which your goods may be shunted about – and become known around the community. On entering one such place in Athens a large rat was the first thing I saw. Consider the effects of heat or damp or cold if the delays may be lengthy. Be careful to ensure that there is adequate insurance cover for any such delays.

Double-check everything on unpacking, ensuring that any marks on the boxes or chests have been noted by the removers before they leave; photograph the damage if excessive. A polaroid film is useful for this: immediate availability, and a copy for each party. You will only have a few days to report damage or loss, so attend to it quickly. If you are pressed for a quick signature before examining your effects, sign 'Unseen' to protect yourself. If a problem is solved but not to your satisfaction, sign it 'Without Prejudice' so as to allow your agent or lawyer to take the matter up.

SOME GUIDELINES

Guidelines have been produced by the British Embassy in Athens. Your embassy will have its own list, but the underlying principle will not vary so it may still act as a guide:

- If you fail to get permission to reside, or outstay your period of residency without permission, you may have difficulties in leaving, and may face prosecution.

- If your passport or related documentation differs from the reality you should get official recognition of the change(s) or a new passport, a special visa, or a new driving licence.

- Your passport is legally the property of the British government. You are *not* entitled to offer it as collateral, loan it, or leave it with any other person. It is your responsibility to guard it; its loss must be reported immediately.

- Contact the Embassy or Consulate if it expires; be prepared for delays for its renewal.

- If you do not have full British status, or if your status is in any way qualified (such as a citizen of British Dependent Territories, a British Overseas citizen, or a British Protected subject) serious difficulties may arise. These qualifications subject you to the special controls of the *Immigration Act, 1971,* and limit your entitlements in Europe. You may be refused entry to Greece, or a residency permit. If already in Greece your return to Britain may be difficult. Check before departing.

- If you fly directly to the islands, ensure that your papers are duly validated before going to Athens to collect your possessions. Ensure that your possessions, if sent separately, have prior clearance.

- Charter-flight tickets may have their return portions invalidated by overnight flights elsewhere. This is especially so of visits to Turkey. Be prepared to buy a full one-way fare to get back.

- Technically, inspection of an EU citizen's possessions during their importation into Greece is no longer required. But concerns for criminality (e.g. drug importation) over-ride this. It is unwise to voice opposition; expect it, and co-operate with them.

- Do not expect the Embassy or its Consulates to support residence permit applications. Nor expect it to intervene on your behalf regarding appeals or challenges in the event of your being refused such.

- Motor vehicles registered in EU countries are allowed to circulate freely within member countries for up to six months from the date of entry. Keep your travel documents handy to prove your dates. Vehicles so brought in should be registered in your passport. (This is a problem, as some control-points are not manned.)

- Should you extend your stay, road tax is payable to the Greek authorities – and only for the vehicle owner, his wife or children. After the second six-month stay the vehicle must be taken out of Greece or cleared through a Customs' procedure which requires the payment of VAT and other charges. A daily fine can result if these conditions are not complied with.

- Vehicles so taken out of Greece may not be brought back into Greece within 185 days. 'Voluntary impounding' is offered for those who break this regulation!

- If you sell your vehicle to an EU citizen, Customs must be informed immediately. If the purchaser is a Greek citizen the sale must be supervised by the Directorate for the Supervision and Control of Cars (DIPEA) in Athens; check with it first.

- You no longer require an International Driver's Licence, provided your UK licence is up to date and valid. You also need to have your passport which, in any case, should always be carried – all Greek citizens carry identity papers. Ensure that the details are current.

- Your UK insurance should cover your vehicle while in Greece; the Green Card is no longer a legal requirement in the EU; always carry your documents with you. Extensions to the cover may be sought at the International Insurance Office.

- You may exchange your UK licence for a Greek one without further examination. This has to be done in your first year in Greece and will involve the surrender of your UK licence. You will be required to show your passport; other demands may be made (e.g. a medical test); these extra demands differ according to time and place. Those over 65 years have a mandatory annual test.

- Despite EU agreements, the transfer of capital out of Greece is illegal save with the express permission of the Greek authorities. But this is a fast changing area, so check with the National Bank of Greece in Athens (telephone 01 3201111 or 3202935) or at its local branch. Outward transfers for commercial reasons should be placed through them or a commercial bank. Personal transfers of 10,000 ecus or over should be advised on your arrival in Greece. You may carry out cash to the value of 2000 ecus in any currency without constraint. Cash to the value of 10,000 ecus must be declared at Customs on departure (they will want to know why); you will need to have your tax registration number. Cash above that figure is subject to stringent control, and requires the tax office's certificate proving that you have fully paid your taxes and that this amount was declared by you on entering Greece.

ALIENS' OFFICES:

		Tel.
• Central Athens:	173, Alexandras	641 1746
• Amaroussio:	71, Grammou	802 4788
• Glyfada:	1, Alsous	962 7068
• Piraeus:	37, Iroon Polytechniou	412 4133

—Chapter Eight—

TRANSPORT:
PUBLIC AND PRIVATE

The usual three means of transport are available: land, sea and air. Because of Greece's terrain, the emphasis is different from that of other countries: sea travel is more common, necessarily so with over 150 inhabited islands. Private transport now predominates over public, the latter having been subjected to fluctuating political ideologies, to no one's advantage. On the whole transport is cheap and reliable when compared with the rest of Europe. We look briefly at each of the main types:

SEA TRANSPORT

The Greeks have been engaged in this for over three thousand years; they are very good at it. They have the largest maritime fleet in the world, greater even than that of the Japanese, and still increasing. You may fly into Greece, but it is certain that your possessions will be moved there in a container ship, probably Greek owned. Your travelling between the islands will be by ferry; it is arguably better than flying, though slower. It enables one to get a view of Greece that travelling at 12,000+ feet cannot; and is incomparably more beautiful.

Ticket Negotiations

Ferry-ticket sellers appear to be a law to themselves, but it is not as anarchic as it seems. It is possible to secure reductions, so ask around. Return tickets are not always available, so most journeys involve two lots of negotiation – frustrating for us, but fairer for them, though over-manning and higher prices result. You will usually deal with agents of large shipping companies who have to buy their agencies. Some ferries allow the purchase of tickets on board ship or on embarkation; in such cases there is no question of discounted prices. The hydrofoil companies have their own offices and agencies, as well as using others'.

Sailing Times and Weather

Details of sailings are obtained from the agents, the travel bureaux, tourist offices, and the port police, who post the dates and times outside their offices. The police will also give weather and sea reports, which is useful if you have a queasy stomach. Booking ahead is not usually necessary, save at rush-hour and national festivals or celebrations (such as at Christmas, Easter, Ocki-Day).

Ferries vs. Hydrofoils

There are two forms of sea-travel: the traditional ferries and the hydrofoils. The former depart mainly from Piraeus Harbour; the latter from Zea, a little further round the coast. The former are slower, sometimes less comfortable – and less expensive; the latter are usually the opposite, their staff not necessarily more polite. They project an air of superiority, carry fewer goods and no vehicles. The seating arrangements are not very good either, having too little space for comfort and significantly less for viewing. In the last few years super-hydrofoils have been introduced – very comfortable catamarans which provide greater stability, more space between seats, higher passenger numbers and faster journeys. Hydrofoils are about two and a half times more expensive than traditional ferries on average; the super-hydrofoils offer a first-class service in addition to the usual one, and are about five times more expensive than the ferries. Hydrofoils are at the mercy of the weather, being unable to go out in windy or rough conditions.

Chartering a Boat

Chartering is big business in Greece. Yacht chartering is endemic, well advertised and managed; it all depends on what you want. Everything is available, from 6-metre yawls to multi-hull, multi-masted schooners, with or without skippers and/or crews, for a single day to a whole season (and more). Depth of pocket will dictate your decision.

It is possible to charter a ferry, too, for both industrial and domestic (e.g. house-moving) purposes. I once went on one of these, which was re-supplying an island's fish-farm. In less than a day we moved enough material to extend and stock the unit for the winter, which would have taken a week of lorry movements and enormous human exertion. The Greeks are never more brilliant than when faced with the need to improvise; they do so in laid-back style and great *panache*.

Sailing Courses

A certificate of sailing competence is usually required but if you do not possess one that can be taken care of too – courses run from the beginning of April to December, often catering for non-Greek

137

applicants. If you intend to make extended journeys check the boat's legal competence against the EU directive COM (95)269, which specifies navigational and safety equipment; boats are no better kept than hire-cars or bicycles.

Expansion of Ports

Sea-power is set to increase in Greece, through the ever-enlarging maritime fleet (over 400 ships were bought in 1993). Merely to cite such names as Onassis, Lemos, Niarchos, Livanos and Pateras is to envisage a world of super-magnates, men who built huge fortunes from nothing. The present aggressive expansion of its ports – notably those in the west, at Igoumenitsa ('the western gate of Greece') and Patras; and in those in the east, at Kavala and Alexandroupolis. Additionally, a host of smaller ports such as Palaia Phaleron near Piraeus, or Rhodes have major extensions in planning and under construction. The Greeks are looking towards, and building for decades ahead, when Calais and the Hook of Holland will be joined by major road systems (see below) to their southern counterparts, and northern Europe will be linked more dynamically to the Middle East and North Africa by a land and sea network through Greece.

Expansion of Marinas

Greece recognised long ago that marinas were destined to be one of the major growth-centres of tourism. They were long restricted, however, by economic difficulties. Their expansion, now, thanks to EU funding, is well under way at Agios Nikolaos, Aghia Galina and Hania in Crete, and on Chios, Argestoli, Ikaria, Kos, Poros, Pylarinos, Samos, Skyros and Zakynthos; others, such as those planned for Alexandroupolis, Kephallonia, Halkidia, Galatas, Iraklion, Lesvos, Lyxouri, Patras and Preveza are already completed. We are talking of over two thousand extra berths for yachts and powerboats – extra places for tens of thousands of sea-farers.

The Corinth Canal was completed at the end of the 19th century

The Renewal of Corinth

One stretch of sea-front that is particularly exciting is a long piece of
reclaimed land from the western end of the Corinth Canal (at ancient
Diolkos) to the city of Corinth itself. No one who knows the past glories
of Corinth, savaged by the Romans and many more since, can fail to be
saddened by this long-neglected area, drab in both architecture and in
amenities. But eyes are now focused on the future. Corinth will yet rise
from the ashes of the past to become great again; the bridge between
southern and central Greece, between the old Island of Pelops and the
former Navel of the World, between the Ionian islands and the capital.
It is one of the few cities in Greece linked by road, rail and sea.

ROAD TRAVEL

Greek roads are hazardous displays of power; the product of a lust for
speed and dominance. In a recent survey, one-in-six motorists were

139

found to be over the legal limit for alcohol – one aspect of the 'anarchy' to which the country is prone. The country has about 41,000 km of motorways and good class roadways, the use of which is contested – the word is used advisedly – by 1.9 million cars, 825,000 lorries, 25,000 buses, and 300,000 motor-cycles. Bicycles are seldom evident except by tourists. The distribution of cars to population is of the order of 173:1000, the lowest in Europe, but the roads are more congested than cities elsewhere. There are huge health and related problems as a result.

Greece's roads vary from the nearly sublime to the crudest form of tracks known to man. I have driven at high altitudes over some of these latter, dodging sheep and goats, shepherds and dogs; rock-faces to one side and vertiginous drops to the valleys below on the other; no railings, of course, not even white marker-stones. At one point I found myself actually driving through cloud, to the astonishment of a peasant – sensibly on foot – who appeared out of it like one of Homer's shades.

Needless to say, the roads are in dire need of attention, and are only slowly getting it. They have one or two motorways almost equal to those across northern Europe – e.g. between Patras and east of Athens, and between Athens and Thessaloniki. Others leave much more to be desired – and they contribute to the appalling statistics of road accidents Greeks notch up year by year. Happily the motorways are presently being given the largest programme of modernisation in the history of the nation. It is part of the EU's Delors II package, designed to provide a truly transcontinental system, as mentioned above. The budget to AD 2000 is 400 billion ecus, 220 billion specifically for road-workings.

Corridor 8 – rebuilding a Roman road

The Romans built many roads, one of which was of supreme importance for trade and the control of their empire: the *Via Egnatia*, which ran between the Adriatic and the Black Sea (from Durres, now in Albania, to Constantinople). It covered a length of some 600 km. The EU has decided to rebuild this, most of which will traverse Greece and will have enormous economic potential. It will run between Igoumenitsa and Alexandroupolis; in Eurospeak it is called 'Corridor #8.' It is expected to be completed by the turn of the century, a formidable advance for Greek industry, transportation and tourism. It is bound to have some major demographic effects as more and more firms align themselves along its route – of interest to intending immigrants as well as those who come for investment and business purposes. The States to the north of Greece have reacted sharply to the plan, well understanding the threat to their own through-trade. They have started to plan a parallel road known as the Islamic Highway; a term which should be understood for its *double-entendre*. It will run from Durres to Istanbul via Skopje and Sofia, with a branch serving Varna on the Black Sea.

Taxis

Public transport exists in the form of taxi, bus and tram services. All are good and inexpensive compared with northern Europe. Taxis comprise one of Greece's largest groups of self-employed workers; they are found everywhere, their owners commonly doubling-up in alternative work-forms. As a result, it means that even if you select a residence in outlying areas, you may get into town within minutes. In some areas (e.g. the island of Hydra) motor vehicles are not permitted. Your taxi will then be the four-legged sort, with its driver at your side, whip in one hand and poopa-scooper in the other.

Fare Regulation

Mercedes limousines are one of the commonest vehicles used, though not necessarily this year's model, with a driver who will get you up to date on the latest news; he will expect to have yours too. Taxis are licensed by the government and their fares regulated by it. At high seasons – Christmas and Easter, for example, there are statutory extra charges, and extra charges for large baggage items. It is imperative that you reach an agreement as to price before you start, especially in the tourist season. Milometers are in place, and they should display the costs as your journey progresses, but they are sometimes out of action – sometimes interfered with electronically! If it does not start to work immediately, ask the driver to start it or pull over so you can get out. If there is a problem, take his number and report him to the traffic police. (Telephone 171, anywhere in Greece.)

Use unlicensed cabs at your own risk. Once you are known in the area, favours may be offered: the highest fares are for newcomers and the incautious. Once the drivers gets to know you, you will find them most engaging fellows, full of interest and keen to help. It is not unusual for some of them to give free lifts from time to time: loss-leaders' in a highly competitive trade. It is usual to pick up other passengers if there is room for them, though they should ask you first; this practice can lead to some interesting situations.

An alternative form of transport!

Bus

The bus services are one of Greece's unrecognised assets, though sometimes old-fashioned, even quaint. They visit places that otherwise would remain untouched; the drivers can be extremely friendly, helpful and sometimes very interesting! I am presently trying to trace the former Scottish girl-friend of one of them – his 'great drama of the heart.' He lost contact with her fifteen years ago through an accident and a misunderstanding. So, Fiona, if you're out there still ....

Buses offer long-distance and local journeys, the former often in first-class vehicles, but not always first-class service! I have known some drivers refuse to open up the on-board toilet over long distances – which they have to clean, of course; refreshments are almost never available. They are more reliable than sea-travel in rough weather, and more comfortable; their journey times may be considerably longer due to mountain passes and country roads.

The national bus service (it was privatised under Mitsotakis, but re-nationalised under Papandreou in 1994) goes under the name of K-Tel, and has departure points in all main towns and cities. In Athens there are two official termini for long distances, known as A and B – from 100 Kifissiou and 260 Liossion respectively. But there are others! Of terminal B the official hand-out delightfully says, 'To get there one can catch a bus from Penepistimiou' – without any sugges-tion as to where that might be. The disorderly queues can be a new experience, and once aboard you may well be crushed like the proverbial sardine. You may have to stand as seating accommodation is deliberately limited. But buses are very cheap, strictly controlled by the government, and excellent value compared with elsewhere. Get there early, and hope some semblance of a queue holds together. You will soon develop 'elbow power' – and you will need it: Greek for bus-stop is *stasis*. That was the ancient Greek word for civil strife or insurrection. Your first queue will convince you of its pertinence.

Unlike ferry services buses offer return tickets, and some of these carry financial advantages. In some places it is imperative to buy your tickets before you board your bus, not least in Athens, where you can buy books of ten tickets – which saves time and queuing for tickets. Make sure that you 'validate' them on the bus by electronically stamping them; on-the-spot fines for not doing so are ten times the value of the journey. In the autumn of 1996 the first air-conditioned public bus was introduced in Athens, a harbinger of cleaner travelling air, hopefully. Services to some of the islands – e.g. Kephallonia, Corfu, Lefkadia and Zakynthos – are available, as are ones to northern western Europe and Turkey (the former known as Magic Bus Tours, a gruelling experience, but worth doing – once). They are often carefully timed to meet ferry arrivals and departures – it is truly a national service – but it is wise to check in advance, and allow time for unforeseen events.

TRAMS

Athens wisely never stopped its tram services, which are now being given extra funding for a major expansion to avoid increasing pollution. By 1999 a thirty billion drachmae renewal scheme will be in place. This is being funded by a direct motor-vehicle tax – the 'green tax,' chiefly against leaded petrol. Non-vehicle users will benefit with a service not quite equal to the buses, and ticketed similarly. Thessaloniki is to introduce them too at some point.

THE RAILWAY

Alongside the roads, sometimes literally so, are the railways – plus an underground system between Piraeus and Kifissia via central Athens (now being extended); one for Thessaloniki is also on the planning board. The mainline system, opened in 1916, offers some 2500 km of track, a left-over from better days. It offers a connection with other countries' systems: to the north (for Bulgaria and Turkey), and to the west via Patras (for Italy). The Athens-Corinth-Tripoli line serves the interests of the Peloponnese.

In such adverse terrain it is not surprising that the Greek railway system (OSE) falls behind sea and road travel. It was laid as an internal means of transport but linked to the international system in the north as late as 1916. It is not a comprehensive service, and has few routes. The best for the connoisseur is the rack-and-pinion line between Kalavita and Diakofto in the north of the Peloponnese, which passes enthralling scenery through the Vouraikos Gorge. The circular line runs through the Peloponnese, from Athens to Patras with a southern extension to Kiparissia, thence east via Tripoli, Argos and Corinth. It is an essential route for tourists; all the better in that one can simply sit back and be carried past glorious views, as well as run alongside the busy Athens-Patras road from time to time.

The centre of the system is naturally in Athens, from which it has two outlets: from Larissa station to the north, and from Peloponnisou station to the west. The central and northern line (Athens to Thessaloniki with an intersecting line from Volos to Kalambaka, and from Thessaloniki to Pithio and beyond) goes to Europe, the Balkans and Turkey. It has great commercial value, though some of its rolling-stock has to be seen, and travelled in, to be believed. An extra line on the Athens-Thessaloniki route is presently being planned. This is expected to reduce the journey between the two largest cities in Greece from six to four and a half hours. It will be a high-speed track, with speeds of up to 200 kph. Speed is exchanged for pleasure, however, on most of the system as the trains are often slower than the roads. But they are also cheaper – by about 40% – a not inconsiderable saving if you locate your residence nearby.

Reservations

It is best to reserve a seat, which can be done at the train's starting point. However, you may not benefit from your foresight as many Greeks believe that possession is the whole of the law and are not impressed with bureaucratic interference. There are two classes, first and second, which are more idealistic than real. Fares must be paid in advance; failure to do so merits a 50% surcharge. On the Super-Express (inter-city) lines between Athens and Volos and Thessaloniki and Alexandroupolis, there is a vastly more comfortable arrangement, worth trying. This is certainly quicker than the buses and is air-conditioned, though much more expensive. A sleeper service is offered for the Athens-Thessaloniki route.

Rail Passes and Travel Cards

Eurorail and Inter-Rail passes may be used by Europeans, or Greek Rail-Passes by Americans; reservations must be made. The Greek Freedom Passes are excellent value; there are extra charges if you opt additionally for the Super-Express service. Travel cards for one to five persons are also useful money-savers, as are group tickets (one to ten persons). Family tickets can also be purchased, offering 50% off the normal price. Concessionary passes for the elderly and for students are also offered. Animals may travel providing they are in baskets; there are facilities for car-transports on some routes.

Athens-Piraeus Electric Railway (ISAP)

A key aspect of rail-travel is the Piraeus-Athens metro, called ISAP: Athens-Piraeus Electric Railway. It is by far the best form of transport in the centre in speed terms, though very restricted as to routing. It runs in a meandering southeast/northwest line from Piraeus through the centre of the capital to Kifissia. It is about an hour's journey from start to finish and is excellent value. The same journey by road would take three times that and more. It is not recommended in the rush hours: 08.00–10.30 and 16.00–18.30. During these times it is extremely crowded, and Greeks are not at their best. It can be blighted by beggars and street-traders working it, though sometimes buskers enliven the scene.

Attiko-Metro

A second line has been under way for two or so years, very largely in the hands of a German-Greek combine named Attiko-Metro. Its budget is 520 billion drachmas; it is scheduled to be ready for 1998, but it will not make that date. For one thing it constantly comes across ancient sites, hitherto unrecognised, which occasion delays for good historico-archaeological reasons; at other times flooding, geological and simple manning problems erupt. It is being cut by a 'mouse,' an enormous boring-machine that takes out completely circular sections as it goes. A curious by-product of the operation is to have speeded up Athens' traffic (which has a three-colour zoning system), due to the closure of some thoroughfares.

Thessaloniki, ever competing with Athens, is also to have its own metro service, which will greatly facilitate the very successful trade fairs and exhibitions it holds each year. It will have fourteen stations, which will cover 9.5 km, commencing at the main railway station and running across the city to its boundary.

AIR TRAVEL

This is the fastest and most expensive way of moving about Greece. In good weather, which means eight months of the year, it is incomparable and essential for the businessman; ideal too for those who travel urgently. Inland as well as island and international flights are offered.

Airports

Greece has thirty-six airports, twenty-four of which are public. Athens effectively has three at Hellikon: the Eastern Terminal for international flights (except for Olympic Airways); the Western Terminal for the internal and external flights of Olympic Airways, the national airline; the Charter Terminal, a purely seasonal one. Agencies and Head Offices serve them; there is a good telephone service (969 9466/7) for enquiries. The airport bus service between the terminals to and from the centre is as good as anywhere else on its good days, i.e. traffic permitting, and is remarkably cheap. Another bus service links the terminals with the two main ports, Piraeus and Zea. A new development is that of Plotin Ait and Karakitzos SA to build a private cargo-port near the Eastern Terminal, which will greatly ameliorate goods handling within the EU and further afield.

Athens airport has been subject to much criticism for many years, not least by the Airline Pilots' Association and certain governments, who regard its security provisions as lax. A new international airport is now being constructed at Sparta, east of Athens, near the historical site of Marathon. Additionally, expansion at four other airports is under way: at Corfu, Crete (Iraklion), Rhodes and Thessaloniki. The last is important not only for its second-city status, but for its position as the 'capital of Macedonia,' now a matter of some political importance.

Olympia Airways

Olympia Airways was the brainchild of Aristotle Onassis. It was wrested from him in the name of the national good, and has been in deep financial trouble ever since. Until recently it had a monopoly on internal flights but this is being relinquished under EU law pressures, which will bring great advantages to those living on the islands and in the more distant parts of Greece. It presently offers flights to nine mainland centres and twenty-one islands. Savings of about 25% can be made by flying at night, as well as by last-minute bookings – about 15%.

Charters

Air-chartering is a growing industry. Olympia Aviation offers both aeroplane and helicopter services. It has a large range of aircraft from 18- to 70-seaters. Other charter companies exist (e.g. Mediterranean Aviation, Aegean Aviation, and South East European Airlines – linked to Virgin Airlines); such competition is now opening up airflight more readily.

—Chapter Nine—

PROPERTY:
BUYING AND RENTING

TO BUY OR NOT TO BUY ...

The majority of those who move permanently to Greece purchase their own property; it was a particularly good investment a few years back, but times have changed. Cheap property no longer exists in Greece and bargains are few. That said, Greece alone in the EU shows a surge of more than 66% in net mortgage lending, up by 10% – confirmation of the very high regard Greeks have for owning their own property. Every father here believes it his duty to provide for his children, not least his daughter(s).

Economic convergence with major European states is now the name of the game. It has triggered rising housing costs, that and an understandable desire to realise their land and property values. House purchasing may not be the best way forward for you, especially if you cannot buy your property outright. In late 1996 the average mortgage interest rate in Greece was 19.4% – the highest in the EU. An additional concern regards the disparity between Greek property law and that of the EU, much of which refers to the principles of freedom guaranteed by the legislation – currently 25% of Greece territory is restricted to Greeks 'for national security reasons.'

Rented accommodation is plentiful in Greece; Greeks prefer foreigners as tenants. Excellent bargains exist, advantageous to both parties. Apart from rent remittances, there are no further responsibilities for you; you are protected by law. A number of my friends who bought property now say they wish they had not. I have not met anyone who did not buy who now says he wishes that he had. Additionally, you have the great advantage that if you make a mistake, or your preferences change, the cost of moving is very much less: you simply give due notice and go.

Searching for a Home

Your primary need is to find a flat or house which suits your preferences. (Note, by the way, that Greeks put the street name first, then the house number; not the opposite. Note also that street numbers start nearest the town and work outwards.) List your preferences. In addition to the desired property – location, views, number of rooms, verandahs and/or patios, garden, garage, approach etc. – bear in mind the seasons, the need for extra storage (because of the heat and the insects many Greeks store their carpets during the summer months), visiting relatives etc. Examine your present needs, and those of old age if you are retiring to Greece.

Negotiating is the Name of the Game

Be prepared to spend time searching and in negotiation. The Greeks are shrewd bargainers; they pitch high; they manoeuvre rapidly; they play for time. It is wise to have a second option. Do not smile too often. Be prepared to compromise. Much is said and done *gia ta matia tou kosmou*: for the sake of appearances. A friend told me that he had been waiting to buy a piece of land adjoining his for ten years. I expressed surprise, and urged that he pressure the owner as neither was getting younger. I was told that this was not how things are done. They enjoy the stand-off; they play to see who weakens first: a matter of personal pride (*philotimia*).

Keep in Mind ...

It is essential that you find the right location – judged by its terrain, climate, amenities, transport and cultural requirements. Books will help you, travel and history books in particular, as will holiday memories or friends. But personal visits are a must; preferably at different times of the year. Proximity to the shops – especially a proper supermarket – or to health-care, for example, or a ferry terminal or airport, could be crucial. Is the area hilly? Too hilly for twenty years' time? The 'spirit of place' is important; it takes time to evaluate that.

It is even more important to get the right type of house and garden. Agents can help you, but they seek to satisfy their own interests primarily, and may apply unfair pressure to obtain a result from you. I have known people who have bought property against their better judgement. It is a useful attitude to go into an enquiry as 'merely looking round at this stage.' That dampens the seller's enthusiasm somewhat, and will give you time to think. There are thousands of plots and properties for sale in Greece. Take your time, make the search an adventure: *enjoy* it. Compare differences, watch the people, taste their food, their water, observe the traffic-flow. I am not suggesting that you make a hobby of house-searching, as some do; but the calmer and wider your search, the happier will be its outcome. Your future happiness is at stake. Unknown territory merits caution, but it also entails delights and surprises. The owner of one cottage met me as if I was a visiting royal. I was conducted to the best seat, offered ouzo and *meze*, given the family

Island delights

history, reminded how much the Greeks owed to the British (*sic*) and introduced to his neighbours. Others have yet to reply to my enquiries; perhaps they were using me to gauge the market.

The best way to search, in addition to using agents, is to drive around your preferred area, with map and notebook in hand. Have a camera at the ready, not only to take photographs of the property but of its outlook, views and special features, neighbouring features and properties. Note the particular items of interest, or aspects of particular potential – an arbour or pool site. Look out for overhead cables – a Greek speciality is aerial spaghetti. First impressions are sometimes inspirational; they can also be misleading. *'The wise tailor double checks his measurements before cutting his cloth.'*

Think Long-term

Think summer and winter, off season and on, when the place is full of tourists; in health and in sickness. Your early years are likely to be your most energetic and expensive, but think in the long-term, not forgetting the possibilities of local developments. Look for tell-tale signs of subsidence (pavements and brick lines reveal much) and water movement – winter flash-floods are dangerous and expensive (as are the flash-flood emotions they engender): a cubic metre of water weighs a ton. A compass is a most important piece of equipment for making sure of the orientation of your property: whether the patio faces north, or your bedroom faces east, and so on. Chart the sun's path over your land and property; remember that it can be blisteringly hot in the summer; shelter is all-important. Study the prevailing wind directions; the rectitude (or otherwise) of trees, do they show regular growth? If not, why not? Look for signs of rain and wind erosion, soil and crop damage and water drainage routes, saltwater damage.

Neighbours?

Look at your neighbours' properties and how they are looked after. They can tell you a lot about the locality – about themselves, too. Do they keep goats, chickens or pigs? Is the fencing adequate, what are the border demarcations? Trees and rocks are often used for this, are they clearly marked? Take photographs, preferably with your agent/ lawyer in tow; a camera with a dating device is especially useful. They will be necessary if a dispute arises – border disputes are frequent in Greece.

Greek families spend a lot of time out of doors. Will they be over-looking you? Will their barbecue smoke drift in your direction? Will their washing obscure your views? Do they have lively young children – or even livelier teenagers? – think ghetto-blasters, guitars, motor-bikes. How and where do they park? What hours do your neighbours keep? Greeks love the late hours, and their parties can be noisy. They love loud outdoor music. I once had regularly to listen to a radio over a mile away, thanks to a neighbour's habit of listening to it while in his garden. Cacophony is a Greek word! Are there rights of way across the property? Have you similar rights? Greek law is

very explicit on these things; you may have 'legalised intrusions.'
Ask you lawyer to detail them and their implications.

Fire Hazards?

Is there a fire risk to you from adjacent property, or from trees and
shrubs on your own property too close to your house? Are they under
protection orders? Is there access to your property for fire tenders?
One town I lived in bought a new fire-tender; everyone was proud of
it – until the first fire, when it was discovered that it was too wide to
get through the narrow streets. The owner of the first house that caught
fire had to sit watching his property go up in flames; the firemen sat
with him, loudly commiserating. The Greek fire service is often
voluntary. I tried to help at a neighbour's property on fire, horrified
to see the fire-fighters disgorging their literally knotted hoses; then we
found we had no water: the electricity cables were down and the
pumps were useless. It was eventually put out, so they said: everyone
went home; the fire restarted the next day and caused twice as much
damage. They brought in the airforce, who did a brilliant job. One
needs to take care: one dropped eight tons of water almost on my head.
This is an especially important matter if you live in woodland areas,
tens of thousands of acres have gone up in smoke every year over the
last few years, and not a few properties with them.

The Good Points

The above problems and habits should not be interpreted too negatively.
The Greeks are wonderfully gregarious, hospitable and generous; they
love entertaining and being entertained. Their society is very open, and
communal. They will expect you to make an effort to enter their world,
and will think you above yourself if you do not. Some national holidays,
e.g. Easter, or name-days, are especially important. Be prepared for them
to welcome you with open arms, with spoon-sweets and a drink; and to
turn up unexpectedly. They will ask a host of questions and attempt to
'sus you out;' it is an important encounter on which much depends.

When to Search

Avoid the high season, when people are too busy and places show themselves falsely. A package-tour plus a hired car is very good value in early or late seasons. One couple known to me has been doing this for the past three years, twice a year, spring and late autumn, each time selecting a different place, using different transport modes: car-hire, bus and taxi. They are having the time of their lives! They know what they want, are gradually reshaping it; they are prepared to wait; and they are making many friends in the process. They will never feel that they have decided too hastily – as others have done, and now regret.

A Hands-on Search is the Best

A hands-on arrangement is essential to ensure that your hopes are properly fulfilled. Commented a leading member of the British-Hellenic Chamber of Commerce, 'Don't expect to do business in Greece by telephone; it won't work. You need to get over there and meet regularly with your agents.' The advice is sound whether your business is a multi-million pound set-up or the purchase of a *stremma* or two of land for a house. Agents are necessary but the buck will not stop with them; it will stop with you. Remember the Chinese proverb: 'He who asks a question is a fool for five minutes. He who asks no questions is a fool for life.' I have listened to many heart-break stories from people who did not follow this advice. Do not leave others to do your own job; do not trust others, cynical as it sounds.

Summary for Property Buyers:

- Plan well ahead; five years is not too long.
- Choose your region and your location carefully; research it from every angle and season.
- Outline your preferred property type and all its intended uses.
- Enter your name on as many agents' list as possible; place an order in appropriate newspapers or magazines.

155

- List your additional requirements, internal and external, e.g. an extra bedroom, a shower, pool, greenhouse, garage or plants.

- Determine your budget; separate the costs: visiting and searching, land, house, lawyer's fees, move, alterations, etc. Add at least 15% for contingencies.

- Shop around, widely and slowly, look out for non-advertised properties – chalked signs on posts and rocks are not uncommon.

- Choose your lawyer and architect with care and instruct them precisely; never give them carte blanche (*en leuko*), always retain control of the direction (and costs) of the work.

- Notify your bank as to imminent cash movements so as to avoid delays.

- Inspect properties carefully, preferably on several occasions: e.g. in the daytime and at night, in summer and winter, with and without expert advisors.

- You are choosing your next neighbours, not they you; look and ask.

- Beware of following the crowd; expatriates' ghettoes can be claustrophobic places: the bigger they are, the worse they can become.

- Be involved at all levels of the transaction from price agreement on, insist on translations of all key documents.

- Negotiate from strength, knowing all the facts: when was the property built, who owned it, the changes to it and to the locality.

- Only accept work-estimates after comparative offers have been seen.

- Insist on a time-schedule for completion, add a time-penalty for delays

- Meet with the architect and builder regularly; diary the meetings; be your own progress-chaser.

- Ensure that legal and technical requirements are listed and discharged – i.e. controls and permission procedures (for water and electricity especially), developments and liens etc.

NEGOTIATING

Buildings marked *POLEITAI* (for sale) can offer the best bargains, and give you direct access to the sellers – no agents' fees, no artificial price increases. They usually state a telephone number to contact. If you do not speak Greek, arrange for a Greek-speaking friend to make the opening call for you. (It is better not to let on that he is speaking on behalf of a foreigner – the price may go up.) Beware of people who volunteer to help you; examine their motives. I have had all sorts of people offer me properties: waiters, shop-keepers, teachers, bus and taxi drivers (the latter are a mine of information as to the locality), often total strangers. Many of them were anxious to help and full of goodwill. Some were out to help a friend – and help themselves. They will make the offer irresistible; that is their method. But it may obscure the problems or raise the price; compare them with similar properties. Always confirm their powers to act for the person selling the property before you get down to serious business. Beware of *to meson*: 'the man-in-the-middle,' the string-puller. Such can be immensely useful – and expensive.

In negotiating you may be lucky and deal with a single person or his agent, but you may have to attend a family conference at a local *taverna*, as a friend did, interviewed by each of them in turn, paying for their drinks, and then having to sit back to listen to the vigorous and incomprehensible arguments which followed – for nearly three hours – before a decision was reached. Except it was not reached: future meetings were arranged, more drinks and arguments; eventually he got the land – and then found it was full of legal problems. Patrimonies are taken very seriously, as sacred trusts, in Greece; they will not easily be let go. The owners will be more ready to sell if they like you, if they feel the family property is going to good hands – and if the price is right.

Avoiding Future Legal Problems

Once the price is fixed, your lawyer will need to attend to the various legal requirements – of search and confirmation, irregularities as to planning permissions, liens or penalties, outstanding bills (e.g. for rates and electricity – which become yours on purchase). Check the original plans with the present state of the building. Have any additions or extensions been made? Were they given official permission? Were they validated after their completion? This is not a theoretical matter. It can seriously threaten not only your life, but your bank balance, even your freedom: Several months ago a hotel balcony in one of the islands collapsed, killing one teenager and injuring two more. The police immediately arrested the owner who had only just bought the property, the former owner, the manager and the builder: they were all charged and brought to trial. A British couple built an extra patio onto their house illegally. They got cheap labour to do the basic work, which was on a hillside inclining at about 45°. Inadequate foundations were laid, and no reinforcing materials were built into the walls to support the metal canopy. Their reaction to my observation about its lethality was to bury the slender foundations more deeply. A few months later they put their house on the market. One day it could kill someone. It is a wise move to ask your lawyer specifically to investigate such extensions in writing – before finalising the deal. If he refuses, your happiness may reside elsewhere. Keep a copy of such letters; they will be needed if problems arise.

Final Steps

A deposit of 10% is required to seal any offer, which must be made through your lawyer and be properly receipted. It will be returned should you fail to complete the contract. Ask your lawyer for a professionally translated copy of the deeds. This will add to your expenditure, but it will give you the assurance of being able to verify the details of your land and property and enable you to see something of its history. Some deeds are written in Turkish (especially in Crete and other islands), a leftover from the Ottoman Empire. Few lawyers read Turkish; its translation will avoid presumptions on their part.

Having confirmed the legalities, ask your lawyer to outline any particular rights or responsibilities devolving on you from your owner-ship of the property. Has your neighbour got rights of, say, an overhang-ing balcony, or have you? Rights of access are a thorny problem; they may involve vehicles or livestock or noisy motor-bikes. Water rights may also be involved; as will any over-hanging rock formations which may threaten your property or that of your neighbour. Will your frontage be subject to road widening? Will there be industrial development in the area? Are there rare plants whose handling is restricted? Or trees subjected to preservation orders? If you buy property that has not been built to the legal requirements, there will be difficult problems in store – and expenses. Voice your concerns in writing, so as to ensure that you do not get caught up in unnecessary litigation, or at least have a defence against it.

Alterations to Buildings

If you propose to alter your buildings, full permission from the local authority is essential. Outline your plans and seek advice early, preferably before making your deposit. If you ignore this you only have yourself to blame. You may be ordered to have changes removed or filled in. The latter point refers particularly to the areas between the support 'stilts' on which many Greek houses are built – a reinforcement procedure against earthquake. There have been many cases of these areas being made into ground-floor or basement rooms, an excellent idea on the surface but illegal. Among other aspects it affects the weighting of the foundations on which your house has been built. If you do not obey the demands of the authorities you are liable to be fined – on a daily basis: and they may remove them or fill them in – at your expense. Don't expect them to take too much care while doing of it. Whole houses have been knocked down in recent years because of this failure to observe the regulations; they are known as *aphthereta*.

159

BUILDING YOUR HOUSE

Dream House or Nightmare?

Nothing is more exciting than having a house built or totally refashioned to your own preferences – your dream house. Alas, some dream-houses have proved to be nightmares, occasioning inordinate worry and expense, breakdown in health, loss of investments, even the abandonment of unfinished properties. 'Take care' is the great lesson of those who tried, and of some who are still trying.

Every aspect must be double checked, like the wise tailor his cloth – only more so. It is a slow process and will demand the co-operation of a number of experts and local authority personnel, many broken appointments, dates and deadlines. It is not advisable to do it yourself; find a first-rate agent. If you have real doubts it is better to seek another property which more nearly satisfies your requirements, one that will not subvert your peace of mind or your finances for years to come. I have known some very good people come gravely unstuck.

A house in the making

Choosing an Architect

Use an architect skilled in Greek ways, who knows the regulations, who can talk to the local people from years of contact with them, who knows what can be expected from workmen and their materials. Unless you know exactly what you are doing, and understand enough Greek to argue with tradesmen and local authority experts, get him to act as your clerk of works. If you do employ your own tradesmen it is worth bearing in mind the specific enactments (under the title 'Contracts for Work,' articles 681-702) of the Civil Code which govern this. Substitution, for example, is illegal: i.e. the replacing of the contractee by another workman. There are many other such details for your protection. In the event of things going wrong without an architect's supervision it could be several times more expensive than his charges, and will incur legal fees and bad odour socially.

The architect must understand your exact specifications, and be aware of how important the time-schedule is to you. A Greek's *avrio* is no better than a Spaniard's *mañana*. One of their favourite exclamations is *agalia-agalia*: 'slowly-slowly.' (They do have its opposite, of somewhat rarer usage: *am epos, am ergov*: 'no sooner said than done;' as they have the equivalent to our 'better late than never': *kallio arga para pote*.) If the timing is interrupted, supply him with a revised schedule, in writing, to make the point. Ensure that his English is really up to it; many Greeks skate by on sparse English – we have no rights to grumble about this! – but it can be costly. He will not be too keen to admit that he does not always understand; labour your points if necessary – as I am doing here. Double-check the plans before submission to the authorities. Advise him of any queries or second thoughts – in writing. This is not the Greek way; verbal communication is the norm; but it is better to ruffle his feathers now than have your own ruffled by huge extra costs later.

Mistakes are easy. I have known architects whose good faith is beyond question still get into trouble. Others make a practice of taking short cuts: their problems are still ongoing through the courts. You

161

will pay for his knowledge, of course. It has been gained after many years of study and experience; but it will be incomparably cheaper than falling foul of the authorities, of having to have part of your dream demolished; of risking the non-supply of water, electricity and the telephone because the right certificates of completion are unavailable. Rectification is far more expensive than the original job, as will be fines imposed by local authorities.

Planning for Earthquakes

Building in Greece poses particular problems. Most of the land is based on rock, with very little subsoil. Blasting is sometimes the only way to clear adequately some sites; that requires expert handling. It can also be very expensive: labour costs have been rising at the rate of +12% p.a. during 1996. Much of Greece is built on hills, with particular wind and water patterns, and structural stresses to match. Conservation requirements are now a very important feature of planning requirements. The country is situated in a region of high seismicity, which is expected to increase over the next few decades. This is especially so in the eastern Aegean islands, in the area just to the north of Crete, and that below the Halkidiki peninsula. Earthquakes will be a regular threat, needing constant watchfulness. Surprises are bound to take place even in these well charted areas.

Emergency plans exist for earthquakes, with back-up contingencies, but forecasting is extremely difficult. Professor Panayiotis Varotsos of Athens, and his colleagues Drs Alexandropoulos and Nomicos, have invented a 'Richter predictor,' otherwise known as VAN. It promises to add more security to our lives but obtrudes another element into nature: the miles of wires and thousands of electrodes that are now being buried throughout Greece to pick up pre-seismic bursts of electricity that formerly only animals and birds felt. Happily though, most of the epicentres are situated at sea.

One of the key aspects of Greek planning and building regulations is to ensure that extra-strong foundations, pillars and walls are built to withstand the shocks. I am told that a factor of 6 (strength to risk) is employed; denial of which is criminal folly. The wisdom of the ancients in these matters is worth keeping in mind: curved or arched lines have been used in the area since Minoan times; they are stronger than straight ones. The beauty and longevity of the Parthenon owes much to this concept.

Costs

Your costs will depend on many things: extent and cost of land, road alteration potential, type and size of the house, the materials used for its construction, its finishings. Cartage costs may affect the supply of materials to your sites, as may the importation of expert labour: cliff and ridge tops are wonderful, as are island sites, but building there (even if planning permission is available) can be extremely difficult, and very expensive. Add to this the cost of your architect. An hour's work may cost you a whole day's remuneration thanks to the distances; more if your property is well off beaten tracks. The supply of services (water, electricity, telephone) may be horrendously expensive, or out of the question. Builders cannot work without the first two, and the absence of the third will be a real vexation.

Site-plans

Before he prepares his site-plan, ensure that your architect knows precisely your views as to house-orientation, door and window situating, and paths and garden plans. Arrange them with him well ahead, not excluding private vehicular access: yours and the builders. Ask where the power and telephone cables are to go; many a stunning view has been ruined by unthoughtfulness. Prior planning, even underground siting – which is very expensive – will obviate such distress. The authorities in these matters have a statutory right of way, which may neutralise your plans – another point worth raising, though the replies are certain to be guarded. You may wish to have a gardening consultant work for you at this stage. Orientation is critically important, not only to attain the best views, but to maximise your use of the natural elements.

Taking Nature into Account

Placed correctly, the sun can work wonders for heating requirements. There are 300 days of sunshine in Greece on average. Be careful not to under-estimate the sun's power. A south-facing lounge or patio may well be impossibly hot between June and August; just as its north facing counterpart may be too cold in December through to February. Correct siting will protect your house and garden from the worst weathering – of sun, wind and rain. Note the orientation of neighbouring houses, look at their trees and vegetation, not only what grows but how it grows. Beware of wind-tunnels, the effect of hills, tree-lines and buildings. Some of these problems can be remedied by careful planting (see Chapter 15).

Watching for Details

The architect will suggest the number of rooms, their type and situation within the over-all expenditure plan; he will expect your input. If your ideas are meagre, books and recent PC software applications permit detailed personal adaptations of house and garden, as do various modular dwellings that can be bought 'off the hook.' Finishings are especially important, and Greece has many very beautiful materials and designs to choose from, marble and stone not least. Its shortage of good wood, however, is a problem. Spend time on this. Careful selection and buying can make enormous differences to the whole job; your sense of taste will be judged by the result.

Watch the siting of power points, lighting sockets and water taps. Sit down with the plans, envisage the use of the rooms, and think of their maximum requirements. Better to have too many than too few; and better to build them in now than later. External applications of electricity or water may be vital; ensure that you have enough to cope with all your needs – lighting and power for the garden, garage and pool; water taps on all sides – and drainage. If you are lucky enough to have your own well, ensure that the pumping house is away from the house to eliminate noise, and on the highest ground available for good pressure.

Do not minimise your storage needs. If you are at a distance from the main centres and supermarkets you will need to buy in bulk. Quite apart from additional freezer, olive oil and wine storage space, wet and dry areas should be planned. Car and gardening tools and commodities also take space, not least bulbs and plants lifted for over-wintering. Seasonal changes require the movement of coverings and furniture, quite apart from seldom used items, guest requirements, and so on. Think of seasonal visitors: insects and small animals will want to move inside with you for the winter months; they can cause enormous damage to edible matter – and matter not usually thought edible. A friend lost many yards of reinforced hosing gnawed through by something unknown. If space is limited, it may be useful to have built-in furniture, beds with underneath storage and cupboards to ceiling level.

The Garden

In the garden area, specify to the architect which trees are not to be touched; if some are to be felled, ensure that their wood is retained for your use. Good olive wood makes lovely furniture and fittings once dried and seasoned; poorer wood will supply your barbecues or indoor fires. Mark their trunks with visible paint, even fence them off so that bull-dozer and lorries do not damage them. Or transplant them. Foundations are dug by mini bull-dozers which require turning-areas and space for the collection of unwanted earth, rock and builders' debris. Delineate the safe areas and ensure that they keep to them. Happily, olive trees are astonishingly resistant to all manner of abuse, but it is better not to tempt fate.

Soil compacting by the builders may be a problem; control and reduce site movements where possible. In particular, have the builders pile stones and rocks conveniently for your dry-stone wall or terrace. It is not a bad idea to import soil and even worms early, which should be well out of the way of things, not least of wind and workmen.

Plant ahead, so that you will have a ready-made garden to enjoy on the completion of your house. Since all plants are at risk at this stage, plant them in tubs placed well out of harm's way.

Other Areas

Remember to plan adequate space for your garage and patio, barbecue and drying areas, as well as ones for composting. Most rural houses in Greece are not linked to an external sewage system; they depend on their own cesspits which have to be situated at given distances from the house, and be given access for emptying. (This is why toilet paper and other requisites may not be flushed down the loo: they block up the cesspits.) Siting the solar-panels is also important; you may have to have them free-standing.

Permits and Utilities

Once the building permit is granted (its criteria are laid down in the *General Building Code* of 1985), and initial bills paid according to agreed stages of development, you will be given a permit number which must be affixed to the front of your property to denote that the work has been approved – and to facilitate police check-ups. The electricity supply people will arrange a temporary supply, as will the water people; each supply being separately metered, the costs for which come down to you. Each stage will be checked by the architect and the planning authority, with the builder in tow, and then paid for. It is not a bad idea to have some beer, coffee or brandy and a little *meze* for these inspections. It is thirsty work, this checking; a little lubrication aids matters. Any deviation from the permitted plan will delay the job; unauthorised work will have to be replaced, and fines may be imposed. The permanent supply of water and electricity and the connection of the telephone, rests on the full implementation and validation of the plans. Be very wary of late suggestions, especially of tradesmen who want to do you a favour, which will 'only cost you so-and-so;' such are almost always illegal, incurring delays and costs well above their worth. If you do take risks, do not expect much sympathy.

Expect Delays

Greek society is still very much linked to pre-industrial revolution notions and practices, e.g. the division of labour: the baker does his thing, the leather-worker his, the butcher his, the carpenter his, and so on. Your building will advance according to these time-honoured divisions: foundation-digger, steel reinforcer, pipe layer, cement pourer, general and specialist suppliers, brickies, electricians, carpenters, plumbers, plasterers, tilers, painters, floormen, roofmen – to name but a few. All this takes co-ordination, and Greeks are not known to excel at that. Expect delays. They may not happen if you have managed to get a time-penalty clause in your contract, but even if you have, expect arguments over acts of God, men, weather, unforeseen circumstances etc. Be patient – and understanding. Culture shock is never so intimidating as at such times. It may well be true that someone's suppliers have let him down. One man I knew kept a friend waiting over three months for his supply of paint from forty miles away. Supplies may have dried up at factory level, the manufacturer may have gone out of business; also ferries get cancelled – and lose goods in transit. As Malcolm Bradbury opined, this is the age when the predominant emotion is one of puzzled frustration.

Greeks build their houses as they used to build their triremes: from outside in, from shell to finished unit. The foundations describe the maximum area of development, in size and weighting loads; once completed it is very expensive to re-work them, and may be impossible. In any case further deep work too close to them may have an unsettling effect, especially if not based on rock. If based on rock, blasting may be necessary, with even greater risks. Internal walls do not usually have a load-bearing function: the essential structure of the house will have been made long before – sometimes years before – the walls are completed. Structures are usually made of poured concrete, reinforced with steel, at which Greek builders are very good. This means that walls and windows, doors and some stairways may be re-situated. But take professional advice on this and get full planning consent before the work is done.

It is not a bad idea to leave fencing or walling until last (apart from security needs), as these are easily damaged during building opera-tions. In any case the final clearing up (which is not done by the builder, nor included in his estimates unless you order it particularly) may require a mini bull-dozer. You may be offered landscaping with the latter. Be very careful as to its meaning and cost, and his ability to do it. Ask to see his handiwork elsewhere. Walls are better than fences as they offer greater security and protection, but they are more expensive. If you opt for them, ensure that their foundations are adequate; that provision for drainage *through* them is made if on a hillside. Public liability will be yours in the event of their collapse. Proximity of the buildings to walls and highways, skyline controls, as well as house-to-land ratios, must be adhered to.

RENTED ACCOMMODATION

The search procedures are more or less the same for renting as for buying property – with the obvious differences non-ownership implies. It is rather more difficult to secure as agencies and advertisements for rented property tend to be thin on the ground. Put the word round your friends and acquaintances. Some travel agents in Greece who let holiday and short-term property in season may be helpful. Be careful to insist on residential property, not holiday. The former is usually better provided, with furniture and fittings, garden and other facilities.

A rental agreement must be drawn up, and translated profession-ally for you if you do not speak Greek. You should get a lawyer to talk you through its terms, clarifying your rights and duties under contract. Printed rental agreements are available at kiosks or stationers. They are standard documents, their terms being the minimum required by the government. Ensure that the rent is payable monthly, and based on an annual (or longer or shorter) basis according to your needs, without seasonal fluctuation. Watch for the ancillaries, especially service charges for the lobby or stairs, electricity and water and other fuel costs and supplies, postal arrangements, security, telephone (if available), garden, fuel storage etc. Insist on having your own meters for water and electricity; shared meters give rise to trouble.

Rents must be clearly stated. They are presently controlled by the government, but you need to see what they include, as well as when they are subject to increase. Watch for matters relating to your personal and possessions' insurance, and keep your receipts. The Post Office and the banks offer payment transfer services, with proper receipting facilities; use them if the remittance of your rent looks like being difficult.

Rooms to Let

Chapter Ten

FOOD AND DRINK

Trogei choris na akoumpa sto trapezi: 'he eats without leaning on the table.'

Food and drink are important in Greece, too important to leave to the experts; though they also accept that there is no accounting for taste: *peri orezeos oudeis ho logos* (or as the French say: *chaqu' un à son goût*). The high proportion of the family budget spent on food compared with other Europeans demonstrates this; food, drink and tobacco account for well over 35% of it.

Every housewife, and not a few husbands, can put their hands to turning out a splendid meal; and they frequently do – though it is still 'women's work' by tradition. Greeks discuss their food, its characteristics and its ingredients learnedly, comparing the sources of meat and fish, vegetables and fruit, their partiality to certain herbs (fewer spices), discriminating even over the quality and taste of the water. Paramount is the concept of *tes horas*: 'the hour or season,' i.e. its freshness; the phrase also describes food cooked on the grill – a venerable tradition. French gastronomic superiority is accepted; but they are not daunted by it and few would want to change for it. They believe theirs is better, and health statistics prove it: 'Greek is best – and Cretan is better,' a matter now of scientific fact. Even as this goes to print, European Commission experts are preparing a 'dietary blueprint' based on Cretan food habits, which will be circulated to all General Practitioners in the EU. Its principal component is 'virgin olive oil.'

AN ANCIENT CUISINE

One of the great successes of recent years has been a resurgence of historic dishes, drawn (if slightly changed) from the old recipe books, and enlivened by the feasts they celebrated.

> We may live without poetry, music or art;
> We may live without conscience, or live without heart;
> We may live without friends, we may live without books,
> But civilised men cannot live without cooks.

So wrote Athenaeus, in the *Supper-Connoisseurs: Deipnosophistai*, one of the oldest books on the art of food (c. AD 175). We may wish to dispute some of his comments, but we have him to thank for preserving some of the best food traditions of the classical age. Archestratos of Gela (c. 325 BC), a poet and therefore a man geared to the peripatetic life, toured the world in search of recipes and food customs. His resultant book, *Voluptuousness*, was translated into

171

Latin under the title *Hedipathetica* by Quintus Ennius (the father of Latin literature), from which it made its way into French and North European culture. As with so many things, the Greeks did it first.

But Greek table interests were and are about more than food. Generally they take a relaxed view of manners *per se*, though the quotation at the head of this chapter suggests otherwise. It has always been a time to enjoy serious talk on big subjects. This brought about the symposia – Plato's *Symposium* is the best known of what came to be called symposium literature – with the main talk following the meal, as did the wine. These ancient meals were drinking parties really, preceded by food and geared to chosen subjects; typified by one as 'the feast of reason and the flow of the soul.' The eastern practice of reclining was introduced at them – a good example of new concepts affecting *mores*, thence house-building and architecture, for dining rooms began to change shape.

The wine and water were mixed – only wine mixed in a particular way was drunk at these functions. Some held that a little wine could be drunk earlier, but never without food, and rarely with the first course. Revelry had its place, as did poetry and song (not then separated of course), music and dancing. Long before this, Greek verse had recorded the delights of *koinonia*, manly fellowship, as we may see from such books as Homer's, Hesiod's, or Pindar. The love-feast (*agape*) was very similar. The Christian Church took over this tradition in its central act of communion, not just with the divine but with each other; a practice that typically deteriorated under ecclesiastical convention and control.

Long gone are the days when a great hellenophile and an archaeologist of repute in Egypt and Greece could describe Greece's cuisine as 'a world of hard-boiled eggs and hacked meat;' more recently another hellenophile (quoting a young Greek sailor) could remark that, 'the Greeks can do nothing without a tomato.' John Pendlebury and Peter Levi, whose words I have just used, both lived in Greece during its days of hardship – Pendlebury before the Second

World War (giving his life for Greece in it), and Levi after it – when the population was literally starving, still trying to climb out of the devastations of five hundred years of servitude, the people-movements, and the military and civil unrests that followed.

A reputation for poor food dies slowly. We should be under no delusions as to its unfairness – a quirk of history, the fruit of other nations' plundering and slander. Homer is to many Greeks what the Bible used to be to many Britons – their guide for life as well its supreme expression. Consider the 'various kinds' of food and drink the divine Calypso set before Odysseus in the *Odyssey* – including ambrosia, nectar and the goddess's 'dainties.' Or consider the food served daily at his own palace: the big sheep, the fatted goats, the pigs and heifers; a regal meal with delicacies of offal as well as the best cuts of meat, and bread and wine. The Greeks had haggis long before the Scots; even as they had their bard. Similarly, they had sausage long before the Germans made of it a national dish – even if, according to one wag, it was made of dog and monkey meat. Plato condemned 'unnecessary pleasures,' i.e. delicate and luxurious dishes, which he believed weakened democracy. But to do so presupposes a surfeit of such things. He recommended properly prepared food, i.e. 'simple food with condiments.' When asked if the latter were really necessary, his reply was vigorous and affirmative: 'Certainly' – so long as they were necessary for health.

This is a people who discriminated between different waters as a vintner might discriminate between wines; who distinguished good olive oil from poor, sporelio from *agourolado*; who could locate the type and provenance of different salts by their colour and mineral content; who could even argue about the difference a twelfth part of a coriander seed makes to lentil soup; who had thirty reputed ways of making coffee. I am not saying that all Greeks so live, of course. Nor that very much has not been lost in the savagery of wars and slavery. But they have not entirely lost their discriminating ways and their cultural predilections. A farmer of Askra in Boeotia once commented:

> I love a shady rock, and Bibline wine.
> A cake of cheese, and goat's milk, and some meat
> Of heifer, pastured in the woods, uncalved.
> Or first-born kids ...
>
> —Hesiod, *Works and Days*

Its simplicity is pure Greek. Even if it omits the pleasure of wholesome bread, of olive oil and succulent olives, it conveys magically the finesse of Greek taste, which is slowly being re-discovered after centuries of servitude, after the rape of their land, the destruction of their herds and flocks, vineyards and olive groves; the loss of very much genuine expertise as its leaders were slaughtered or led away into captivity. Sadly, the plunder is ongoing – in the name of the fast food take-aways. The French were glad to serve a *maçedoine* (the very name is Greek, at least Macedonian) of vegetables or fruit; they have borrowed very much more from their eastern benefactors.

GREEK CUISINE TODAY

Markets

To understand Greek cuisine one needs to visit large central markets, such as the one in Athinas Street near Omonia Square, Athens. This market, dissected by the street dedicated to the goddess Athene herself, is the place to see food of every type and description. It is now being rebuilt on modern lines, but still reflects something of the excitement, the odours, even the bloodiness of a rural market. Here you will encounter a riot of colour, shapes, fragrances – and noise; from white bait to sword-fish, from quails to turkey, from snails to huge sides of beef; plus vegetables, fruit, pasta, rice, nuts and herbs of every description. To watch what those intrepid housewives purchase – or their husbands, for Greek men do not consider shopping beneath them; indeed, they often arrogate to themselves its responsibilities – and to watch *how* they purchase it, is to understand their relationship with food. They scrutinise, handle and smell the

Greeks prefer fresh, local produce

produce; choosing and matching it with care; they note signs of age or bruising; they argue with the stall-holders over price, and reject the uncomely. They know their wants, their cuts, the items which will best accompany them; they will keep searching until they have found these, at a price affordable by them.

Eat Fresh and Local

There are four principles relating to the eating and enjoyment of food abroad: eat local, eat in season, eat carefully, and give it time. The first two are in line exactly with the Greeks' own habits of freshness. Even today, with the advantages of refrigeration and modern transportation, they prefer to eat locally, i.e. what is produced locally. It is for this reason that their regional food is so varied and interesting. The micro-climates of Greece's regions produce quite different foods and eating habits. They have always sought self-sufficiency, and their genius for improvisation has enabled them to produce economic, tasty and adventurous dishes. For this reason much of their food, and not a little of their wine, is quite unknown: it is consumed before it reaches the wider markets; they are content with this.

It is a wise rule to follow suit; they will be delighted to see you thus respecting the sweat of their brows and the ingenuity of their minds. They will be offended if you do not. It is even wiser, and certainly more economic, to eat in season. Those who go for unseasonable choices pay through the nose for their wants; their table will not be respected; rather it will be held in suspicion. To buy in season is to buy fresh, and therefore to buy well and to eat well. Fresh produce looks better, smells better, tastes better and is healthier. Vitamins in food, for example, decline with ageing. It is true, of course, that the seasons are tending – even in Greece – to merge. Modern farming methods and fast distribution are making big changes; and the Greeks are being pressed into competitiveness as members of the EU. But the average Greek is not impressed by having his tomatoes of one shape, size and standard if the taste is below his expectations. His wife takes pride in selecting her vegetables and meat and fish, and preparing them in a way which highlights taste and enjoyment. The restaurateur is not concerned that the vegetables he places before you lack geometrical symmetry. The daily collection of bread is still crucial. The knowing spurn the quick-food standards of others for the inferiority they offer.

Food Produced in Greece

A brief look at what food Greece is self-sufficient in underlines the point: wheat, rye, maize, very nearly all its potatoes, veal and poultry; all its vegetables and fruit, save for the exotic. In surplus (and exported) are some fundamentals, such as the aforementioned, plus citrus fruit, white sugar and wine. It has to import oats, cheese, butter, beef and pork, plus many of the 'extras' foreigners insist on – many of which are doubtful food items, directly responsible for disease and early deterioration. We feel sorry for the tobacco addicts; all too often we are similarly trapped ourselves – by food indiscretion. Wine is cheaper; its moderate daily intake very much to your advantage, especially red wine. Best of all is the Greeks' reliance on olive oil, their avoidance of animal fats – butter and lard, cream and the related cheeses. Some Greeks still believe, as the ancients did, that drinking milk is a barbaric practice.

Oil and its Multiple Uses

So keen are they about their oil that oil tastings are organised – on the same basis as wine or whisky tastings elsewhere. Oil comes in three general grades: Extra-virgin is from the first pressing; Virgin, from the second pressing; the third grade is from the rest. The oil extracted from the stones is called *sporelio*, it is not usually used in cooking; *agourolado* is similar, a speciality of Hania in Crete, made from unripened olives. One of its central uses is in the lamps of wayside shrines and churches, though some of these now get vegetable or corn oil. At first olive oil shows a beautiful green aspect, which turns golden with age – a useful point when purchasing it, which is best done in volume as it keeps well (in cool conditions). There was a time when olive trees were a major export item for Greece – she once exported 2000 to Egypt; that at a time when she boasted of having twenty-seven varieties.

Culture Shock for the Newcomer

It takes time to adjust to different tastes, and a different diet: another form of culture shock. Some people are better suited than others. Practice and time are the two essentials for a resistant palate. You are re-educating your system. Most people fear the unknown; strange food is not exempt from this protective reaction. Both your physiological and your aesthetic sensibilities have to adjust. I shall never forget a friend's horror on being offered a delicious octopus stew which had its suckers floating all over it like so many eyes! Or my own aversion to being offered the head of a splendid fish. 'The best part,' my generous host enthused, 'are the cheeks and eyes.' Happily the Greeks are good hosts and make allowances. However, keep in mind that 'Oh, I could never eat that!' is the remark of the defeatist, and very offensive to your hosts. Remember the need for what the psychologists call 'cushion collisioning' at such times: 'I'm sorry, but I don't think I can manage that just now' etc. Also, a point worth bearing in mind should you be offering hospitality is that there are many Greeks who refuse to eat tinned or frozen food, believing them to be a source of cancer.

The Morning Meal

One also has to adjust to the timing of Greek meals, and the tendency to be unpunctual. Wine was once consumed in Greece at breakfast, as food, not as 'the hair of the dog.' Theirs was traditionally a two-meal a day rhythm, the meals being taken at noon and late in the evenings. Modern life has affected this, breakfast is now taken by many – and sensibly, to make good the blood-sugar losses of the night. But it is still a token affair, often taken 'on the hoof,' on the way to work, or actually at work itself, which might entail popping out of the office to visit the local *taverna* – which often visits them: a piece of bread or cake, a large biscuit, some fruit, the essential cup of coffee – with or without water. It is not a highly social meal in this highly social society; Greeks are not at their best in the mornings, a time to tread with care.

The Midday Meal

The Greek equivalent of lunch, a brunch, was taken mid-morning: the farmer's breakfast. The peasant character is still present in rural communities – bread and olives and cheese, perhaps a cheese pie, *meze*, sardines or sausage, a *souvlaki* or hamburger, with beer or wine – *medan agan*! (nothing in excess!) And coffee with water. Generally speaking, this meal has now been replaced by breakfast, and is now from 2 to 4 p.m.; usually taken after work has finished for the day and just before siesta-time. It can be a large meal with several plates.

perhaps with guests; preferably out of doors. The food may all be served together, regardless of consecutive courses. You will have your own plate, but an old custom is for the food to be eaten directly from the serving-plates or tureens, small amounts being taken onto your own plate.

The food will probably be served cool, if not cold. Greeks do not care for hot food, believing it is bad for health. An irate visitor once criticised a waiter for his slowness of service. The rejoinder – not an apology, for apologies are few and far between in Greece – was that it was not the cooking that was slow, but the cooling. In ancient times a cold course always ended the meal, usually fish and raw vegetables. When it was moved to the beginning of the meal Plutarch judged the change a sign of decadence. This decadence takes a different form today, and a truer form, especially in the holiday season. Your 'Greek' salad may not have olives, not even feta cheese; your *taramosalata* may be made with mashed potato; corn or vegetable oil may well have been substituted for olive.

Taverna life

The Siesta

The siesta is sacred. It is bad form to make a noise during this (e.g. with your strimmer), or to go visiting during it. It lasts until 5 p.m. or even a little later; and then time must be given for a shower and mind-focusing.

The Evening Meal

The evening meal is no longer the main meal necessarily, though the more serious entertaining is usually done then. They are late starters, 10 p.m. is not considered too late, but 7 p.m. is definitely early. Greeks are nothing if not generous when throwing a party, and you can expect your host and hostess to pull out all the stops, even if it means the family eats less for the next few days. Ouzo is the traditional *apéritif*, with *meze*, though any spirit (e.g. *raki*) can be offered; this can take some time, an hour is not too short. 'What's time?' cried Browning in a Greekish phase, 'Leave now for dogs and apes! Man has for ever.'

The main course may also be served with the rest, the soup or starter, fish and meat will compete with each other, and vegetables, pasta or rice will jostle side by side. On the whole Greeks do not care for mixed dishes, so you should expect several single ones to be on the table. There will be fruit – the hostess insisting on peeling your orange, or cutting your peach; your host may already have led the way by cutting or breaking your bread for you. Pastries or cake may follow; and coffee, with water. The wine will flow (beer is considered somewhat *outré* at this meal, though there are few rules), and the talk will quicken. Greeks are not like the French, who take half the night to consume the good things prepared – I have been at many dinners in France which took three or more hours. But the Greeks' will also be lengthy, and even after they have finished eating, the talk will continue across the table – cleared or otherwise. Bear in mind that your hostess may have spent the whole day, even longer, preparing her food. Greek cooking is traditionally slow, and if she does not have her own oven she may well have had to reserve time at the baker's; it adds meaning to the phrase 'a labour of love' – one of the origins of the *agape*, the love feast.

LEARNING MORE ABOUT GREEK FOOD

To know Greek gastronomy well is no easy task. The fast food outlets of the tourist spots are a world away from Greek food, though, ironically, their premises are often more enticing than the traditional ones to the incomer. It takes years of experience – in all seasons, around the regions, in restaurants and homes – to know Greek food well.

Choosing your Location by its Food

Those looking for gastronomically linked areas in which to settle could do worse than to look at the location-list of some ingredients: the tomato-belts of Syros, Nafplion, Argos and Thessaloniki; the sheep, goat and cow pastures of the Peloponnese – or its venison and poultry riches; the fruit trees of the Argolid; the olives of Kalamata; the walnuts of Cynouria, the fresh fish of Epirus; the famous granaries and orchards of Thessaly; the wild game, dairy produce and poultry of Macedonia; the grapes of Santorini/Thera and Corinth, and so on. There are many more.

Greece is a kaleidoscope of good things for the alert and active mind, a never failing source of mental, physical and spiritual vitality. Before settling down it is well worth taking a thorough look to ensure that the ideal location for your interests has been found. If already settled, consider a produce-tour in which you pack your car with the fruits of regions and seasons to be frozen, bottled or stored at home. Greek jams are not to my taste – too sweet – and no one there has mastered the divine art of marmalade, though its citrus fruit is superb (especially its red grapefruit, which they do not seem to like).

THE DELIGHTS OF WATER

The famous German epicure Karl Friedrich von Rumohr commenced his book *The Spirit of the Art of Cooking* with a whole chapter on water. Many older Greeks could follow suit, and often give vent to their resentment over the flat taste of so-called pure rain water.

Somewhere Strabo opined that water from Eulaeus actually weighs less than other waters. Henry Miller became positively obsessed about the glass of water in Greece. A more cerebral view is found in Leigh Fermour's comment that the water of the Roumeli is 'chewable': chew on that! It is unquestionably a matter of importance for cooking and wine-mixing. It contributes much to the taste of some of its products – herbs and olives, citrus fruit and grapes – whose over-watering (to increase weight, and therefore profit) has had disastrous effects. Greece's appreciation of water lies in its sparsity in some areas, in the mineral deposits underground and in its pride of its spas

WINE

One cannot think of water without thinking of wine; the two were inseparable in old Greece; soul-mates indeed. Greece's wine is of the greatest antiquity and the most venerable influence. The wine and its usages have produced social and religious *mores* as well as literary interests which will continue as long as mankind does. (We should not forget that it was the Greeks who took wine to France. They may have actually been beaten there by the Phoenicians, but it was the Greek colonists who laid the foundations of viniculture at Massalia/Marseilles and in the Rhône Valley.) The imperiousness of Rome has obscured many of the Greeks historic contributions. In their own country and through a vigorous export trade the Greeks established themselves as *the* vintners of the Near East. Their industry – if we may use an anachronistic term – went into decline under the Turks, as did much of its cultural know-how. It is now reviving itself – a painful, long, and expensive business in an impatient world.

There are many very good Greek wines; some of world-rank. The destructions of history are slowly being overcome, though it cannot be claimed yet that Greece is a great wine-making country. It does, however, have great riches in grape varieties, some of which are very old. In ancient Greek there are at least thirty-eight specialist wine words; a poem of AD 1601 lists no less than 34 varieties. That list can be extended today. In 1992/3 Greece produced 4.05 million hecto-litres, but exported 0.69 – a sign of its disinterest: why export when one can drink it oneself? There are about twenty wine producers of international standing; offering nearly eighty varieties with over two dozen *appellations controllés*, nineteen of which have been given Certificates of Superior Quality.

The fact that so much of Greece's wine is drunk by its own people suggests an untapped source. About 2.65 hecto-litres per annum is drunk according to *Eurostat*, i.e. an average of 5.1 litres per week across the whole population, including tourists. A report in *The Times* of London, of November 1995, gives the daily average for males of up to seven glasses per day; widely extrapolated, this would call into question the reputation of Greeks as moderate drinkers, perhaps. It also underlines their healthy diet.

Discovering Greek Wines

Greek wine is not easily apprehended; its reputation is under-rated by those poor souls who have not outgrown French and other influences. Part of the problem lies in the Greek character, which is fiercely protective of its own and often slow to co-operate with fellow professionals. They have their co-operatives, of course, but the wider spirit of co-operation is often lacking. This does not impede their productivity, now at the level of 500,000 tonnes a year. A complete range of types – red, white and rosé; dry, sweet and sparkling – is available though you may have to travel long distances to acquire some of them. Additionally, there is *retsina*, an acquired taste that wine snobs and the mentally rigid write off all too readily. (The idea is catching on though. In the early 1980s I visited the vinery of a Scottish laird just outside Inverness, who was launching 'pine wine.' Today his business is booming.) Mass distribution is practised by only a few companies – such as Cambas, Kourtakis, Tsantalis, Boutari. To savour the delights of smaller companies and their usually localised wines, one must travel – and enquire, persistently. Their wines are not top of the charts – there are few charts; but the wines are highly serviceable, and sometimes modestly priced.

The more humble table wines (*vins ordinaires*) should not be overlooked. One of the joys of touring the regions for the purpose of this book was to sample these, often offered at the barrel per litre or in three- or five-litre jars, all of them at remarkably low cost. Some were rather rustic in taste, but the majority were good. The best was *BASDABANOY* of Larissa, in bottled form, a delightful fruity red. By the time I came to drink it I was over a hundred miles away – I almost turned back to stock up on it!

Adding Water to Wine

The less palatable wines are improved considerably when water is added – a Greek tradition of very great age, as we have seen. 'Mixed with three nymphs' was how Evenus described the process; though proportions varied from 1:1 to 1:20 and higher. Aristotle, depending

Vineyard in Nemea

on five, a magical number, thought 3:2 best. I think so too, generally speaking. Incidentally, it was a breach of etiquette in the ancient world to add wine to water; one must always add water to wine; the former alters subtly the taste.

Buying and Storing Wines

Northern European wine rules do not apply, in my view, to wines in Greece. The temperatures being so much higher, alcohol performances are changed – dangerously; more than one visitor has been fished out of the sea as a result of this, and not always alive. Watering the wine is thus a health procedure. It affects both the keeping and the serving of wine. You will soon discover who best keeps their wines. Never buy wine that has been shown in a shop window – an astonishing Greek custom, given their 300 days of sunshine per year; never buy wine whose colour is brownish. The old adage 'at room temperature' is usually much too hot in the summer; many wines – reds included – are definitely better for refrigeration.

The old principle of reds for red meat, whites for poultry does not work well either – but only the pedantic believe that anyway. There is something enjoyable about breaking the rules and finding wines and food are better for it. Do not forget that it is the red wines that best induce good health.

Beyond the Grapes ...

Compatibility is one of the most important keys in cooking; it affects particularly the inclusion of wine, especially if one keeps in mind the old tag that wine is the product of 'vine and pine and brine.' (Yes, brine!) Greeks were not slow in making additions such as herbs, lime, even gypsum. The herb and tobacco flavoured *Limnio* , a favourite of Aristotle no less, is still available on Limnos. Europe has now the old custom of spicing wine – with cardamon, cinnamon and/or cloves – which 'warm' it, though sometimes physical heat, supplied by a poker, was applied; these drinks are excellent when taken on wintry evenings. A variety of this which has come to us from the Greeks via the Romans is *conditum*, a wine spiced with honey and pepper. Honey, of course, has an enormously important role in Greek food, especially as a sweetening agent and a garnish. In wine, and as a distillate in its own right, it has a proud place, not least in offering definition to the Homeric 'ambrosia' and 'nectar' (mead perhaps?) Antiphanes discriminated between it and 'nectareous wine, oldest of the old.'

FORTIFIED WINES AND SPIRITS

Ouzo is rightly famous. In addition to this are Greece's various liqueurs. Fortified wines such as port or sherry are not very popular, and often difficult to acquire. The times I have offered them to friends have not been successful, usually on the grounds of their 'heaviness.' *Raki* (or *tsipuro*) – similar to schnaps – is widely enjoyed and distributed, especially in rural Crete. It is my belief that a type of *raki* is the oldest spirit in the world, its production pre-dating the generally recognised Arab practice of distillation, absolute proof of which is wanting. *Raki* and its types are especially popular in the mountainous areas of Greece, where the biting cold calls for something strong. This is quite possibly its original source; heated beer or wine producing the distillate by accident perhaps. If it is a mistake to underestimate modern Greeks, how much more their ancient forbears!

Suggested Readings

- Sofia Constantinidou-Partheniadou, in her travels around Greece *A Travelogue in Greece and a Folklore Calendar.*
- Daniel Spoerri's comments on the food of the island of Symi in *Mythology and Meatballs.* His writing however, is not as balanced and is more limited than hers.
- Miles Lambert Gócs' book, *The Wines of Greece* is indispensable. Not least of its many strengths is his emphasis on the historical

dimension, which cannot be ignored in modern Greece. Another is his recommendations of the foods best suited to the wines, in which the sensitivities of a true gourmet are redolent.

- A recent book by Professor E S Canallakis, late of Yale, *Ygeia kai Makrozia*: (Health and Longevity), is first-rate, already in its second edition and establishing itself as the manual for the careful eater. Unhappily, it has not found an English translation.

Chapter Eleven

HEALTH AND INSURANCE

STATE HEALTH CARE – THE IKA

For EU citizens, health provisions are written into EU guarantees of
their rights of changed abode. It has to be said that some Greeks,
including government agencies, resent this. It is incumbent upon you
therefore to follow the rules absolutely. Provide documents from your
home country and acquire a medical record from IKA – the *Idrima
Kinonikon Asfaliseon* (Social Insurance Foundation); the regional
offices are known as the *Ipopkatastimata*, its branches the *Parartimata*.
It is responsible for the collection and administration of welfare

contributions. To this every just-registered person should apply, having seen their own embassy/consulate first.

Attend only doctors or dentists registered under IKA's scheme. Free hospital services are included in this, though not always to the standard you might expect, and with long queues. Medicines are 75% free and on the whole are relatively cheap. Greece has one of the highest doctor-to-population ratios in Europe: 4.3 per thousand; dentists are even more widespread at approximately one per thousand; so you should have no difficulty in finding one that suits your needs. Insist on having receipts; keep them for possible future reference. The practice of *fakalakia*, cash-filled envelopes used as sweeteners for medical or surgical services, is illegal. Avoid such practitioners.

Another concern of note: in the *Athens News* of March 1994 a third of all patients were said to be seen by inadequately qualified doctors. No less than 300 people each year are rendered paralysed by poor medical care – either at the scene of accidents or as the result of their hospital treatment. This is curious, considering Greece's high percentage of doctors, though it is in line with its lack of specialists and emergency practitioners.

Do bear in mind that all governments are dedicated to driving down health costs – which means transferring as much as possible to the private sector. Any possibility of finding a reason for not accepting you through a technicality is likely to be seized – except in extreme cases. The average spending on social protection (as a percentage of GDP) throughout the EU fell from 28.8% in 1993 to 28.6% in 1994; it will be reduced further. Greece's was only 16% – the lowest figure; even Portugal managed 19.5%. Support for the elderly takes the largest cut; that relating to sickness, disability and accidents is set to decrease.

PRIVATE HEALTH CARE

If you have private health-care insurance its agents will advise you of the procedures to be followed. Other insurance matters should also be talked through with your insurers – to cover your getting to Greece. your possessions and future needs. There are many schemes today. some of them immensely complex. Magazines such as *Which?* or *Oldies* make it their business to offer unbiased critiques of these; they are well worth reading.

LIVING OUTSIDE THE CITIES

If living in rural areas, the choice of your home and its situation regarding steep paths and precipitous inclines, exposure to sunshine or damp, its proximity to shops and friends will be important. If you choose to live on a small island be aware that it may not have full medical provision. I have seen sick and aged individuals – and young ones – carried onto ferries, bumped around during the voyage. sometimes in great pain and/or distress, and off-loaded like cattle. Think ahead. Preventive medicine is not widely available which. when added to deficiencies in water supply and drainage in some areas, as well as rodent infections (e.g. Weil's disease), means that great care must be taken. Even if there is help the doctor may not work within the government's scheme, forcing you to go private; the costs for this could be considerable.

ALTERNATIVE MEDICINE

For those with a yen for alternatives, Greece has much to offer – not least in homoeopathy. In the Athenian School of Homoeopathic Medicine, and the International Academy for Classical Homoeopathy, Samuel Hahnemann's brilliant medical insights are well represented. Giorgos Vithoulkas, who founded the foregoing schools, was recently made one of the four prize-winners in the so-called 'Alternative Nobel Prize of Sweden.' However, be forewarned: there is a tendency for some herbalists and salts' manipulators to call themselves homoeopaths. Worse, one character in Athens displays an alleged homoeopathic qualification from 'the University of North West London.' There is no such institution; at least no one has heard of it in the UK.

The spa in Methana

MEDICAL ROUTINES

Some routines are available outside medical centres. For example, Blood-pressure and other tests are available at your local pharmacy – that is, if you don't mind sitting in your shirt-sleeves while mothers fuss round you looking for nappies or whatever. We are talking culture shock, remember.

GREEK DOCTORS

'Bedside manner' is not something that every Greek doctor cultivates. Be patient with their attitudes; what may look like offhand treatment may simply be shyness or pressure of work. Language difficulties may give the appearance of unconcern; better for you to learn a little Greek than expect them in their busy lives to do it for you, although some will already have some knowledge of English. It is a different health service that exists in Greece, and you will have to come to terms with it.

191

A HOSPITAL STAY

Should you go into a state hospital you will have to arrange for someone to feed you; food is not part of the services, nor are laundry requirements. Ask carefully before you enter to ensure that adequate provisions have been made. Make full arrangements before you go whenever possible, emphasising that you are an IKA patient, if so. Most hospitals advertise their emergency admission information in the press (e.g. in the *Athens News*). It is wise to keep a copy of the latest one handy. Emergency treatment is usually free for everyone, which may involve air-transport to the mainland. IAMAT and MASTA are the organisations dealing with this.

Hospital treatment can involve expensive extras: e.g. if you travel, for the upkeep of your partner staying nearby (to feed and launder for you), and so on. Some nurses offer to do these things as a private service, but their food and other choices may not suit you. Be very careful of entering into such agreements. In commenting on such things one has in mind 'the worst possibility perspective;' it is wise to be prepared. That said, many have enjoyed excellent conditions, treatment and care. Greeks are very jealous of their reputation, so providing that you plan ahead there should be few upsets beyond the bearable.

SOME TIPS FOR BRITISH CITIZENS

Before leaving the UK you should obtain the form E 111 from the DHSS at Newcastle. This must be validated by your local Post Office. It is also recommended that you obtain their booklet SA 40: *Before You Go*. If you are a pensioner it is form E 121 that you require; if you are unemployed but looking for work, it is E119. These have to be presented to the nearest office of the IKA, *Idrima Kinonikon Asfaliseon* (Social Insurance Foundation). The forms will be processed, and you will be given a Medical Book.

If interested in private care, it is worth mentioning International Express Care, which is available to everyone who has access to a UK bank (for the payment of its premiums). It is part of the Norwich Union Healthcare Schemes and offers cover for Europe and the rest of the world according to need.

MEDICINE PRESCRIPTIONS

Medicines are obtained by prescription, 25% of which is payable by you. Obtain receipts for these, as you should be able to obtain refunds from your health insurers. It is worth asking the chemist about the medicine you are taking; he may advise you differently, and there may be savings from the doctor's recommendations. But be watchful; the doctor may have good medical reasons for so prescribing, while the chemist may have his financial considerations in mind.

One drug that should not be left out of any comment on health today is aspirin. It is under no legal prohibition and is quite safe, given certain medical cautions. Research has established it at reduced dosages as a most useful aid to sound health for those in or moving into the at-risk sector of heart and stroke disabilities. It was once outlawed, due to its ability to exacerbate internal bleeding – it is for this reason that it should not be given to anyone who is bleeding, anyone menstruating, or anyone suffering from snake-bite. It has now been rehabilitated. Follow your doctor's prescribing; recommended dosages between countries vary. Regularity is the key; all those at risk should see their medical advisor before commencing this regime, particularly women, and especially the menopausal.

BRINGING MEDICINES INTO GREECE

Great care should be taken when taking drugs into Greece, even for strictly personal and medicinal use. The laws are very rigorous, and rigorously enforced. They were reinforced in 1987 by the provision of extreme sentencing: even the possession of small quantities of forbidden substances can elicit a sentence of fifteen years *and* a fine of up to 100 million drachmas. More serious offences carry sentences of up to twenty years and a double fine. It is also illegal to grow any drug-related plants; there are stiff penalties for law-breakers. Greek law classifies more than 100 prohibited drugs, including:

• Amphetamines	• Cocaine	• Codeine	• Demoral	• Hashish
• Heroin	• LSD	• Marijuana	• Mescoline	• Opium
• Morphine	• STF	• Methodone		

Note that all synthetic narcotics are prohibited; as are all opium derivatives. Such laws change from time to time; your embassy will have a recent list. If in doubt, contact your lawyer. If you have to take prohibited drugs for legitimate health reasons (e.g. Codeine, a component of at least six proprietary pain-killers), you should ensure that they are within the permitted scope. If you are prescribed any of these by your medical advisor, it is imperative that you contact the nearest Greek embassy or consulate *before* you travel to Greece.

HEALTHY EATING

The so-called 'Mediterranean Diet' is a key to good health. Its essence is oil simplicity – i.e. virgin olive oil. One study to bear this out (late 1995) comes from the united efforts of the universities of Harvard, Melbourne and Athens, whose carefully mixed team of researchers, doctors, epidemiologists and health workers confirmed many similar studies over the last fifteen or more years. As mentioned earlier, the EU Commission is presently preparing a blueprint based on such research which has been confirmed on a world-wide basis.

The diet recommends the consumption of unsaturated oil, i.e. olive oil; plus fresh fruit and vegetables – potatoes, leaf vegetables and pulses; a small amount of red meat, a regular use of fish (especially), chicken and game; also fibre-related items, good quality bread; and a regular moderate amount of red wine. It restricts the use of animal fats, white bread, and cholesterol dominated foodstuffs – such as eggs and dairy products; some cheese and yoghurt may be taken regularly. The Harvard-Athens researchers based their findings on two parallel studies of three villages in Greece, the first between 1988-90, the second between 1993-94. They remarked on the lack of 'adventure' in the diets, which perpetuated the village diets of yore; they called attention particularly to the fact that it was the over-all balance which gave the best health protections and increased longevity. One should remember that cheese and yoghurt are made from sheep's and goat's milk in the villages, that villagers have a high activity level compared with northern Europeans, that their consumption of sweets and confectionery is usually much less, though honey is a firm favourite, that white sugar is taken in moderate-to-high quantities in coffee. Important technical factors are the high levels of betacarotene, the vitamins C and E, plus some mineral content. Supplemental intake of these is encouraged, as is that old world cure-all, garlic. 40% of Athenians take supplementary vitamins according to a recent survey, only 10% elsewhere. They are a vital part of our food regime, whatever its precise orientation.

Photo courtesy of Life File

Fish shop at Amarinthos, Evia island

195

Slipping Into Bad Habits ...

Sadly, Greeks are now slipping in the international health-charts, resulting from their westernisation. The Greek diet has shifted, especially in the fast food centres where cheese and other pies, rich in fat, are almost the only choice – ferries are notorious for this – and white bread. Red meat intake is increasing: bacon, sausage and salami particularly; as is the ubiquitous toast: two layers of white bread with slices of cheese and ham between them. Even the near-sacred intake of olive oil is on the wane, actually being beaten into second place by meat in some areas. According to the figures from the 20th Pan-Hellenic Medical Conference, 33% of Greeks have unacceptably high cholesterol levels, a rising figure. Pressures on the food chain itself are bringing about other changes; for example, fish stocks are declining and chicken meat is registering high fat levels due to battery farming.

ENVIRONMENTAL HEALTH HAZARDS

There are great benefits to living in Greece: its sun and warmth; low humidity; low industrial effluent – except in the large centres; its fresh air and clean water; relaxed culture; the lack of rush-and-hurry attitudes – and much more. However ...

Air Pollution in Athens

For those living in or near Athens there is the disturbing problem of its infamous *nephos*; a 'smog' which collects over the greater urban area and continues to envelop it under certain warm weather conditions. It precipitates heart, vascular and respiratory complaints and is, literally, a killer. Merely to walk through Athens on certain days can be discomforting, even for the fit and healthy. Radio and television bulletins warn of its dangers, and a public display is mounted near the National Library in Eleftheriou Venizelou Street, which is updated automatically and shows specific contamination levels.

On bad days child admissions to hospitals increase by 15%, heart conditions by 14%, respiratory ones by 16%, asthmatic attacks by

35%, chronic breathing disorders by 12%, and actual deaths by 5–10%. Some experts have warned that it can lead to as much as a 40% increase in liability to certain cancerous conditions. If you suffer from any of the foregoing, keep away on those black days. The government and the universities are working hard on the problem, but the pollution is due to the fact that there are too many motor vehicles and factories too close to the city centre, and the geographical make-up of the area augments the problem; it is similar to Los Angeles. The chances of any real reform are strictly long-term.

Smoking

Smoking is on the increase, too, not least among women and children. The figures are worrying among school children: 5.3% admit to occasional use, but 5.4% admit to smoking twenty cigarettes a day, or more. The statistics for smokers in Greece are the highest in Europe and the second highest in the world (next to Argentina). According to figures from 1996, 700 million drachmas a year are spent on the habit. The number of tobacco-related cancer patients registered each year is around 7000, a rising figure. This produces a mortality rate of 87 per hundred thousand for males, 13 for females; three million have died through it since 1960. Under-30s are now the chief population of concern. Social smoking with peer pressure is mostly to blame, plus the vigorous, previously unhampered advertising. Greece now has a total ban on all broadcast advertisements of tobacco. There is very little protection against passive smoking, however.

UV Exposure

Greece's ozone layer is believed to have been reduced by at least 15%, i.e. about 0.5% per annum in less than thirty years. The sun is now a much greater menace to health than it was but five years ago. This rapid reduction in the ozone layer has produced an increase of about 10% of the ultra-violet rays which are very harmful. Temperatures over 95°C are not unusual in Greece. Hospitals automatically go on alert when the temperature touches 100°C. In addition to the usual dangers – of heat-stroke, sun-burn and dehydration – there is a real risk of skin-cancers which may lead to other forms if not treated quickly, and to the formation of cataracts leading to blindness. Records show that breast and cervical cancer are also on the increase in Greece – against the trend compared with Europe and the USA. Those at greatest risk are light skinned and/or hairless individuals, but all should take precautions against prolonged exposure. The most dangerous point in the day is between the hours of 12.00-3.00 p.m., a traditional time for 'mad dogs and Englishmen.'

Adequate clothing is the answer to sun and UV exposure. It should be light (in colour as well as weight); a sun-hat and sun-glasses are also advisable. Mid- to high-level barrier creams are required to filter out the dangerous UVA and UVB light rays. These should have a factor of 15 to 20 at the beginning. The principle is controlled exposure – to heat as well as sunshine; to which end one should keep in the shade, avoid strenuous exercise, eat little and drink much (but not alcohol), take frequent showers, and use air-conditioned rooms and transport. Note that even on cloudy days dangerous exposure can be unwittingly suffered. Any skin lesions should be notified to your doctor immediately; virtually all skin cancers respond to treatment if caught in time.

Dehydration

Be careful of those apparently cooling outdoor exercises which take place in direct sunshine – swimming and sailing, for example. Great harm can be suffered through them as the water washes and the warm air dries off perspiration before high heat levels are noticed. This can have a major effect in dehydrating the person, quite apart from the risk of sun-burn and sun-stroke. A fiercely dehydrating agent is alcohol; every year lives are lost in Greece through swimming after its consumption, usually in the daytime. Babies, young children and aged people are particularly at risk from dehydration, and should be kept from prolonged exposure to the heat, and given plenty of liquids. A daily intake of three litres is considered the minimum for an average adult. If caught by the sun, cold showers and ice packs must be quickly applied. Use a bathing or other hat filled with ice if nothing else is available – even a packet of frozen peas is useful. Yoghurt mixed with water is a great thirst-quencher, and may be the only food sustainable in emergencies; it is also an excellent burns' ointment. When skin has been lost, a mixture of anti-biotics (purchased at the chemists) and yoghurt is highly recommended – so long as the person is not allergic to the former; always keep the tube to show the doctor.

Siestas Instead of Sun

The siesta is not a habit to be despised in the hot months of the year, if ever. Indeed, it is to be encouraged, if not for sleeping, then for light activities such as reading or the enjoyment of music, videos etc. A recent study showed that an hour's sleep on average was taken in the afternoons by Cretans; I suspect that it is rather more elsewhere. Its benefits are numerous: absenting oneself from pernicious sun-rays, an aid to digestion (but never lie back fully after a large meal, which can cause reflux oesophagitis or hiatus hernia etc.), breaking the stress-pattern, time for family and personal relationships, and time to meditate.

Diarrhoea

Diarrhoea is another cause of fatalities in the very young and aged. Rehydration tablets (a compound of salts and sugars) should be in everyone's medical cabinet during the hottest months, and checks on their 'use-by' dates made regularly. An increase in salt intake is advisable, save for those suffering from raised blood pressure or related ailments. Contaminated water or bad food is the usual cause of diarrhoea; there are plenty of specific tablets to overcome this. Careful washing of hands after toilet usage – a provision not always found in Greece – and of food should obviate this. It is important not to mix frozen meats with fresh, or allow blood from the former to drip on the latter. Do not eat old fish, shell-fish in particular. Persistent diarrhoea should be reported to your doctor.

Living in Northern Areas

If you choose to live in northern areas their comparative coldness should be taken very seriously. This is especially so for the aged. Chilling can precipitate cardiac arrests and brain haemorrhages as much as intense heat or the dreaded *nephos*. Waiting for a bus, sitting about in the garden or simple queuing should all be avoided if not adequately dressed – hatted in particular. If you are subject to high blood pressure or other vascular problems you must keep warm, indoors and outside.

Follow the ground-rules for protecting yourself against hypothermia: keep your home properly warmed; eat nourishing warm food; do not rely on alcohol to warm you, it does not do so beyond an initial rush, when its effect becomes the opposite; warm drinks are best. Wear appropriately warm clothing outside.

HEALTH ISSUES AMONG GREEKS

Stress, in fact, is becoming one of Greece's main health problems, for which the famous 'worry-beads' are not the answer. As many as 10% of the population – 1,020,000 persons – confess to suicidal thoughts. Every third woman and every fifth man is treated for some form of mental disorder, according to one report; Athenians more so than any others. So much for the *'Don't worry! Be happy!'* tee-shirts. Thirty-one percent of all health problems in Greece are stress-related. Administration statistics of mind-caring drug use are interesting: 13% among adolescents; 26.9% of women between the ages of 18 and 24; and 19% of men of the same age. The figures for those over the age of 24 years soar: it is reckoned that 40.8% of women and 24% of men are habitual users of psychotropical drugs.

Such figures give statistical weight to the oft repeated comments on the 'nervy-ness,' instability and insecurity of the Greeks and their paranoia. It could be because they know they live in a potential war-zone, and are subject to devastating earthquakes, as well as an unforgiving sun. It is bound to affect their behaviour, national and personal. Their sensitivity to criticism – or assumed criticism; their refusal to be conventional; belief in people's double motives, overt paranoic forms are also further indicators. To live close to some Greeks is to risk being bounced emotionally in all directions by them; 'smiling one moment, raging the next' as one exhausted expatriate expressed it.

Rising Temperatures, Rising Tempers

High summer sees a rise in the number of accidents and illnesses, displays of bad temper and futile arguments. Road-rage is also becoming a problem. The month of June is said to be Hera's month in old Greece. This bad tempered and cantankerous goddess is renowned for her sulks and perversities. Be that as it may, this is the month of atmospheric changes and of violent storms, quite often electric – brilliant cosmic firework displays which are sometimes matched by the human condition. It is in June that the highest level of suicides are recorded, when many other features of imbalance – criminal and other – appear. This is attributed to the sun's power; a power that should be taken very seriously by those engaged in inter-personal difficulties. Little wonder that every hilltop was dedicated to Helios, the sun-god!

AIDS in Greece

Greece is not free from 'the scourge of the century' – AIDS. As elsewhere, it has gone through the pattern of homosexual activities, thence blood transfusion errors, to hetero-sexual activities. The statistics for women are causing particular concern. The blood transfusion service is now well regulated. It is, however, at the bottom of the European blood-donor league, with a mere 19 donors per thousand people: the international target is fifty. There are said to be over 12,000 HIV-positive cases in Greece, with a figure just below 10% for fully developed AIDS' patients. It is set to rise.

Sexuality is much vaunted in the major cities. Thessaloniki is reputed to be one of the pornographic centres of Europe. Condoms are widely and descriptively advertised; prostitution is constrained by law, as noted earlier; a relaxed view is taken of sexual activities in public toilets and sex cinemas. Because of this sexual crimes are limited, rape is comparatively rare, kerb-crawling practically unknown. But beware of the harpoons – unmarried men who stalk women for sexual advantages.

Drugs

There is a growing drug culture in Greece, as there is in the rest of Europe, hence the rigour of the authorities towards it. The main age-group is young people. The figures are disturbing: 46% of all illicit users are below the age of eighteen according to one report by OLME; a further 43% are aged between nineteen and twenty-five years. The evidence is that these ages are lowering. Some drugs are available in schools and colleges; nearly 20% of all young people acknowledge having had some experience of them. One young person dies every day from such abuse in Greece – actually about 400 per year; between 1985-92 a mortality increase of 800% was registered. To influence minors towards drugs carries a sentence of life imprisonment and a fine of 200,000,000 drachmas.

Infant Mortality

Infant mortality is a matter of grave concern in Greece. It is recorded at 14-15 per thousand, which is very high – seven times greater than in northern Europe and the USA. Between 1980-90 it decreased by about a third from an intolerably high position, but it still accounts for 1500 infant deaths per year – against a falling birth-rate of nearly 30%.

—Chapter Twelve—

LANGUAGE AND EDUCATION

'When you understand the point of view of another race
you are a civilised human being.'
—T E Lawrence (Lawrence of Arabia)

It is possible to live happily in Greece without acquiring facility in its
language; but it is not possible to live fully without it. Language
creates national character; it is not possible therefore to understand
Greeks well without knowing their language. Even a smattering will
help. Faced with a proliferation of courses and private tutors, as

intending settlers are, it is worth learning the language. Greeks take easily to foreign languages, though their expertise generally speaking is not of a high order, and is seriously vitiated by Americanisms – a tendency increased by computerisation, the use of spell-checkers, and the Internet.

Learn some in your home country, if possible, before you go. The very minimum should be to know the Greek alphabet and those 'Key Words and Numbers' that preface tourist manuals and guides. 'Kitchen Greek' comes readily enough as one does the shopping, travelling about, and passing the time of day with neighbours. If you have been lucky enough to have studied some ancient Greek (classic or *koine*) it will stand you in good stead, but you will find many differences – of words and structures, and especially of pronunciation. You may well feel that modern Greek is somewhat inferior to those elevated delights. Do not be put off by Greek radio or television presenters, who often seem imbued with an extra facility of speed. I have heard Greeks say that they also have difficulties following them.

The ancient Greeks called their writers *p[h]oinikastas*: Phoenician; for their early letters came from the Phoenician script, which was symbolic, i.e. pictographic. Knowing the history can help the memory. For example, *theta* – the first letter in *thanatos*, death – was scratched onto pieces of broken pottery at capital trials to denote the death sentence. A whole abercedarian – from ABC – can be made up to aid you. Why not make one yourself? Even a little of such goes a long way, and will enable you to get over those first fences of culture shock safely.

COURSES

There are many courses – daytime and evenings, and correspondence – for you to enroll in. Linguaphone heads the list; its threefold emphasis on hearing, seeing and repeating supplies the golden key to confident advancement. Additionally there are organisations such as the Berlitz Language School, The Institute of Linguistics, the Modern Language Association, the National Institute of Adult Education, and the Centre for Information on Language Teaching and Research, as well as courses run by the Open University and Local Education Authorities, some of which offer excellent introductions to cultural aspects of Greece in addition to purely linguistic ones. *Yellow Pages* will give you their details. The effort could be the best investment in your new future that you will make; it is the pathway to friendship, understanding, safety and ready communication – and a thousand and one delights.

Photo courtesy of Life File

Road signs are a helpful learning tool (but do not trust their spelling!)

Residential Courses

Nothing can beat the 'total immersion' concept of language learning offered in some residential courses. While expensive, they offer expert tuition and guidance by highly qualified people. 'Direct method' courses – in which only Greek is spoken – are best, for they force one to *think* Greek by advancing from one level of cognition to another, and not to rely on translation which, however accurate, never quite has the subtleties of genuine Greekness.

Part-time Language Schools

In Greece there are many part-time language schools (such as summer schools; see below), and they are not that expensive by British standards. Most of them prepare their pupils to London, Oxford or Cambridge standards, and are checked from time to time. Others prepare to American standards. The British Council offers good advice in such matters; if living in or near to Athens you have the use of their library and other facilities. Do ensure that your teacher is properly qualified. Beware of those enthusiastic amateurs who, even out of the goodness of their hearts, will misinform you and waste your time and your money.

Practice Makes Perfect

Whenever possible, opt for courses which provide language laboratory facilities; these will protect you from making those initial mistakes of pronunciation that are so difficult to remedy once ingrained. Preferably, your tutor should be a native Greek speaker, from the central – i.e. Attica – area to avoid regional variations; for no matter how good some foreigners are, few have perfect inflexion and grammar. You can always improve your grammar; it is very difficult to relearn the other. Only by hearing the language frequently and reading it, will you become fluent; tuned to those important nuances. Speaking it often is essential if your tongue and throat muscles are to get around the new sounds – and the earlier the better.

Experts reckon that for every hour of tuition you receive you should expect to put in at least two more to master the material provided. Vocabulary learning is the easiest part. One extremely busy archeologist known to me, who had the habit of learning new languages for the pure fun of it, started each day by learning ten new words. They were written on little cards and learned by his placing them on the shaving mirror, repeating them as he went along: every cut a step to competence! He kept them in his pocket, making use of them in queues, while strap-hanging in the tube, etc. Try it – at the washing up, sweeping the drive, while travelling; a month of this, at only ten a day, means three hundred new words – a good starter to your new way of life.

EDUCATION

Education in Greece is 'a basic State mission' according to the Constitution. It has a very long history, albeit one often interrupted by invasion and captivity. In the classical age its proponents recommended the study of mathematics, astronomy, literature, music and philosophy (then a much wider subject than today), and gymnastics. It has often been said that Sparta stood for the healthy body, Athens the healthy mind – an over-simplification, but one that holds enough point to be useful. The Greek word for it – *ekpaideutikos* – is interesting in that it suggests that the process draws something from the child, a very modern concept.

Education is free to all Greek citizens, and by treaty extended to those of EU citizenship. One of Greece's great virtues is its emphasis on equality for women educationally – its record is better than that of Germany, the Netherlands and Austria (according to the EU report of April 1997). It lasts for nine years and is mandatory for all children between five and a half years to fourteen. In a popular poll conducted by MRB for the newspaper *Ta Nea* in June 1994, education was declared to be the sixth most vital issue confronting the Greek people. (Pride of place was given, respectively, to inflation, unemployment, foreign affairs, drugs, health and pensions.) Its 'importancy factor' was 69.8% – more important than economic growth, crime rates, public services and taxation.

The Ministry of National Education and Religion

The Ministry of National Education and Religion is in charge of education; the law requires the affairs of the Orthodox Church, in this respect, to be under governmental supervision. It is the fifth largest ministry in expenditure terms; the ratio of education to overall budget expenditure is increasing: An increase of 20% was recorded in the nation's general expenditure between 1985/6 and 1989/90, whereas that for education was 42.37% – a good indication of its importance. These figures include private as well as public expenditure. The system is divided into the normal tripartite divisions of primary, secondary, tertiary; the primary division occupies a voluntary place as it is not required by law.

Greek Primary Education

Primary education usually commences at 3.5 years and continues to 5.5 years; the shortage of places in some areas limits this, however; with later commencements becoming necessary. Many parents make a private provision for primary education, usually on a part-time basis. By 1993, 31.4% of the population had received primary education.

Secondary Education

Secondary education commences at 5.5 years. It is divided into three groups: General High Schools and Lycees (known as Gymnasia); Technical Lycee and Vocational Colleges; and Ecclesiastical Colleges. Attendance is required at these over three years, four if evening courses are taken. The first group of these covers the classical model of education – the three R's (reading, writing, and arithmetic), with 'multi-branch' courses widening this in the Lycees. The second group also offers the basics, plus specialised courses for trades, crafts and professions. The ecclesiastical division's interests are appropriately defined, though a fourth year is essential due to the breadth of learning required. By 1993, 12% of the population had received secondary education.

Tertiary Education

Tertiary education is divided into four divisions: General; Technical; Vocational and Ecclesiastical, and Higher (i.e. the universities). Technical students are prepared for TEI and SELETE/ASETEM qualifications, i.e. those of the Technical Institutes, the Teacher Training Colleges and the Technical Engineering Teachers' Colleges. TEI courses last over six to eight semesters; SELETE and ASETEM last over eight to twelve semesters. Vocational students prepare for those relating to 'personal services,' the merchant marine and the arts; the Ecclesiastical students prepare for the theological colleges. Those in the Higher division prepare over eight to twelve semesters for graduation in a wide range of subjects, including HEI qualifications which rank above Teacher Training Colleges. By 1993, 7.2% of the population had received tertiary education.

YOUR CHILD'S EDUCATION

Children's interests in this matter will be of great concern. Happily, they learn more readily than adults, and usually more accurately. The earlier they start learning the language, the better, even if it is for just a few minutes each day. One friend's child is perfectly bi-lingual at twelve, and is given to correcting his parents' faults in Greek, as well as extending their vocabulary somewhat colourfully.

Adjustment Problems

Some children have socio-cultural problems that they may not let onto. To change school is hard; to be thrust into one in an unknown language is *very* hard. Cushion their difficulties by breaking the ground in advance, by being aware how cruel other children can be, and by asking the teachers to watch for signals of distress which manifest themselves either positively (i.e. aggressive behaviour) or negatively (i.e. becoming withdrawn). Some preconditioning before you actually move is a vital element in this, perhaps a holiday in Greece – especially if you can stay with Greeks *en famille*. The school counsellor will also have useful advice and will be even more willing if you show your concerns considerately.

Choosing British or American Schools

For those looking for British or American schools in Greece the choices are rather limited. This option also has its own disadvantages. For one thing these schools are only found at Athens, which may well mean some dislocation of family life, increased travelling (and therefore stresses on your child), and your child's alienation from nearby friends. Worse, he/she will not be nurtured in a Greek *ethos* but a British or American one, which may be confusing. Your decision to move to Greece must have been made in the light of your best judgment as to its all-round advantages; why reduce these for your child? Once over that admittedly large hurdle of initial acclimatisation, he/she will make rapid progress; why limit that now? Other advisors may offer you contrary advice; it is for you and your child to make the decision which best suits his or her long term needs.

For British schools you have a choice of but one primary school, at Kifissia, in Athens: St Catherine's British Embassy School. Below this age group Pooh Corner offers kindergarten facilities which are run on British lines and with an all-British staff. The same applies for Early Learning, the British Nursery (sometimes known as the 3-4-5 Nursery), and the Montessori Nursery. American children have Agapeland, Stepping Stones and Peter Pan.

For older children Campion School is the best known. It offers educational facilities for the full range up to eighteen years. It also provides primary care, but not on the British model. Preparation is made for both British and American examination boards – 21 subjects at GCSE, 17 at A-level; as well as CEEB; it also provides private tuition and summer schools, the latter for academic subjects, computing, sporting and handicraft interests. Four other schools exist in Athens: the American Community School, Byron College, St Laurence College and the Tassis Hellenic International School.

Specialist Schools

There are also some specialist schools which may be of interest to you and your children: Pooh Corner, mentioned above, is based on an adapted version of the Montessori method which emphasises freedom of choice, spontaneity and the importance of movement, to which it now adds modern concerns such as ecology and environmental issues. Elizabeth Mamas, an Austrian artist, offers an emphasis on self-expression, which she bases on a philosophy of 'good vibrations'; all tuned to classical music. The Old Mill School concentrates on children with learning disabilities, including dyslexia and Down's Syndrome; numbers are restricted to ensure personalised education.

Greek Summer Schools

Greece has long been known for its summer schools, of which it boasts a great number. Part-educational, part-holiday, they can be an excellent introduction to Greek life in all its aspects, ancient and modern, and an incitement for imminent examinations. It is important to ensure that your child fits into the type and programme offered, especially in age terms, and it must have twenty-four hours' supervision with properly trained teachers and medical staff. The ratio of staff to the children is critical; 1:10 is too high, especially for the younger age groups; 1:8 is tolerable; 1:6 is ideal. Food and safety matters should be checked, and special attention given to the dangers of sun and heat. Non-gregarious children are best sent to them in the company of a friend.

Further Education

Further education is very highly regarded in Greece, but formal institutions are behind those of north Europe and the USA; they are supplemented by institutions such as the Goethe Institute, YMCA, YWCA, British Council, British School of Archaeology, or the American School of Classical Studies. These offer lectures and courses of all sorts of length and description; they are usually well advertised (in the English-language newspapers and in *What's on in Athens?*); some will put you on their mailing lists for a small charge. Most are centred on Athens.

Special mention of the Open University (a British institution, open to all) should be made as it has recently set up an Athens branch. No matriculation requirements are made, and a wide range of professional qualifications can add to the credits it awards for progress through to graduation. It works on the basis of a system of carefully presented lessons, tutorials, and set work. It has been an enormous success in the UK, and looks like following that success here in Greece. A study commitment of about fifteen hours per week is required. The average cost for a full degree course is approximately £700 per annum. Shorter non-degree courses can be taken for recreational and educational reasons.

Pursuing Your Own Interests

Beyond the interests of further education lie evening lectures, exhibitions and *soirées* of every description. Athens is an exciting place culturally and offers the perfect counter-balance to the body awareness of Greece. Whatever your interest, there is bound to be an outlet for or an expression of it in the capital – music, philosophy, art, politics, sport, religion, drama, literature, dance and so on. If not, why not start one? Other cities come poor seconds to the capital, but it does have 40% of the population.

Decisions ...

Some opt to leave their children at schools in their home country, but thought should be given to the damage this does to the family relationship, as well as the missed opportunity for your child's involvement in Greece's rich cultural inheritance. It is a more difficult decision for those on short-term stays in Greece, but the disruption this will cause your child has to be set against the vital broadening of their experience and knowledge. Holiday visits are in no way comparable to living in the country. One of my friends was taken from Greece to Germany and then to Britain during her father's rise in academia. She is now a very elegant European, with a facility in three languages and a very broad cultural base – the envy of her peers, highly sought after by would-be employers. It is hard to think of comparable gains had she stayed in her own country. Despite the difficulties of so moving one's children, I have yet to meet anyone who has done so and regretted it. Some have been startled at their children's emergence as excellent linguists. There are, of course, particular difficulties for adolescents in such moves, an age-group already replete with problems. Careful advice and pre-counselling are essential, on a one-to-one basis, but the advantages are still large, and the young are very adaptable given the right handling.

WORK, TAXATION AND RETIREMENT

HIGH UNEMPLOYMENT

It has to be recognised that Greece has a severe unemployment problem. In May 1996 it stood at 9.2% of the work-force, slightly up on the same period last year. This acts like a drag-anchor on the economy. According to *Eurostat*'s (1993) figures a massive 21% of the (4.1 million) work-force is in agriculture – easily the largest in the EU; a mere 24% in industry; and 55% in the services' sector. This is in considerable contrast to many EU countries where agricultural employment ranges from 2% to 6% and industrial from 28% to 38% of the work force.

Greece has a self-employment rate (which includes the employers) of no less than 47% – only 53% work for others, a disproportionate number cushioned in the civil service. This condition restricts the jobs' pool and tends to favour selection in the direction of one's kith and kin (the *parea*), making employment more difficult for those outside the circle. Kinship in Greece is an elastic term, which moves in concentric circles: immediate family, extended family, locality dwellers, fellow-nationals, expatriates.

Greece's statistics for young people show unemployment of about 28% (autumn 1996 figures); for women of that age group there was an average of 64% unemployment in 1992, the worst areas being Macedonia, Central Greece and Attica. The real wages' index in Europe, based on the usual 100 standard, for 1993 show Greece's workers as the lowest paid by a considerable margin: at 90.2; it had actually *fallen* from the 1989 figure by no less than 8.1, a considerable decline. Even Portugal had produced a figure of 113.3 – an increase from its 1989 figure. When these are placed alongside the well known fact of agricultural workers' poor pay, it shows how much worse off half the work-force is compared with their northern counterparts – to say nothing of the plight of the unemployed.

Convergence with the EU is the present economic issue, to which the government is straining every muscle and sinew. In May 1996, it met the EU's budgetary objectives – a remarkable achievement. However, it is still technically in 'excessive deficit,' with Portugal and Spain, unable to join therefore the single currency – the goal of the painful exercise. This will restrict further its economic development.

WORKING IN GREECE

Company Job Transfers

In cases where one's company arranges an overseas transfer, the paperwork and related requirements will be completed at its Head Office. Care should be given to the adequate safeguarding of all your rights. Merely the provision of a job, a wage and perhaps accommodation are not enough; incremental aspects should be provided, and insurance and tax provisions also made, particularly relating to health-care; relocation and re-entry to your original country should also be provided.

Seeking a New Job

Where employment is sought on the open market, particular care as to the standing of those advertising and/or offering the job should be taken, and a proper contract of employment, which includes the provisions just mentioned, should be included. Precise duties must be outlined, along with the place of employment, hours of work, days off (including holiday provision), salary and residential aspects (if any), and notice periods. I have known so-called 'area managers' sent out from the UK without these.

Unhurried work

217

Employment Agencies

Employment agencies are not technically illegal in Greece, but their work lies within the remit of the Ministry of Labour (OAED) offices, which has a proprietorial interest in it. It is a good idea to see its officers first, then to enquire at the (few) agencies (such as Executive Services Ltd, on Athens 7783.698; or Link International, on 3222.858) who offer (paid) help. Press advertising offers another option. Use only the best sources. They will usually retain some information about their clients, and they may insist on your rights and be willing to stand up for you should you be misled in any way. Embassy guidelines for those seeking employment are not enthusiastic: all too often they are asked to pick up the pieces, a job they usually decline. There is some political sensitivity here, unemployment being what it is. It was rated the second most crucial issue facing the nation in a 1994 poll. Warnings are issued regularly against employment bureaux which fail to meet the required standards in their stated promises and fulfilments. This is particularly so in live-in jobs, e.g. child- or home-care situations. Good opportunities for such work do exist, but the *bona fides* of all those involved should be checked. The recommendations given above apply here too.

Temporary Employment

Temporary jobs may be found anywhere and are usually seasonal, for the tourist and harvest periods particularly, but also in baby-minding, on construction sites, even in shops. They may offer little more than subsistence, which may create problems for you when they end. Ensure that you know when this is to be, and that you have enough money to get you back. Opportunities for part-time employment have been worsening of late; competition is much stiffer than a few years ago. In 1990, 4.1% of the work-force had them; by 1995 the number had doubled.

It is essential to report to the police for registration on arrival. The maximum period presently allowed for casual work is three months.

Any changes – of work or location – should also be reported. If you are in full time and regular appointment, any such changes should also be reported to the local Ministry of Labour office.

Insurance

It is your employer's responsibility to pay your insurance contributions to IKA – *Idrima Kinonikon Asfaliseon* (the Social Insurance Foundation), and this must be confirmed by him. Accepting this responsibility will help to validate his *bona fides*, but it is the paying of the contributions, not the promising which is important.

Self Employment

Self-employment is possible, but you may encounter official opposition to your scheme if your ability with the language is not sound. Even if it is, you will have to go through a number of careful vetting procedures – of registration, tax compliance and banking. For some jobs a good knowledge of Greek history will be required. Registration with the appropriate professional body is *de rigour*. It will impose on you its standards and routines, and will not be over-interested in your own. It may not recognise some of these, particularly non-graduate ones. If you intend to set up your own business you will have to follow the routines laid down by the government, to the letter, through Ministry officials. A lawyer and an accountant will be required. The principles regarding the establishment of professionals from member states in EU countries have recently been clarified by the Court of Justice (in *Gebhard v Consiglio dell'Ordine degli Avvocati e Procuratori di Milano*; Case C-55/94). National measures which hinder or make less attractive professional establishment are now subjected to four conditions:

- The conditions must be applied in a non-discriminatory way;
- They must be clearly justified in the national interest;
- They must be appropriate to the end for which they are formulated;

- They must not go beyond restraints necessary for the attainment of that end.

Compliance with the host-state's rules is mandatory; they include the elucidation of the professional's activities, and their performance in manners becoming; the comparison of knowledge and qualifications – the equivalence of diplomas and degrees – is specifically enjoined.

Teaching Languages

An area that offers above average opportunities is English and other language tuition. This has many full and part-time places, but these are protected by a Presidential Decree of 1994. *Qualified* teachers may work in and even open FLT (Foreign Language Teaching) schools – they are classed among the *frontisteria* (i.e. preparatory schools for part-time students) – but the procedures can be slow and arduous. Greek teachers have pride of place in the jobs' list, and these are appallingly lengthy as Greece has been producing too many teachers for years. Further, they can obtain these places on relatively low qualifications – e.g. a teacher training college certificate. Non-Greeks, however, must be graduates. Those with unusual, modular, mixed or composite degrees may be refused. Despite its splendid emphasis on education, teachers are poorly paid in Greece, and many have secondary jobs. Applications for acceptance have to be made to the Director of the Ministry of Education.

Nursing

Similarly, graduate nurses may find good employment opportunities, though not all those advertising such turn out to be for pure nursing – *caveat lector*! Application has to be made to The Association of Graduate Nurses. It is recommended that you apply to your own professional bodies, stating your intentions, before you apply to the ones in Greece.

RIGHTS OF EU MEMBERS

A central aspect of EU law appertains to the rights of non-Greeks to work in Greece; other nationals are naturally being squeezed out by this convention, save for those selected for unique skills in particular posts and industries. Originally the EEC was a 'common market;' thence an economic community; now, increasingly, an integrated community in the widest sense of that term, with quasi-federalist interests. The freedom to work, to enjoy the fruits of one's work and related protections, is secured by its treatises which bind the member states. Those rights are extended automatically to the spouses and children of the workers.

Among the rights and protections that are specifically guaranteed by Article 51 are social security and tax benefits; also the rights of aggregation, association and collective bargaining; plus equal opportunities as to sickness, industrial accident, retirement and death provisions. These are subject to some phasing for economic and political reasons. For example, employment in some public services has been specifically excluded (Article 48 of the Treaty of Rome): in the judiciary, police, armed services and the diplomatic service, also the Post Office and the civil service. These are now under review, but it is not likely that Greece will be the pace-setter for change here, though great pressure is being brought to bear on the question of foreigners' involvement in the health service, education, some research bodies (excluding military or defence research) and organisations which manage or affect commercial services – i.e. transport, energy, navigation, post and communications, radio and television.

TAXATION

Tax Avoidance

Tax avoidance was once a virtual sport in Greece. The black market was said to be of the order of 50% or more of the economy. Such behaviour did not carry the social disadvantages that crime does –

221

which can have enormous detrimental effect on a family or an individual; it was regarded as a particularly Greek thing to do – an Odysseus-like aspect; a sport.

Cracking Down

This is now being courageously uprooted by the government, under intense pressure from the international banking community. It has corporate as well as individual bearing. In one sampling in August 1994 no less than 42,000 tax law transgressions were revealed; at another time it was claimed that 91% of all business transactions involved some form of business irregularity.

The government's responses have been called draconian, beyond the rules of fair play. But crisis requires radical diagnosis and action. The authorities now have the right to assume tax irregularity unless you can prove otherwise; appeals against their judgments are extremely difficult to make. The very old system of *pothen eskhes*: 'where did you get it?' is in force. This means that if you have got, say, a house, a car, a boat it will be assumed that you must have earned the money to pay for it and its upkeep. This principle includes all purchases above a certain value, except for one's first home, state bonds, and shares listed on the ASE. If you have not declared such notional income, you will be fined and taxed for it – even if it was your aunt that left it to you.

Moreover, the banks have now lost their right of privacy – the principle of *aporito*: 'no passage.' Tax officials may gain access to any account within Greece if they believe false statements as to investments and/or earnings have been made. This new access covers not only bank accounts but all public agencies that hold information germane to tax enquiries, including credit card companies and financial consultancies.

Paying Taxes

Tax is payable by all residents over the age of twenty-five years who have an income from within or outside of Greece. Non-residents or short-term residents are required to pay tax on income earned from within Greece. Assessments are based on total income to the end of the last financial year, less duly recognised allowances and exemptions. Recent laws to counter double taxation and evasion have come into force via EU machinery. Intending immigrants to Greece must see their local taxation officers; a visit to the DOY – the Greek equivalent to the Inland Revenue – is strongly recommended. Your taxable status in Greece becomes operative at the point of residence permission; new procedures are now in force to ensure that this process is tied into the taxation system – as is the registration of vehicles, houses etc.

Tax Offences

The non or late declaration of your affairs will result in fines (a grace period of two weeks is allowed), as will any fraudulent declaration. Late declaration incurs a fine of 2.5% surcharge per month; unpaid tax debts up to 200,000 drachmas carry a three-month jail sentence and a fine of 500,000 drachmas; debts to 1 million drachmas, a six-month jail sentence and a fine of 500,000 drachmas; and those over 1 million drachmas carry a year's jail sentence and a fine of 1 million drachmas. These figures are all subject to change; please see your local advisor. As is usual in Greece, jail sentences can be satisfied by the payment of stiff penalties in substitution. Should the offences be repeated, the penalties are automatically doubled and the business premises closed down via the withdrawal of licences and permissions; this can be temporary or permanent. Moreover, those convicted of such offences may be black-listed from all government agencies and contracts, and refused access to grants and allowances.

VAT (Value Added Tax)

New laws also cover the payment of VAT. Most of these are chargeable at source by the supplier. Should you be a supplier of goods or services, a VAT statement must be submitted. Again, you should seek professional advice on such matters. To withhold the

223

payment of VAT will result in criminal charges being laid against you, which could involve the seizure of your goods in addition to fines and imprisonment. Even the transportation of goods without fully paid and receipted paperwork (i.e. VAT certificates) can be liable to seizure and fines. Electronic tills are required by law in all businesses, their rolls being an integral part of the accounting/auditing system. Shoppers are obliged to demand receipts in the event of their not being offered, and can themselves be prosecuted should they be found emerging from a shop with goods without a valid receipt. A pricing bureau works under the supervision of the tax authorities, and maintains some prices according to government policy. It keeps a check on all imports and vets invoicing and related tax procedures, especially under-invoicing. To withhold the payment of VAT is to risk incurring fines and the seizure of the goods in question, as is any fraudulent arrangement of the paperwork.

Tax Forms

Tax assessment forms are required by law to be completed and filed with the chief officer (the *prostamenos*). If you work for a company registered in Greece whose Head Office is out of your area – there are over three thousand middle and large foreign companies presently in Greece – then your form must be filed in that area, not that of your residency. Final submission dates differ according to status: for the self-employed, the salaried, the pensioned etc. All supporting documentation (receipts and records etc.) has to be filed with the form, and all have to be professionally translated into Greek by a recognised translator of the Ministry of Foreign Affairs. It is not a cheap operation.

You will be taxed on the (new) principle of *antikeimenika kriteria:* 'objective criteria': what the tax assessor can see and discover about you, as mentioned above. This now assumes minimum income levels for various professions, even failed professionals. Self-employed people, of which Greece has a very high number, and merchants, are the chief targets of this new regime. Over a thousand employment types are listed by DOY, with their presumed incomes.

Indices of Wealth

Imputed wealth is a corollary of this attitude. Residences, domestic staff (including children's tutors), motor vehicles and motor-cycles, boats and crew members, aircraft, all forms of investment (bonds, securities and shares etc.), land-holdings, and capital obtained from the sale of assets, all come within this purview and are taxable. If you live in your own home, a rent-value (*tekmarto*) will be given to it, based on the objective criteria. Should it be less than 200 sq. m it will not be taxed; above that, or if you have a second home over 120 sq. m, you will be taxed for it (them, i.e. their conjoint size). Houses in excess of 300 sq. m are subject to a special tax. As there is yet no adequate Land Registry, officials have been given the job of preparing lists of real estate properties in order to secure the most complete inclusion under the law.

A further list of presumed expenditures on your motor-vehicle's maintenance is also being brought to bear on one's presumed wealth, despite the fact that vehicles in Greece must be among the worst maintained in Europe (an aspect the government is also seeking to overcome). The size of the engine is the chief point in this; as it is with boats, whose age and length are also taken into account.

The size of the office of the self-employed is also taken as an index of wealth, along with its location and notional value. Additionally, the self-employed are tax-indexed according to their qualifications, their length of experience, the number of services or employees used, and the average earnings of similar professionals; even the living standards of their clientele is brought into the equation. The tax level for those earning over 15 million drachmas per annum is presently 45%.

Pensioners and low wage earners (to 800,000 drachmas) are exempt from mandatory declaration, as are those whose homes are less than 60 sq. m. A special reduction of 40% for pensioners and low wage earners (up to 400,000 drachmas) is in force providing they can produce the receipts of their purchases (to 1 million drachmas). These figures are also subject to change; you should check with your accountant or financial advisor as to the latest schedule.

The golden rule in this area is: if in doubt ask an expert; remembering that it is often cheaper in the long run to pay more now than to risk second-rate or criminal advice. There are large internationally based accounting companies in Athens and other large cities who have specialist departments for this (e.g. Price Waterhouse PLC, Coopers and Lybrand PLC, or KPMG PLC); some banks also offer this facility.

A Word of Caution

Organised criminal activity among financial advisors has been uncovered by the police; several hundred cases have so far come before the courts. Should you suspect that you are being fraudulently advised or black-mailed on any tax matter, it is your duty to report the matter to the police and the tax authorities in writing; complicity charges may well be brought against you if you do not do so.

RETIREMENT IN GREECE

Most people who retire to Greece do not have work on their minds – apart from the duties of house and garden. But for those still active and with time to spare some opportunities exist. It is one way of contributing something to the host country. This is especially so in the tourist industry which has got itself into a rut in recent years and is witnessing a very sharp down-turn as a result. It has the advantage of being largely seasonal; with many offices protected from the heat by air-conditioning it is not an unpleasant way of spending a few hours per week. Other possibilities lie in environmental or charity work – which are likely to be voluntary. Such organisations as the WWF are always promoting schemes that call for extra help, and that of a particularly satisfying kind.

You will be even more welcome if you come with capital to invest, or come with managerial experience. Regarding the latter you may be especially useful, though not necessarily more welcome, as others' ways, especially an abundance of paperwork, is not the Greek way. Whether you work or not, life for the retired in Greece is not without responsibilities to the State authorities, especially in regard to tax.

Chapter Fourteen

CONSUMER AFFAIRS AND FINANCE

akribos sta pitoura kai phtenos st'aleuri: 'penny wise, pound foolish.'

Greece is now a country in a hurry. It suffers from the contradiction of being the oldest civilisation in the west with the economic muscle of a third-world country – the result of countless invasions, the devastations of wars, the machinations of foreign governments, the catastrophic handling of its economy by dogmatic and self-serving leaders, of not a little corruption, and that selfishness of the wealthy and go-getters which makes huge fortunes with very little going to either the state or the workers. A study from Athens University has found Greece to be one of the most corrupt countries in Europe; four out of ten Greeks admit to bribing officials. These bribes cover everything, such as health-care, car licensing or schooling. Greece has not been helped by some of its best brains emigrating, then keeping their wealth overseas on their return. Many of its consumer affairs are subsumed under the problems governing these fiscal aspects, a point recognised by the world institutions.

THE NATIONAL DEBT

In 1994 the national debt was assessed by IOVE (The Foundation of Economic and Industrial Research) as 138% of the country's GDP. In 1995 no less than 21% – over a fifth – of the government's income was said to be required to finance it. The President of the Republic, the nation's saviour in 1974, spoke of 'the social and economic morass' into which it had fallen. Mr Karamanlis further warned that it 'faced disintegration' unless urgent and radical steps were taken. The duel between Papandreo and Mitsitakis had cost the country dear. At a different level the Mediterranean Research Institute declared that tax evasion represented 50% of the country's fiscal deficit; the government itself complaining that black economy dealings constituted 50% of GDP – with some startling details. For example, 90% of all building activities were said to involve 'moonlight' operations; between 60-70% of all tourist activity was similarly inflicted. Inflation was rampant, an unprecedented rise in bounced cheques occurred, and bankruptcy figures reached unprecedented levels. The EU, voicing many concerns, warned that 'the disparities were set to increase': the poor to get poorer, the rich richer. And that while personal debt increases horrifically. In the last ten years it has increased by almost 40 times, from 12.5 billion drachmae to 512.8 billion.

RADICAL CHANGES

From 1994 onwards, radical steps were taken to reverse this state. Socialist economics were abandoned, a very austere budget introduced, inflation (at over 12%) set to be curbed, along with foreign debt, some age-long principles of private rights abolished, huge tax reforms introduced, public spending pruned, price controls eased to allow competition, incomes subjected to stiff limitations, and huge injections of cash made by the world authorities – the World Bank, the International Monetary Union and the EU. As a result the country is now on an upward curve, converging more readily with the EU but the harsh restraints are continuing. Infrastructure investments of importance are once again under way, which have decreased the jobless figures and laid the foundation for the amelioration of Greece's wider integration into Europe in banking, transport and communications.

Social conditions have worsened, however. The poor are getting poorer, students and trade unionists are angry, professionals resent having to pay their taxes after years of cheating. The country has entered a period of deep unrest, exacerbated by the frailty of the government's reputation in the popular mind. And tourism has dropped away.

A NATION OF ENTREPRENEURS

The Near East has always produced monetary skills and carefulness. The Greeks have never been far behind in this; often they led the way. An interesting change has taken place in the language. The old Greeks used to say, *dei chrematon*: 'money is needed;' now they say, *chreiazometha*: 'we need money.' Under the Ottoman Empire they all but ran the economy, some of them emerging from it with enormous wealth. Others have accumulated such even in the darkest days of the twentieth century, as marine merchants, entrepreneurs, etc. Greeks are shrewd and tough negotiators; they enjoy the business of bargaining. All this has produced a very materialistic nation, the standard of the good life being that of possessions and status: a long way from the thinkers who laid the ideals of the nation-state 2500 years ago and despite the maxim that 'money is the root of all evil.' The principle of 'go-getting' is intrinsic to Greekness; necessarily so considering the poverty of the nation's natural resources, the difficulties of its terrain and climate. Odysseus 'the wily' is regarded as the great icon. It is not only his physical strength and the determination of his character which is admired, but his ability to pull off a *coup*. He was the 'Smart Alec' of the Bronze Age. His nimble wits are applauded, even when they are seen to be flagrantly dishonest.

This does not mean that one can never get a fair deal in Greece; far from it. Generosity is also part of the Greek way. But be warned that established customs do not traditionally require a negotiant; be warned of the weaknesses and the problems you are about to obtain with your 'bargain' purchase. One couple known to me were sold a damaged gas-fire that could have killed them; on complaint no one wanted to know. The principle is still *caveat emptor*: let the buyer beware.

Tremendous bargains have been gained by foreigners buying into Greece – in land and property notably. It is done at the expense of Greeks whose young people are faced with escalating house prices and mortgages of impossibly high rates. Greece has now taken her place in Europe; her economy is converging with its partners. In some matters Greece is now more expensive than elsewhere. But the balance is still in her favour. For example, the cost of purchasing a house may not today be much cheaper than in northern countries, but what you get for it, the views and the climate, its produce and their benefits – not least lower fuel and repair bills, easily outweigh those of the north.

COST OF LIVING

The advantages of lower costs in Greece were confirmed in the round a few months ago by the Swiss Banker's Union, which selected a hundred standard items of consumption and service and investigated their price ranges among the leading cities of Europe. It was based on the standard of 100. Athens was found to be in the lower part of the analysis, scoring but 60.2 – as against Zurich which scored 100, or Copenhagen (the most expensive) which scored 102.1. The lowest scorer was Lisbon, at 55.6 – only 4.6 below Athens. So long as Greece's inflation rate remains high (it stood at 12% during this investigation) the threat to its cost of living index will remain high. But the inflation figure has been reduced by 6.5% since the SBU did its research and it now stands at 7.5%. If it can continue this excellent work through the present political unrest the omens are good, for at least a steady position on prices' inflation.

THE RETAIL INDUSTRY

Major changes have been taking place in the last fifteen or so years, which have brought Greece's retail industry nearer to north European or USA standards (the latter, of course, are still well ahead of the rest of the world). But there are differences. On the whole Greek supermarkets, and the even fewer hypermarkets, tend to go for range rather than price and quality, their competition being differently slanted, in line with Greek demographics and terrain etc. The 'pile it high and sell it cheap' philosophy has been largely ignored in Greece; as has the loss-leader concept. This means that their prices are not substantially less than the corner shop; though one has more choice, better packaging, and extra freshness – sometimes. This is a factor which doubtless affects the very high food expenditure of families. It remains to be seen whether they will shift the centres of shopping, as they have in the West. Discount stores are almost unknown in Greece, especially away from the urban areas. As more supermarkets are built and as better roads are opened, competition is bound to increase, though one wonders at the presence of cartels. The heavy hand of government intervention is still at work. In the annual sales, for example, dates and times and prices are controlled; occasionally relaxed or extended, but the full freedoms that signify an open market economy are not yet completely installed. Other areas of control include school supplies, books and children's clothing, and tuition fees.

Retailing takes place between the hours of 8.00–2.00 p.m. on Mondays, Wednesdays and Saturdays; and 8.00–1.00 p.m. and 5.00–8.00 p.m. on Tuesdays, Thursday and Fridays, though local variations apply. In the tourist season much longer hours are in vogue even on Sundays, though by and large 'the Continental Sunday' has been withstood in Greece. The usual threefold division is evident, to which we must add the kiosks (*peripteroi*), which are open at all sorts of hours, selling almost anything. (Their licences were a special concession after the war to aid veterans; they are quite often very valuable.) The big three are: hypermarkets, supermarkets and sole traders, with much over-lapping. Hypermarkets sell almost anything; supermarkets tend to sell within the traditional grocery lines, with the addition of meats and vegetables, some kitchen and stationery items. Some of these are little more than well stocked corner shops – and not always that. Mini-markets are but corner-shops with big ambitions.

A local supermarket with ambitions

Hypermarkets

Hypermarkets *per se* are of recent date in Greece. The first, Makro, was opened at Egaleo West in the capital in November 1991. (This is actually a cash-and-carry warehouse catering for the needs of small traders, restaurants, hotels and kiosks; they require strict passes stating the purchaser's status.) The number of hypermarkets has increased; they are led by the big four: Prisunic-Marinopoulos (sometimes simply Marinopoulos), Sklavenitis, HellasSpar Veropoulos and Alpha-Beta Vassilopoulos. Other contenders are: Atlantik, Continent, Masoutis, Metro, Niki (a subsidiary of Marinopoulos), Paschalias, Promodes, Tresko, Kreta Markets, and Le Lion. The activity is now mature enough to sport its own association, GSOA, and its own journal *Self-Service*.

Sole Traders

The sole traders continue to function traditionally but with an eye for expansion wherever possible, which in these competitive days is not easy. Many have been forced out of business; doubtless many more will follow. Unlike the supermarkets and the hypermarkets, they are not setting standards, save the few specialists such as the confectioners (*zacharoplastes*).

Direct Marketing

A fourth element is beginning to emerge – direct marketing, now very big business, here as elsewhere. The already cacophonous airwaves are being injected with the bombastic voices of salesmen, including that cat-call of the late twentieth century, 'If the lines are busy try again, but do call.' The alluring enchantments of ancient Medea have deteriorated into those of the media. These are mixed into radio and television programmes without art or artifice, mouse-bait appearing with Mozart, Ravel with ratatouille – to name two examples. To this must be added an even more disconcerting aspect, the introduction in 1993 of network marketing.

Hot telephone lines and slick patter have never been hotter or slicker; it became a booming business almost overnight. Often portrayed as 'clubs,' the only clubbing which is likely to take place is on the pockets of those drawn into schemes which are not yet controlled by law.

CONSUMER PROTECTION

The customer here is not 'always right;' one can fall foul of badly trained and ill-mannered staff. Shoddy workmanship is more of a problem, however. But consumer protection is rising, albeit slowly. Retailers are now required to give written notice of defective goods – which reminds one of their law prohibiting pavement parking! But the law is there, and that is a first step. Greek shoppers are mostly very well informed in fresh food matters. The housewife knows what cut of meat or type of fish she wants, and she knows what it should look like if fresh. If you show ignorance, expect to be taken for a ride; show knowledge, and you will be respected – and you might even get what you want. Your local butcher may even agree to hang your joint for you – a common fault being to sell meat off too quickly.

Labelling

Labelling is now slowly catching up with EU regulations, so watch the labels as well as the quality and the prices. Food preservatives and colourings – the infamous E numbers – are particularly important if you or your family suffer from any of the allergy-related ones. Sell-by dates are not always observed; any infringements should be avoided. It is a good idea to 'go Greek' and buy loose goods, e.g. dry commodities (beans, peas, rice, herbs etc.) which offer excellent value and easy storage. Some sifting will be necessary. I have spent many an hour throwing out teeth-breaking objects among chick peas, but somehow the resultant dishes always seemed to be more enjoyable for that. Some markets have market-police (*Agoranomia*) in attendance, who will offer advice or re-weigh your goods.

Consumer Rights Organisations

Private and public consumer protection is on the increase. There are about fifty such organisations in Greece, such as the Consumer Rights' Association. The over-arching body is INKA – the general Federation of Greek Consumers. In March 1994 *Ta Nea* published a list of the top ten complaints made to INKA which I repeat here in their order of magnitude: telephone (OTE), power supply (DEH), inflation, contamination of foodstuffs (e.g. foreign bodies, cereal-bulking in corned beef; colourings and preservatives), water supplies (EYDAP), mass-media, recreation and tourism, public administration (the impoliteness and ignorance of its officials in particular), transport (especially in the public sector) and environmental damage.

Thanks to the EU, consumer protection is now an international matter. Once properly installed, its Consumer Price Index will be an additional help, though Greece's historic waywardness with figures will doubtless be a factor to watch. Of even greater help is its *Green Book*.

BANKING

EBTA (The Hellenic Industrial Investment Bank) claims that Alexander the Great started the first bank, including the principle of secrecy, at Susa in Persia (Iran) in 324 BC. *Trapeza* is Greek for bank; also for 'table;' the point relies on 'the tables heaped with gold' that Alexander set before his men to relieve them of their debts. Whatever the truth of that story, it is certain that Greece has honoured both aspects. Perhaps only Switzerland has preserved as much independence in banking as has Greece. However, since January 1994 the EU regulation concerning 'the free movement of capital' has been in force, though this has not proved to be quite as open as was promised. Greek banks have responded somewhat unwillingly to the EU in this regard, though it is getting better. It is still important to retain your 'pink slips' – receipts of imported capital – as these will be required for both tax and transfer reasons.

The National Bank of Greece

The National Bank of Greece has always proved very helpful. Accounts are opened swiftly, with the minimum of fuss and paperwork – your money and your passport are all that are required. Its usual hours of opening (their branches are to be found in all the main centres, linked electronically to each other) are from 8.00 to 2.00 p.m. Mondays to Thursday, 8.00 to 1.00 p.m. on Fridays. In some cities they are open for additional hours, which should be checked locally.

Investing

Interest rates are high, so loans – when available – are expensive; but investment is good, yielding highly, thanks to the Greek tradition of thrift. As this goes to Press the official rate is 15.50%, by far the highest among EU nations, plus Canada, Japan and USA; its nearest neighbour is Italy, at 6.75%.

Many country people do not trust banks and Greece is still a cash economy to a large extent; but this is altering under modern pressures. One friend who transferred a modest sum to Greece under her local manager's guidance, has lived happily and well ever since.

It is wise to get professional advice for investments. The main accountancy companies all have their money-managing and tax departments, as do the banks; for the large investor, recourse should be had to EBTA, whose *Investment Guide* and *Business Directory* are standard works; it also produces particular and annual reports. For those with a yen for excitement, the Athens Stock Exchange exists to fulfil your every need. It is always wise to take corollary advice in such matters; and the legal aspects should be confirmed by your lawyer. If you have international interests, currency movements will be of great importance, as will the fluctuating inflation rates. The imminence of the single currency – thirteen countries out of a possible fifteen have recently been given the green light from Brussels; excluding Greece – is another factor to be kept in mind. One friend has a profitable retirement pastime in playing the stock-market, most of which is done by telephone-link with the UK. Internet facilities are now making of this a superior and more sensitive undertaking.

INSURANCE

This is big business in Greece, with all the large companies angling for a share in its market. Whatever your needs, they can be met, but the secret for the best deal is to shop around. Again your financial advisor or bank manager will help; Greek banks have a long history in this involvement. New regulations which legalise the activities of the brokers place them and their agents and activities under close scrutiny, but the small print is always to be watched.

—Chapter Fifteen —

GARDENING

TRIGG.

Greece can be an intoxicating delight for those who love gardening; it can also be heart-breaking misery – thanks to its impoverished soil, abundance of rock, limited water and burning sun. You need not only 'to know yourself' but your plot of land, too.

Those who want a large and beautiful garden and are building their own house must make their plans early, to ensure choosing a place with the best soil, water supply and climate. Greece offers a great range of plants, shrubs and trees for the enthusiastic and adventurous gardener, but what you may grow in the north will be very different from what you may grow in the south, and the eastern part of the country will limit you more strenuously than the western. What you can grown at sea-level is very different from what will barely flourish at 1000 feet. Note *what* you see in your area, *how* it grows, and *when*. It is unlikely that you will alter the natural preferences of plants and soil, still less the seasons. You can choose lushness or aridity, but you will not be able to convert the one into the other easily.

FIRST A FENCE

Start with a fence or wall. These are important both for privacy and for protection, but also characterise your garden to a certain extent and determine part of its use. A chain-link fence is cheap and quick to erect, but unless you cover it with foliage it will not give you privacy nor your garden protection from wind or sun. Anything with a small snout will also be able to enjoy what grows on it or near it. A wooden fence is better, but is subject to the weather and will require a certain amount of upkeep – though not as much as fences do in wetter climes. If worried about security, fences can be broken and chain-link cut by the very determined. Walling is best, but the most expensive.

SOME POINTERS

Which way does your garden face? At what points does the sun rise and set? What are the prevailing winds? Are there any wind-tunnels from neighbouring property or hills etc.? What altitude is it? (This will have a very important bearing on what you grow.) Is there likely to be water movement across it, in winter or spring especially? Are there frost-pockets? Do not forget the local bird or animal population. Well-worn tracks suggest an oncoming problem, say from goats, or badgers, or moles – or birds with a sweet beak, so to speak. You may be delighted to have frogs about, but snakes will be grateful, too.

Have you allowed enough space for the trees to grow? Will your views be obscured by your favourite trees, or your walls endangered by them? Five years can make a world of difference in Greece. A fig-tree is a wonderful shade in the summer months, and keeps its colour delectably, but it will grow huge – and it will not take too kindly to your pruning it.

In thinking of plants one must think of function and over-all effect as well as subtler aspects such as leaf shape and texture, height and colour, fragrance, seasonal growth and usage. You may wish to use the services of a consultant – a relatively new concept in Greece, but one now expanding. But it is much more fun to do it oneself, reading up from the manuals, talking to the experts, laying it out according to one's exact preferences. Think of the effects carefully: vines or ramblers grow at phenomenal speed in the right conditions in Greece. A Greek friend planted a vine in a one-metre gap between his tall building and the perimeter fence. I laughed at it and said it would never grow in such conditions; three years later he had a superb green canopy two floors up to two roof-top arbours, from which dangled succulent grapes in season.

SOIL

An important factor to keep in mind is the soil – or its absence. Experts reckon that 95% of Greece's topsoil has disappeared since Plato's day, through water and wind erosion. Even in Plato's day he wrote of Attica's soil as 'the bones of a body wasted away with disease.' Walling, as opposed to fencing, offers better protection against erosion. You will need to plan ahead if the soil is thin or exhausted. If building your own house you will need bulk deliveries early to avoid remaking access points for the lorries, and for over-coming the problems of soil-impaction that deliveries and building make. You may need to import worms, minerals and fertilisers (the three principal ones are phosphorous for roots; nitrogen for leaves and stems; and potash/potassium for flowers, fruit and seed). Manure may be available; it is wise to get this laid early too, so that the worst effects of its odour have passed by the time the building is completed. The best is pigs', followed by goats', sheep', cows' or asses'. Unfortunately, the odour level seems to keep pace with the nutrient value, which may render pigs' manure out of the question if you wish to enjoy good neighbourly relations. Wood ash should not be forgotten – burn it on site when possible; fig trees like it particularly.

Test your soil, and start working towards the ideal pH-levels you need for your choice of plants. Check on the drainage to ensure that it is neither too dry nor too wet – or vulnerable to flash-flooding.

Nature abhors a vacuum; you will be amazed how quickly your ground is covered by a green sward, which you can dig in as green manure. Having this planting gap carries an additional advantage: you will be able to see what grows there naturally. You may be pleasantly surprised to find quite unusual plants, some of which have a very short life but are very beautiful while they last; some may be protected by law. If you have brought in extra soil all sorts of plant-life may come with it; better to see it now while it is in a weak and disturbed condition than later when it has put down roots.

OTHER GARDEN STRUCTURES

Plants and tertiary structures come next. Some of the latter will already be high on your agenda, and will take shape from the outset of the building. Others need to be put in position as early as possible, for reasons given above. Any that are not laid – pools or sheds etc. – should now be done, in outline at least; plus extra paths, walls and terracing. Siting a greenhouse, for example, is important and must include the protection of your views, and its protection from the sun, children's play-areas, trees and the weather. If you are able to do these things while the builders are working it offers several advantages: you can keep an eye on them; and they will offer you advice as to how they would do things and what materials they would use; they may help you to move heavy objects, and you will be able to extend your involvement with Greeks and thus make some useful contacts. A bottle of ouzo and a plate of *meze* go a long way in this connection.

CHOOSING PLANTS

'There is nuthin' like a tree' crooned Paul Robeson rapturously, the great singer of Negro spirituals; and that is especially true in Greece whether you regard the stately growth and stature of the cypress, the prolific generosity of the fig, the dense green of an orange or lemon tree, the loftiness of the palm – or their brilliant colourings.

Be creative in your planting. You can think body-shop, for example, by planting juniper, bay, cassie, orange, storax etc., and have your own perfumery-on-the-hoof. Make your own carrier: oil from almond, apricot, avocado, sesame, wheatgerm or calendula, grapeseed even. It is not more difficult than making your own wine. Or think functionally, with wine and resin, pitch and broom, heather and thorn-bush, flax or turpentine etc. Or pharmaceutically, with ephedra, peony, bongardia, leontice, eruca, etc. The choices are abundant, though one should bear in mind the danger to young children of some of these choices – of *Agrostemma* or *Delphinium staphisagria*, for example, which have poisonous parts. Best of all, think nutritionally, with lemons and oranges, apples and pears, quince and persimmon, plum and fig, olives and grapes, nuts and seeds, salads and peppers, cucumbers and melons, herbs and spices – the list is endless, and the delights – to eye and palate – voluptuous. Do not just swallow your vitamins; grow them; and enjoy them as nature intended – off the plant and as fresh as the morning sun.

Many of the trees we now regard as Greek have in fact been imported to it, albeit centuries ago. Examples of these are: the olive, vines, orange, lemon, fig, pomegranate and the date palms. Some of these have political as well as historical overtones. (The pomegranate, for example, comes from Phoenicea, and is rich in folk-lore and mythological aspects.) A few decades ago the government ordered the palms in Omonia Square in Athens to be cut down as they were too 'eastern'! Greece's original trees include the carob, myrtle, plane, oak, lentisk (or mastic) and so on. It would be foolish to exclude the olive or vine whose coming to Greece is celebrated in the – sometimes contradictory – mythologies and are now an irrefutable part of Greekness.

Inspiration from Ancient Lore

If you have a bent for history, you can delve into the horticultural lore of ancient Greece. For example, why not plant a *Laurus nobilis* - the Greek *dafni* (from Daphne, the mythological nymph who changed into a laurel tree) as a windbreak or shrubbery item? Then they will truly say of you *anapauetai eis daphnas tou*: 'he is resting on his laurels,' as they did of winners in ancient Greece.

Should you be near water then the classic tree in old Greece – much in evidence today – is the willow. If not near water, then the plane tree. The willow is fast growing, seven metres in four years is not unknown, and its wands have many garden uses with cricketing overtones. Like the olive, it may be pollarded when too energetic. Alders alongside these give a stirring visual note, offering the further advantage that both do well on degraded soils.

Creating a Functional Garden

Think radical as well as traditional, and do not forget the functional. Every Greek garden should have olive trees, fig and pomegranate trees, oranges and lemons. And what incomer would pass up the chance of having a vine arbour? A friend was once scathing about my suggestion to establish one. 'Pure banality!' was the damning verdict. Well yes, in one sense. But to enjoy its fragrance and shade on a late summer's day, to be able to stretch up and savour its sun-warmed sweetness, to enjoy your own 'Beaujolais' in the late autumn, cannot be judged on purely 'artistic' (and to that extent artificial) merits. The vine plant is also one of the chief ingredients for dolmades. You will never regret planting your vine, and if it loops its way around your balcony so much the better.

The vine is also a useful source of mulch. I have been struck by how many gardens do not bother with this very important component, particularly useful in Greece where the many narrow-leaved or spinous trees offer little mulch value.

A Kitchen Garden

The kitchen garden should best be kept to the kitchen side of the house, and the items of most usage, e.g. herbs, placed within easy distance of its door. Drying areas – for laundry and for vegetables or fruit – will also be required, each requiring particular needs: wind for laundry; sun or shade for the others. Beware of growing foodstuffs that quickly become inexpensive in the markets, e.g. potatoes, onions or tomatoes, unless you grow non-commercial varieties. 'Buying local' is an important principle: what the local experts can grow you can, too – given a little luck and much hard work. Keeping your soil in first-rate condition is expensive – fertilisers are not cheap in Greece, even less your time. So why grow products that can be bought cheaply and in tip-top condition?

Aromatherapy at Your Door ...

There are all sorts of herbal or medicinal plants, those famous for their leaves and those for their flowers, those useful for insect attraction and those for their repelling, those for food and those merely for the eye, those that do best on land and those specific to wet conditions, and so on. One especially nice use of herbs is to use them for paths. Chamomile, for example, makes a superb garden path, the walking of which is to shroud oneself in fragrance – the best form of aromatherapy. Merely to think thyme and rosemary along one's path, or orange blossom at sunset, is to capture another essence of Greekness, which you can have at your very door – to say nothing of roses, pine or oregano(one of the few herbs whose fragrance actually increases by being dried). Another idea is to build a sitting or picnic area in the herb garden, that way you can taste as well as smell their fresh delights.

Careful Planning with Trees

Trees should be considered un-moveable (some may be under preservation orders in any case), so care as to their siting and future growth is essential. Their roots can block drains and damage walls, and their canopies might be a fire hazard if placed too close to house or garage. Some trees 'leak' substances that will spoil your patio or car; very tall trees may attract lightening, and some (e.g. the olive) are ground-root feeders which will prevent the earth underneath them from being used for other production. Very large fig trees may need to have their boughs propped up to prevent splitting which looks unsightly. The access needs of harvesting must be kept in mind: oranges require ladders, olives a large plastic sheet, and so on. Cordon-trees require good fencing and light. Many trees have natural habitats that you may try to alter at your peril: palms love dry sandy soil, silver leaved plants are generally good in salty dry and windy areas, most trees grow best in groups – which also provides insect and bird cover as well as good fertilisation. Some plants do best under such conditions too; it is not always wise to go for open designs.

Flowers

Unless you are a martyr to hard work, perennials are best. Once rooted, they will almost look after themselves, and if chosen carefully you will have colour the year round. In Huxley and Taylor's book, *Flowers of Greece*, the authors distinguish flowers in four useful categories: seaside, hillside, mountainside and island. At one read, therefore, one is given a panoramic view of what is possible in any particular location. Their book is a tour of delight, but that is nothing compared to the realities that careful selection, sowing or planting will produce; to say nothing of the culinary by-products, the birds, bees and butterflies which will add sound and colour to your garden.

Oleander

The oleander is one of the best known shrubs, often used as a hedge. Grown to two metres or so, it can also be a useful and picturesque form of privacy. Curious customs also appertain to this plant. For example, sprigs of oleander are placed in fig and pomegranate trees to enhance their rooting growth in some places. In others they are actually attached to the roots. Again, the plant plays part in the 'coronation' days of figs and pomegranates whose crowns are made of oleander and marjoram. A more interesting use is that of its sap, which is used as a styptic.

Bougainvillaea

Who can resist the sheer splendour of that famous Brazilian import bougainvillaea? It comes into its own as a covering for garage walls or villa extensions. So long as it has good soil and space to climb in, it will expand riotously, offering colour and shade almost the whole year round. Its branches are an elegant internal decoration. Its spikiness is also useful for keeping children and animals away from prohibited areas.

A Lawn

Because of the heat and aridity you will have your work cut out to keep up a lawn, but special grasses can be bought which fare better in the Greek climate, especially South African varieties. A friend bemoaned his foolishness in laying a lawn near his house; its upkeep was exhausting and he often thought of having it removed. Then the adjacent land was caught in a hill-fire which spread with awesome speed up and across the mountain. We simply did not have sufficient hoses to fight it, and in any case the overhead power lines soon came down so that water pumps failed. Others in the area were reduced to a fevered and crude chopping of trees and vegetation to preserve their houses, even bull-dozing some parts. Not all of them, alas, were successful, and many painful losses were suffered, human and otherwise. Life was genuinely at risk; some simply fled. My friend's lawn proved a very special blessing that day and justified the hard work that had been put into it over the years.

PLANT CARE

Greek habits of tree-care should be studied. You will note their reliance on a circular method of watering at the base. All vegetation to about a metre's length from the trunk is dug away and the soil loosened; a ridge is then formed around the trunk at that distance. This prevents water and dew from running off, as most is drained back towards the trunk. Water soaks into the root system and is protected from evaporation by the leaf canopy; what natural water is available is thus maximised. Other plants are similarly treated, especially in large areas such as vineyards; ground-cover is left to grow naturally, kept in check by grazing animals, usually sheep, pigs or goats (beware of these latter; they will eat everything in sight). Deals can be struck with the shepherds by which rent in kind – chops or cheese – is paid for grazing rights; thus only the plants need attention. Another method of preventing water loss is to cover the loosened area with small stones or a heavy mulch, such as bark if available.

If you are daring and decide to have a goat or two, remember that they are very aggressive in their demand for food, and will not stop even at climbing trees in order to satisfy their hunger. Fences for such have to be strong enough to withstand their ardour; thorny or spiky plants are best, such as hawthorn.

COMPOSTING

It is never too early to start composting. You should have at least two areas for this so as to allow adequate time for decomposition. Start now, ensuring that it is well away from the house and patio etc., and not too close to combustible materials or plants. Situate them on the lee side of the garden to avoid odours; add all leaf and other vegetable matter and newspapers to it, layering it with earth from time to time. If you can find them, add worms to encourage good soil growth.

WATER FOR YOUR GARDEN

A word or two about water supply is necessary here. It is one of Greece's direst problems, and its lack can wreck your life. I have seen pleasant personalities badly deteriorate under the strain of insufficient water, and heard sad tales of unending disputes with neighbours, and huge lawyers' bills in consequence. Ensure that your supply is safe and dependable, and make sure that you do not contravene others' rights in its enjoyments. I know of water-theft being practised, and not just by Greeks. In some areas rationing comes into force under certain conditions, the penalties for whose ignoring are tough. Most people will be either on line with the national supplier or have their own well. But the latter may be shared, even rationed to certain daily amounts or hours of usage. If it is restrained, steps can be made to make it go further. Domestic irrigation systems are inexpensive.

Cisterns

One of the oldest structures in the Near East is the cistern – you will see them abandoned all over Greece, though many more lie out of sight and functional. If you think your site will sustain such, why not have a cistern built at the same time as the foundations are dug for your house? They are relatively inexpensive, but the savings – of time and energy etc. – are enormous. I speak as one who once had to transport water, 10 x 35 litres of it at a time, halfway up a mountain, and then pump it into a cistern. If you have a cistern you may have natural drainage into it, or you may lay out plastic sheets and catch the water that way, sailor-like. A large sheet can be put on a roller alongside a house wall and brought into use at a moment's notice; it can also double up as a sun-shade. Have the guttering and down-pipes so placed that the roof and the patio aid its filling; even the roofs of sheds and garages can be so utilised, if only for gardening purposes. One acquaintance cut a joint into his bathroom and kitchen outlet pipes and joined them up to piping leading to a large barrel which was secreted behind some colourful bushes. The result was an unending supply of (soapy) water that helped to nourish and protect his plants. Another, if small, gain is to use the waste that comes from having defrosted your fridge; at a certain point in the operation you can chip off the ice that has formed and place it exactly where you wish it to be most useful. Be careful not to leave untreated water exposed, as insects will quickly take over – never so quickly as the mosquito.

Pools

A million hectares of wetlands have been destroyed around the Mediterranean since the end of the Second World War. It behoves us all to do what we can to preserve both plant and animal life. Pools are ideal for this. Their careful siting can have a great effect on the local environment, and ameliorate one's lifestyle. Some build them for swimming, others for water-life, others for show. Evaporation is the key problem; up to 70% of your water may be lost through it. Take steps to limit this loss, by means of a roll-back covering or by building a pergola over it; alternatively you may plant trees or large reed-type plants to shade it. Where there are young children, spiky plants – such as berberis – are essential to safeguard them.

OR A GARDEN GONE WILD ...

It is sometimes helpful to ignore the artificial distinction between flowers and weeds. One couple known to me, who only manage to attend to their garden for three or four weeks per year, have a magical 'wild patch' which is no stranger to tortoises and snakes, rabbits and birds, all enjoying its untamed qualities. It is not a habit that will necessarily go down well with your neighbours, but its pleasures are very many including its relative lack of upkeep effort.

EXPLORING GREECE'S UNIQUE FLORA

Greece has an abundance of flowers, herbs and grasses, to suit every locality, season and taste. They number 6750, of which 600 are unique to it. Space does not allow the listing of these; suffice it to say that the well-known ecologist W B Turrill (author of the 1929 classic *Plant Life of the Balkan Peninsula*) lists 700 species specific to the Balkans' area, of which Greece has over three hundred; Crete offers 131 unique plants; the Attic peninsula and Mount Olympos each have 16. It is for you to consult the manuals and determine your preferences, but you will have the time of your life planting and enjoying them, and thus giving back to Greece something of her own rich heritage.

Chapter Sixteen

YOUR FAMILY AND OTHER ANIMALS

TRIGG

PETS

There are few restrictions on the importing of animals into Greece and fewer still for taking your pets with you and keeping them there. No licences are required, but you must have a suitable collar (with name, address and telephone number) for your dog; without this, if found, it will be judged *adespotos*, masterless, and may be taken or destroyed. A veterinarian's certificate is crucial, certifying good health, i.e. as well as confirming the usual inoculations and vaccinations.

Trauma

Bear in mind the trauma your pet may suffer on moving, both from the move itself and its new environment. If moving from a colder climate, remember that some dog breeds are not suited to hot climates. It will be necessary to keep your pet under some restriction at first, to keep it from wandering off or being attacked by the local animals. It will have lost its territorial base, and will need to make a new one. Allow it time for this; expect fur to fly if it comes into collision with other animals and their territorial ideas. This is especially so for cats who will not be restricted by fences.

Keep the heat in mind and ensure that your dog always has a shady and cool place to lie in and a full bowl of fresh water. In moving you will be radically changing your pet's feeding habits. Even if you buy the same brand of food it will not be from the same meat or fish, as local suppliers are licensed to substitute local types for the original.

Author's pet dog outside cottage in Mt. Ares

A little extra pampering is in order, and possibly some doctoring of the food during the transitional stage. In some areas pet food may be scarce; village people do not generally use it. Their method is to use stale bread (either their own or specially bought pieces) which is soaked in water and thrown out for the animals; meat needs are left to their pets' natural instincts. One neighbour kept thirteen cats on this basis, and I cannot say they looked much the worse for it.

Gifts from your pets!
Be prepared for your cats bringing their lunch home. Rats and mice and birds and crickets etc. are easily – if carefully – handled; but snakes are a different matter, cats love to bring them in. One friend kept his long-handled coal tongs handy for such gifts; another a spade. The good news is that the majority will be grass snakes, and harmless. But be careful of the horned-lip viper which loves gardens and water barrels. Cat-traps in the house are a great idea, but they can be used by others.

Veterinarian Services
If living outside the large cities in Greece, you may want to do some extra planning; veterinarian services are not easily available outside the cities. If you want to have your cat neutered for example, do it before you go. A vet may also be willing to give you some medication to cover various possible diseases your pet may pick up, to ward off ticks and other parasites, and some elementary equipment for do-it-yourself treatment (for medication measures such as a hypodermic needle, eye-drop applicator). Greeks often medicate their own animals, and even put them down brutally when the need arises.

STRAYS
Greeks are, generally speaking, much harder towards animals, even to the point of cruelty (as some would judge). This is not to say that many do not love and look after their pets; they do, some of them very expensively. But on the whole, there are very many *adespotoi,* strays

in Greece and they can be a nuisance. Every town and port has them. Dogs band together naturally, which can be daunting. Both cats and dogs are often disease-ridden; be very careful of handling them. It is not unusual for some to be killed deliberately by the use of rodenticides which is illegal. Dumping is another way unwanted animals are got rid of. Most of them in public areas are wild in the full sense of the word, afraid of humans thanks not least to the kicks and stone-throwing they receive. Some sights can be truly disgusting.

The number of strays can be amazing. For example, there are said to be over 400 cats at large in the National Gardens near Syntagma Square, Athens; of every sort and shape imaginable. Not a few people feed them daily, and do so sacrificially. I have seen this at many other places in Greece. One lady on the Apollo Coast used to drive up in her very expensive car at 6 a.m. every day. She would empty a sack of feed into four or five bowls and shout; a dozen or more dogs would appear instantly. She then stood guard over them, fending off the large and greedy for the sake of the small and weak and refilling the bowls as necessary. She then collected her bowls and disappeared. Fishermen often keep a string of cats who do useful work in clearing up their catch debris, seagulls competing for the fishy remains along the quayside. They are given to quarrelling – the animals I mean (well, the others, too) – and if a female is in season the noise can be horrendous.

ANIMAL WELFARE GROUPS

The late *Greek News* did sterling work for the strays, bringing the problem to the attention of people generally and the authorities. It frequently offered free advertising space to animal welfare groups, and supported their work in many other ways. One excellent scheme is run hand in hand with the Council of the Cultural Centre of the Municipality of Athens; George and Othonas Vardas offer an Animal Lovers' Award in the name of their parents to children between the ages of eight and sixteen. Thoughtfully they include the disavowal of hunting in any form – from children and their parents.

Others are PETA – the People for the Ethical Treatment of Animals; a Greek branch of the charity called The Friends of Cats; the St Francis of Assisi Animal Shelter; GAWF – the Greek Animal Welfare Fund; and HAWF – the Hellenic Animal Welfare Fund. There are a number of organisations that offer specific interests: SPMS – the Society for the Protection of Monk Seals; the Sea Turtle Protection Society of Greece; the Arcturus [Brown] Bear Society (a branch of MEDASSET); IAPPEA – the International Association against Painful Experiments in Animals; and the Aegean Wildlife Hospital. Some of these receive government and other official backing. The SPMS, for one, works in collaboration with the Greek Tourist Board.

ILLEGAL TRADE IN ANIMALS

The commercial use of animals, wild and otherwise, is of continuing concern. Some are traded for private and often temporary amusements, some for research purposes, some for their body parts – fur, horn etc.; some for taxidermy, which is not out of date here. Greece is one of the 120 national signatories to the Convention on International Trade in Endangered Species, CITES, which looks after flora as well as fauna. But the government does little itself to stop the trade, even though it has set up a department (TRAFFIC) to monitor it. It has to be said that Greece's attitude towards endangered species leaves much to be desired. As *The European* tartly observed, 'There doesn't seem to be much control.'

THE WWF

The WWF, the World Wide Fund for Nature, an international body, has a branch in Greece, though it finds itself frustrated at the obese bureaucracy which undergirds government initiatives. All too often a public statement is believed to be enough – the Greek belief in words – as opposed to action or legal imposition. The WWF has been active in Greece since 1969, and now has permanent representation here; it received charitable status in 1994. One of its first actions in Greece was the programme of reforestation on Mt Hermettus.

The WWF is a growing force in the country, energetically pursuing its objectives of 'preserving genetic, species and ecosystem diversity; ensuring that the use of renewable natural resources is sustainable ... and promoting actions to reduce pollution and the wasteful exploitation and consumption of resources and energy.'

Theirs is a high-minded campaign, but not a high-brow one. It is about sea turtles (*Caretta caretta*), the Mediterranean tuna (*Thunnus thynnus*), brown bears (*Ursus arctos*), Mediterranean monk-seals (*Monachus monachus*), wolves (*Canis lupus*), eagles (*Aquila heliaca*, now reduced to ten pairs) – to name a few of WWF's projects. At root, however, is the determination to preserve and improve the quality of life for humans and all life-forms, under deep threat in Greece, as elsewhere.

Over thirty full-scale projects have so far been completed throughout the country; twenty more are under way. Potentially the most important project is with the Ministry of Education: the distribution of an information box, beautifully prepared and illustrated, to every primary school child, teacher and mentor in the country, challenging them to take seriously nature's heritage. It includes a series of nine 'work-notes,' mini-projects that can be enjoyed, which promote the ends of the WWF. It is already being test-marketed in some schools, and it is hoped to be sent to every primary school in the country.

Another five major projects are under way:

- Attention to the forests of Greece.
- Improvement of Greece's water supplies.
- Amelioration of marine life, on the coastlines and at sea.
- Preparation of 'the Red Book;' a complete elucidation, with coloured pictures and carefully researched text, of all of Greece's 300 endangered species of flora from its natural bank of 6750 species.

• A Law Manual which will gather together all the regulations and laws of Greece and the EU concerning the environment, and offer practical guidance as to how these can best be implemented. (A hugely successful precursor to this was produced between 1987-92 on the threatened vertebrates.)

GREECE'S WILDLIFE

Greece offers a veritable Noah's Ark of birds, fish, reptiles and mammals, and has its fair share of the EU's 100,000 species of invertebrates and 408 varieties of birds (60% of which nest locally). The mammals are breath-taking – from the near-human dolphin (which gave its name to the famous oracle centre at Delphi), to the wild brown bears of Rhodope and Pindus, of which eighty survive. It is an unforgettable experience to find oneself in the middle of a school of dolphins, as happened to me at the end of a night-watch in the Gulf of Patras once. Greece also has a significant pelican population

RARE TURTLES

Greece also boasts of the very rare sea turtle, *Caretta caretta*. This turtle has made the beach at Lagana Bay, Zakynthos, world famous (the Venetians called it 'the flower of the orient') – despite the mindless construction work of the 'get-rich-quick' entrepreneurs and their conniving political allies. There are other turtle colonies on Crete and the Peloponnese but this one, of 800, is very special.

It is curious that Greece, whose pre-Olympian and Olympian deities had animal or bird associations (such as cow-eyed Hera or owlish Athene, etc.) has not preserved to itself such a figure for their national emblem. The Americans have their eagle, the Russians have their bear, and the British had their bull-dog – until economic reality pulled its teeth. The early Church did not ignore the usefulness of this sort of thing, symbolising three of the Gospels as lion, ass, ox and eagle – though not consistently. Perhaps the turtle should be considered for Greece: it is very ancient, durable, a great traveller, a persistent colonist, with long associations with the arts and music, crafts and gastronomy. As Byron commented:

> Know ye the land where the cyprus and myrtle
> Are emblems of deeds that are done in their clime;
> Where the rage of the vulture, the love of the turtle,
> Now melt into sorrow, now madden to crime!
> —*Bride of Abydos*, I.i

'The love of the turtle' smacks true of Greece: the male stays at sea, leaving the female to fend for herself in producing her young – as every packed *taverna* or *kapheneion* demonstrates. As for sorrow and the disposition to 'madden to crime,' they are the very substance of Greekness, its history and its drama, which ever reasserts itself.

SNAKES AND OTHER UNPLEASANT THINGS

Greece is a land of snakes and scorpions and things that go *bzzz* in the night; but their numbers and ill-effects have been hugely exaggerated.

Snakes

You will rarely see the former, but you only need *not* see one for problems to arise; so walk with care. Be careful not to put your fingers under wall edges or rocks without looking. Be careful also, when walking in isolated places or among ruins. I myself was looking at some old remains at Varsiki during the writing of this chapter; in stepping between some fallen stones with open sandals I all but put my foot on a viper, which quickly slid away – as they usually do unless cornered. I was moving slowly, and that is the secret: *festina lente.*

Snakes love to sun-bathe, but often do so out of sight, in very dry conditions; beware of them when walking off the beaten path. The horned viper (adder) is the only dangerous variety according to most, though Greek friends have warned me of a very small brown string-like snake – which they themselves have never seen. A friend recently saw a large one, possibly eight feet in length, at the bottom of Ares mountain; but it disappeared before he could get it in focus. If bitten, do not panic! Try to remember the colour, pattern and shape of the snake for identification purposes; horned vipers can be green, brown, smudge-green, grey and blackish. Restrict all physical activities such as walking, climbing, especially running; they cause the circulation to quicken. Restrict the blood flow higher than the bite, though do not apply a tourniquet unless you are skilled at doing so. Tourniquets must be released every ten minutes, to prevent gangrene. If you have splinting material – a rolled newspaper will do – splint the affected limb. Remove all rings, bangles, necklaces, and loosen tight clothing. Get to a doctor or hospital quickly. Snake serum is well distributed in Greece, in addition to which you must have an anti-tetanus injection.

Despite the above words of caution, snakes are part of the glorious past of Greece and an integral part of its mythology; we need to re-appreciate them. Sarakatsans, a nomadic people in Greece, actually feed them with milk. Contrariwise, April 25 is sometimes celebrated as the day to get rid of them. It is marked by noisy celebrations. Some ceremonies are quaint, such as displaying viper's heads in Trikorfo or Argithea; or throwing garlic heads on the fields in Tinos. In the church of Markopoulo, Kephallonia, the church is said to fill up with them between August 1-15, and then they disappear.

Scorpions

I have never seen a scorpion in Greece, apart from an innocuous type. If you are bitten by one the treatment is more or less the same as for snakes. They love to rest just out of sight, under ledges etc., so keep your fingers clear of such places. They are seldom fatal, despite their reputation. In the Gulf War over fifty such stings were reported; none was fatal. More damage was done by the prophylactics!

Bees and Wasps

A small practical point is to watch what you eat. Bees and wasps settling on apples and such being eaten *al fresco* have accounted for more than one life by occlusion of the trachea; a point especially important with young children.

Mosquitoes

Mosquitoes are likely to be the commonest nuisance. They are night creatures and loathe the light, hiding under beds and furniture during the day if trapped indoors. A party trick is to close all the doors and windows for a few minutes and put out the light. Light the adjacent balcony and set going an anti-mosquito device. Give it five minutes, then open the door or window nearest to the light: you will see them streaming out. There are many devices to ward them off: mains-electrical, battery, combustible, indoor and outdoor, creams and sprays. You will find the effect of their bites lessening the longer you stay in Greece as your body builds up its anti-bodies. It is vital that you do not scratch them – an exquisite torture – which makes them far worse and may leave you with festering scars. If you have severe reactions to them you should take medical advice. Often a single course of anti-histamine is sufficient.

Chapter Seventeen

PASTIMES AND THE MEDIA

Kane kati: 'Do something.'

THE ANCIENT GAMES

It is untrue to say that the Greeks invented games, but they certainly institutionalised them. They are as endemic to its culture as myths, heroes, poetry, drama, argument, forest fires, retsina and ouzo. An anonymous poet in *The Greek Anthology*: indicated that there were four games in Greece – two sacred to mortals, Palaemon and

Archemorus, and two to immortals, Zeus and Apollo. Their prizes were wild olive, apples, celery, and pine.

The four games were held at Olympia, Delphi, Corinth and Nemea. They are known to us as the Olympian, Pythian, Isthmian and Nemean Games, respectively. The first, of course, is the most famous and the only one to continue still. It was, however, outlawed in AD 393 by Theodosios the Great, on the grounds of its paganism – one of the degenerative acts of Christendom in its attempt to control men's minds by controlling their bodies. The Olympic Games were finally re-introduced after several false starts at the end of last century .

Nature used not to be in opposition to deities, science or religion, and the Games were thoroughly religious. What the wild-olive was to Olympia, apples (formerly the laurel) were to Delphi, pine to the Corinthian Isthmus, and celery to Nemea. Behind these emblems – once the acclaimed prizes – were their respective gods and goddesses who were notable for their sporting interests. We should not think only of these four games though; games were endemic to Greece long before 776 BC, as the bull-jumping in the ancient city of Knossos or the competitions mentioned in Homer's writing demonstrate. In addition to running, horse racing, strong-arm displays, boxing and wrestling, there was archery, song and poetry: the mind and body were both the focus of the ancient world, in proper and harmonious relatedness.

SPORTS TODAY

The Greeks are still at it today – in promoting competition, in acquiring physical skills and athleticism, in furthering speed and agility of mind; ever mindful of the body beautiful as well as mental excellence. The sense of fun which they exude is at its best in their games and pastimes which number many a dozen – on land and sea, under the sea and in the air, up mountains and down pot-holes, at card tables, on chess or backgammon boards. Fun is surely the right word to characterise the irrepressible, joyous element in their nature; a fun that is at the same time serious, and includes a determination to win.

Winning is everything in Greece, whether in bargaining, sealing a business deal, or scoring the decisive goal. The fun permeates the playing, and becomes a crescendo in the celebrations. It is this which differentiates them from over-serious Westerners, whose sporting interests are thoroughly regulated, usually corporate, often class-related – and unambiguously commercialised. The religious element is nowhere to be seen, perhaps happily. Robert Browning – a winning poet if ever there was one – made this comparison, 'the whole tone of Byzantine Christianity was optimistic, elastic, occasionally Panglossian, and very different from the more sombre, guilt-ridden Augustinian of the Latin west.'

Whether it be in *jeux d'esprit* or great feats of strength, Greeks love physicality as much as intellectual conflict, and are occupied by activities anywhere and at all ages: the old men splash around in the shallows on the coasts, or argue fiercely at cards; the middle-aged jog or fling themselves about the basketball courts; youths compete at everything, but mainly football – the second-most favourite Greek activity, or pit themselves against electronic tests of brain and hand; the very young are put early to learn and compete in the grace of movement and its strengths. Best of all perhaps, and in line with the society's traditional emphasis, families participate in these activities together, as any visit to parks (even car parks), harbours, marinas, beach or countryside can prove. Ball games and electronic models, speedboats and sailing boats now compete with the more sedate *volta* – the evening family stroll to show off children and clothes – and the old-time kite-flying.

Greece has taken to its feet, and its fun is thoughtful and energetic. Alongside the traditional activities, newer ones are taking their place: sailing and skiing, hill and long distance running (the marathon is quintessentially Greek), para-gliding, wind- or sail-surfing, water-skiing and scuba-diving. For equestrian types, horse-riding is available, even hippotherapy (healing through association with horses) in at least three centres near Athens. For those who like to spoil a good walk, golf is becoming the in-game of the newcomers, as it has always been. A championship course now exists at Porto Carras. The human frame is no longer sufficient: power-driven activities – on bikes, cars and speed-boats, with or without wings – are all being pursued. Obesity and unfitness are scorned, as are couch-potatoes; there is a like derision for those who indulge in more effete pastimes, e.g. *einai nautes glykou nerou* – 'he is a fresh water sailor.'

Physical fitness centres and health clubs are also proliferating around the country, where men and women exert themselves side by side at the bars, the weights and the rest of the equipment; trainers often standing by to give expert advice in the pursuit of tone, muscle and posture. Motives are mixed; a high commercial instinct lies behind many fitness centres. But the ego is still there: the more public the exercise, the more they seem to enjoy it. Sports' equipment shops are widely distributed, offering the latest items of torture for indoor or outdoor zealots. It is no idle thought to consider that without the Greek *gymnasion* (from the word for naked, in which condition the Games commenced) Rome may not have fallen; perhaps, even, Apollo may not have quarrelled with Athene.

Fitness is all: they laud *nous hugines ev somati hugiei*: 'a sound mind in an healthy body;' though now lamenting *kano diaita*: 'I am dieting.' Mental agility and physical aptitude usually go together. Greeks are changing shape; or, rather, they are re-finding their traditional and Olympic slimness. Fat people are less common than hitherto, especially among women, whose contemporary wasp-waisted descendants would honour the ancient cities of Thera or Knossos. Their Apollo-like counterparts proudly exhibit their frames, jostling with each other for pride of muscle; not too displeased over the continuing compulsory military service which makes fitter men of them. (One of my friends was furious that the main part of his military service was spent in the diminutive control- room of an exocet missile launcher, contemptuous of the computer expertise he was acquiring. He wanted muscle! He already had more than his fair share.) This new trend is leading to bold dietary and fashion changes; but most of all in changes of the expenditure of their leisure time. All this activity, however, seems to have had little effect on their smoking habits!

Anyone who has lived on the coast or islands near to Athens or Thessalonika can bear witness to the weekend *eisodos*, influx, that takes place, as the city-slickers move in, change, and splash and run about. Some go to the warmer areas, others to colder; some look for sand, others look for snow; some go for the fishing and swimming, others for the hunting and shooting; some go bird-watching, others seek out the grasses and plants; some plumb the depths while others scale the heights. Some come by ferry, some by their own bikes, cars and boats; but come they do, in their thousands, the spring, summer and autumn through; not always pleased to find so many tourists clogging up the *oikotropheioi* and the *tavernas*, but gaily determined to recreate themselves on land and sea, indoors and outdoors.

Sunny weather in the Corinth canal

TRIGG

THE MEDIA

In speaking of pastimes we cannot omit the electronic ones, of music, radio and television. The media in Greece are very powerful and freedom-loving, with strong commercial interests. Cacophony rules! But it rules OK – provided you have the ear-muffs and the will-power to switch it off.

Music

Music is to Greece what religion is to the Vatican. It was inspired by the Muses – by Euterpe (flute), Erato (lyre) and Polymnia (sacred music) – long ago. Today it is more reliant for inspiration on folk and classical music and the disharmonies of pop culture than on the Orthodox Church, for in the latter instrumental music is banned. All tastes are catered for in Greece, and there are many musical delights. Whether you like pop concerts or chamber music, the fiddle, guitar, or the *bouzouki* of the wandering or *taverna*-based folk-singer, great choirs or orchestras, you will find them all in Greece. Radio offers twenty-four hours of classical music of the highest order, particularly delectable on those moon-bathed nights, when the sea is as still as glass; and nature cools from its heated activities.

One of the happiest sounds is the often un-melodious noise of the local church bell which summon the faithful to worship. It is the Church's single public indulgence, adding piquancy and rhythm to life by its atonal clanging. Sometimes its voice is very different – when it tolls of death or burial. But even then it is apt – a reminder of our frailty in this old-new land.

Radio

The traveller, Leigh Fermor, speaks of the ubiquitous radio sounds in Greece, even more evident today thanks to car radios and ghetto blasters. His words are not an exaggeration, and these radio sounds are an integral element of modern Greece:

> Even the remotest Arcadian or Epirote village rings from sunrise to midnight with swing music, sermons in English, talks on bee-keeping in Serbo-Croat, symphonic music from Hamburg, French weather reports, the results of chess contests in Leningrad or shipping signals in morse code from the Dogger Bank; and, as the instrument is nearly always faulty, all these sounds, turned on full blast, are strung on the connecting thread of an unbroken, ear-drum puncturing and bat-like scream. Nobody listens, but it is never turned off....

Why is the radio never turned off? Is it because modern Greeks have lost the art of silence? Because they fear it? A social or intellectual element without which they cannot do? A substitute for such? Here as elsewhere, it does not do to generalise; though where it is left on, mercilessly destroying the peace of others, its role as substitute is difficult to gainsay. Leigh Fermor omits two crucially important elements in this wave of sound that washes across the country from dawn to dusk, from Sunday through Saturday and then some: sports commentaries and 'the ads.' They are the real menace, and they are incessant and inartistic: the ultimate culture shock. The one pays for the other, and the other justifies the many: a loud cycle of madness. Worse, advertisements are fired into the programmes willy-nilly, without regard for context or timing; often without warning that they are advertisements; sometimes without altering the flow or sense of the broadcast. Time is money; an acceleration of gabble may be the only indication of a change in subject.

Sports commentaries can be positively healing sounds, though the huddles of excited men surrounding the loud-speakers (an exact description) shouting encouragement and curses, throwing themselves into even more excited commentaries on the commentaries, adding arguments, threats and recriminations, contorting the body sportive, may not make this seem likely. This is not unique to Greece, of course, but it is as definite a characteristic of Greece as elsewhere. Be warned in choosing your residence and neighbours, even in the siting of your picnics: the demon of the decibels may be around the corner.

There are over a thousand radio stations to choose from, twelve are national stations, offering news, sport, music, plus drama and current affairs. Sky at 100.4 FM or Antennae at 97.1 FM are probably the most popular. The BBC World Service can be heard at 93.4 FM, a twenty-four hour service – if you can get it; reception is difficult outside the areas of central and southern Athens, Piraeus and the Saronic Gulf and some coastal areas. Some newspapers carry a schedule of its services, which is very useful. The Greek Channel Three offers excellent classical music programmes, though the introductions to them often go on longer than the pieces they front, plus they have the annoying habit of switching off prematurely because the scheduled time has run out.

Television

Television consists of the three State-owned channels (ET I, II, and III) and about one hundred private or municipal ones; it does not always earn the respect of serious broadcasters and viewers, though it advances more purposefully the concept of 'a people's television.'

Television is a somewhat less aggressive medium than radio though the Greeks' use of it outdoors – on their balconies and in their gardens, and even via portable sets in the countryside – can render it intrusive. There are forty-seven channels from which to choose. The ten most important channels are ET1, ET2, Antenna, Mega, New Channel, Seven X, Star, Sky, Channel 5, MTV and CNN.

Greek hunger for the 'soaps' is inexhaustible, in all languages; a main constituent of modern culture. Satellite dishes convey the world to Greece, and there is little that cannot now be seen thanks to their ubiquity. News, current affairs and sport come high on their list too; the widespread use of 'talking heads' is unashamed. Actually, it is indicative of something that Greece can boast of: its willingness to sit and listen to conversation on serious subjects without the intrusion of alleged artistic or pictorial aspects which the BBC and others think we need – not least their use of hackneyed 'library shots.' The problem is that the West has largely lost this ability to talk and listen, is too transfixed on the American notion of concentration lasting no more than seventeen seconds (or whatever the latest research figure is); too reliant on the visual being more important than the meaningful: a picture is only as good as the intelligence we bring to it.

Greek programme-makers have not followed the West in this (its cheapness is not ignored!); some discussion programmes are highly entertaining and informative. Their worst habit – Americanisms and Australianisms apart – is unpunctuality, a Greek vice. The timings are seldom accurate, and often inflict programme change through their indiscipline. This can be particularly annoying if you wish to record something; it frequently happens that you get a large portion of the preceding programme and only half of the one you want. Again the newspapers offer the schedules, the English-language films and soaps in particular.

As of 1st January, 1998, telco-monopolies will cease and a new era of free-for-all may obtain; it may not be an improvement, though the EU's 'Television without Frontiers' scheme will ensure that events of national importance are not side-lined by commercialism.

The Press

Hard news and its curiosity factors are well served by radio and television, but the newspaper industry still makes an important contribution to Greek life and entertainment, despite heavy losses. Between 1988-91 their circulation in the Athens and Thessaloniki areas fell by no less than a quarter. In 1991, with a population of about 10.2 million, the total sales of political newspapers (including the satirical ones) was over 277 million; sports' papers achieved sales of 40 million, and economic ones 1.3 million. Foreign language papers for a constituency of 229,156 in 1990, had sales of 701,000. There is a wealth of choice, for every taste: 120 newspapers and 17,000 magazines according to EBTA. The problem for outlying areas is distribution; the further from Athens or Thessaloniki one is, the longer one will have to wait and the more disruptive is the service. English language papers tend to be more expensive; for example, they cost about 2.5 times the price in the UK.

Periodicals are plentiful, and of every type and description. In Athens alone in 1991, 94,247 were sold, of which 2516 were 'pocket books' (i.e. paperbacks), 146 were parts-magazines, 48,947 general magazines, 26,932 specialised matter (technical, historical, etc.), 980 concerned sport, and 17,265 were for children. Multiply this three times across the country and you have something like the total picture for Greek reading of this sort.

Books

The importance of books is not something Greeks need to be told, though they have a well known tag: *mega vivlion, mega kakon*: the bigger the book, the greater the evil.

Books have always been expensive in Greece; today is no exception despite foreign publishers offering booksellers discounts of 45% and more. A mark-up of 50% on the original price is not unusual, and can be higher. I have been offered five-year old stock at ten times the original price, and re-wrapped to disguise the wear and dirt of countless fingerings. *Caveat emptor* here (let the buyer beware), as elsewhere. One reason for this, and it appears to be worsening, is the number of bookshops in the main centres. The over-manning of the general retail trade is obvious. I once did a survey around the bookshops of Athens and found on average they had slightly more than double the average staff compared with the UK. Many British ex-patriates buy directly from the UK (via friends or directly). I have tried this myself, but it is curious that the only losses I have suffered through the postal system in Greece have had to do with books 'lost in transit;' it worked out at an average of 1:7 lost. Perhaps bookworms have bigger appetites here.

Those with libraries of any size or significance should think carefully about the many advantages of air-conditioning. Books are susceptible to the dry heat one gets in Greece, and care must be taken to ensure that the glue used in binding does not dry out or crack and cause the book to fall apart, or that the heat does not warp the covers of the hard-backed books. Direct sunshine is a killer, for books as well as humans. If you have to keep them in a room facing the sun and you do not wish to keep the curtains closed, a separate light-reflective blind is recommended for your book cases; plus a wide bowl of water to offset evaporation.

Theatre

Drama reached its *apogee* in classical Greece, a tradition which is still continued vigorously today, notably in the State theatres. The principal venues are: the National Theatre, the State Theatre of Northern Greece, The National Opera, the State Orchestra of Athens, the State Orchestra of Thessaloniki, and the Municipal Theatre of Piraeus. But many private theatres are to be found, not least of which is the open-air theatre at Epidauros. The English-language newspapers offer the main attractions to theatre week by week, with ticket sales offices being found locally via agents.

With this, appropriately, our tour of *Culture Shock! Greece* comes to an end: a glorious, mystical arena, in which gods and men met and nurtured each other, the ripples transcending history and geography, politics and nationalism: its finest endowment.

Theatre at Epidauros

CULTURAL QUIZ

Greek culture locks easily into others'. For many, it is the root from which they grew, a point argued not only by linguistic affiliations and historical ties, but by many individual aspects – in literature, the arts, sciences, medicine, religion, law, etc. The Greeks make great allowances for the ignorant, for those who tread on their cultural toes, and very frequently go out of their way to solve problems. They pride themselves on their courtesy, their eclecticism, the welcome they give to foreigners, their ability to solve or ease difficulties. Nevertheless, their culture, their habits and their customs must not be taken for granted; it is not a good thing to labour your viewpoint in the face of their expressed antagonism in their own land. That mainstay of psychologists – 'cushion collisioning,' the ability to deal with adverse reactions and not retaliate – will save you from many an awkward situation. Here is a quiz to help you through some everyday situations which may be perplexing.

SITUATION ONE

Greeks love parties, and enjoy throwing them expansively. Your neighbours are not very well off, but invite you to one of their parties. You discover that you are guest of honour, and that great expense has been lavished not only in the birthday person's honour, but in yours as well. You know the family budget will suffer for weeks to come. Do you:

A Draw attention to their great generosity.

B Offer to 'go halves' with the expenses.

C Simply ignore the cost and 'eat, drink and be merry' as an old Greek enjoined.

Comments

Option C is the more acceptable, as Greeks have a high sense of personal and family pride (*philotimia*). But it is usual to take a gift to such parties – a personal one or a bottle of wine, for example. Recognise the sacrifice for what it is, and enter into its spirit. A little later you can invite them round to your place and help ease their pressures by having them to dinner, or by 'discovering' that you have bought too much of x, y and z, and would they help you by taking some from you? But do remember that your Greek friend will regard it as a matter of honour to match *your* generosity – and thus the circle will continue!

SITUATION TWO

At this dinner you are presented with a beautiful octopus stew, in a large pot with its suckers floating over the surface. It is not beautiful to you, alas; you are a lifelong vegetarian, but in any case the sight of all these apparent 'eyes' staring at you fill you with horror. Do you:

A Put your serviette to your mouth and rush from the room.

B Refuse to accept your proffered portion.

C Accept it, but leave it.

D Try and slide it unostentatiously onto your partner's plate.

Comments

You may have no control over the first point! though you will hopefully exit in as dignified way as possible, without embarrassing your hosts. B is probably the safest way, as long as you do so without rancour and their embarrassment (again). But it would have been better to have informed your hosts of your position *when the invitation was made*, suggesting for example, that a piece of cheese or a simple omelette would be very welcome instead of meat or fish.

Vegetarianism is not well understood in many parts of Greece. A simple spaghetti-with-tomato-sauce dish for example (Greeks often call spaghetti *macaronia* by the way), should have no meat in it. But Greeks often put kibbled ham in their sauces to increase enjoyment – as a friend found to her cost in ordering one, and had to send it back three times for that very reason! Veganism is even less well understood.

SITUATION THREE

A young woman known to you falls head-over-heels in love with a Greek boy. She is no *Shirley Valentine* figure, seeking to relieve the boredom of her life with a short fling. This, she believes, is the real thing – she has found her *Kurios Dexios*! He has a reputation for being a ladies' man, however, and his mother is xenophobic. Do you:

A Try to break up their romance.

B Warn the young woman that she is heading for disaster.

C Take the young man on one side and lecture him on your ethics.

D Tell his mother what a superb match they make; how much the boy will benefit the girl.

Comments

Probably no issue save matters of the heart causes such distress to *all* those involved – save for the boy, *if* he is simply taking advantage. Many Greek boys do wish for a non-Greek wife; and some mothers do believe that such is likely to bring much needed capital into the family (business) and may accept her provisionally – the provision being her willingness to accept Greek ways. Many families are still 'extended' technically; the mother-in-law has great say in their running; the Greek housewife often runs her household by extension from her.

A frontal assault is unlikely to get very far; and you may well suffer for interfering. A quiet and sensitive chat *may* help the girl, especially if it comes from someone involved in a mixed marriage. She needs to know that few male Greeks will give up their mother's for their wife's peace of mind; and even fewer Greek mothers are likely to be happy unless the girl shows a decisive willingness to conform to their ideals – especially when babies arrive. At the very least an aptitude in the language will be required, great forbearance, possibly conversion to the Orthodox Church; and much else. The ability to see matters from *their* standpoint is essential: it is their country; she is their guest. Very many hopeful girls have had their lives ruined by failure at this point. The mayor of one locality know to me even offered the community services of a psychiatrist to ease tensions in several such families – tensions that were common knowledge. In this regard many priests will be against the marriage; and not much help when things go wrong. Mixed marriages can work superbly, and the children of such are most fortunate in having dual cultural insights; but they require hard work and perseverance.

SITUATION FOUR

You are taking a pleasant walk out of town when an accident occurs. To your horror a tourist couple is knocked off their motor-cycle by a careless Greek driver taking the corner too fast. He, the Greek driver, rages at their stupidity, their bad driving, etc. On arrival he so informs the police. Do you:

A Call the driver a maniac and a liar.

B Argue with the driver in front of the policeman.

C Tell the couple to take legal action against the driver.

D Tell the policeman to accept the tourists' statement.

Comments

This is the sort of involvement best avoided! As a good citizen you know that your responsibility is to truth and the law. You should bear in mind that the driver and the policeman *may* be related; in any case most policemen automatically favour their own countrymen. Take no direct action against the driver. Quietly inform the policeman that you were a witness. (Assure yourself of the facts before doing so: *were* the tourists on the right side of the road? *were* long skid marks left by the Greek driver which demonstrate his speed? *do* the positions of the vehicles vindicate your claims? and so on.) Offer to report to the police station to make a statement. If refused, make your own; sign and date it; and entrust it to your lawyer or a good friend. But be prepared for the worst. Possibly the best that can be expected in such a situation is that the tourists are not charged; any indecisiveness is likely to be settled in favour of the fellow-Greek or quietly forgotten – after all, by the time the matter comes to court, you may well be thousands of miles away.

SITUATION FIVE

A man sidles up to you off the main street and offers what he claims to be a rare antiquity, for sale at a bargain price. Do you:

    A Buy it without more ado.

    B Bargain with him to get the price reduced.

    C Tell him to go away; the offer is illegal.

    D Call the police.

Comments

Under no circumstances should you enter into any discussion on the subject. Antiquities are rigidly preserved by the law; fierce action can be expected from the police should you purchase any such object, even from a legitimate authority. Only a government ministry can authorise such sales – and they are unlikely to do so. Calling the police

can involve you in difficulties: the man will almost certainly have disappeared by the time the police arrive; he may have disposed of the evidence and may accuse you of trouble-causing; the police may become suspicious of your activities and want to search you and your possessions. This same situation may arise over drugs. Be vigilant. Keep your distance from anyone purporting to offer such for sale.

SITUATION SIX

You are chatting to folk casually, when the question of Greek pre-eminence in matters of civilisation and culture come up. Yours are denigrated in favour of theirs. Do you:

A Agree with the absurd claims being made.

B Argue against the assertions on the basis of the current state of Greek economy and government.

C Point out the historical failures of the Greeks to uphold civilising aspects of humanity – such as democracy, the arts and sciences, law and morality, etc.

Comments

In all such oppositions, cushion-collisioning is the rule; that and the recollection that you are a guest in their country. In such cases *philotimia*, personal honour, takes over. Unwisely handled, you may find yourself at the centre of a public brawl. The majority of Greeks are very open to reason and evidence, and will thoroughly enjoy a verbal engagement of wits – but be attuned when subtle (or not so subtle!) changes of atmosphere take place, when discussion becomes argument, the weight of evidence looks like defeat, considerations become personal accusations – and smiles become artificial and intensify. 'A soft answer turns away wrath,' as the saying goes.

SITUATION SEVEN

You take a taxi, naming your destination and asking the price (the two fundamentals to be exercised *before* getting in one). The driver points to his timer, and takes you off. After a little while you observe that the timer is switched off, or behaving erratically. Do you:

A Wait until the journey ends and pay what he demands.

B Ask why his timer is off.

C Tell him to stop.

D Threaten to inform the tourist/traffic police.

Comments

Avoid the problem by ensuring that he switches on the timer the moment you enter his vehicle. If he refuses, get out. If you have cause for complaint, keep your money in your pocket/handbag; insist that he stop; take his license number and call the police immediately, noting the time and the location. Huge swindles take place every year over this; the police are very concerned – they will investigate and act.

SITUATION EIGHT

You agree with a business colleague (or friend) to meet at a certain time and place; or promises are made for a certain task to be completed by a given date. At the appointed time nothing has happened; no one appears. Do you:

    A Mutter to yourself *avrio!* and patiently wait.

    B Give him and/or his colleagues a piece of your mind.

    C Take your business or friendship elsewhere.

Comments

It was a Greek-speaking Jew who said that 'love covers a multitude of sins;' and a French monarch (Louis XVIII) who commented that 'punctuality is the politeness of kings.' Punctuality is not a Greek virtue, and kingship is bitterly rejected by the majority. Even those Greeks who have spent decades in the West will quickly slip back into their preferred ways once re-ensconced in the homeland.

Accept the attitude for what it is, not a personal slight, not even an outrageous character defect; but more a profession of faith: that there are more things in heaven and earth than are scheduled in our time-conscious living. The spirit of Greece is *freedom;* the Greek feels free to make and unmake the pattern of his life – at whim. He will change, but slowly, under the pressure of modern society. It you want to be happy in Greece you will have to come to terms with his anarchic and anti-monarchical view of time and promise. Plan ahead: take a book, prepare a back-up plan, philosophise over his absence. But don't give up on him: he could be your best contact; your best friend; and that friendship will be very rewarding.

FURTHER READING

The inducements to live in Greece come best from personal knowledge and first-hand experience, and through listening to or reading the experiences of others. Among the best loved books one can count those of Lawrence and Gerald Durrell, Patrick Leigh Fermor, Henry Miller, Dilys Powell, Peter Levi, John Hillaby, Nicholas Gage - to name but a few. Greece is itself rich in modern writings, as in radio and television, theatre and cinema, poetry and fiction, all of which will stoke the fires of interest and add to your cultural contentment. Some writers have contributed to the topography, history and literature of Greece - e.g. Peter Levi, Patrick Leigh Fermor and C M Woodhouse, to which must be aided the surreal writing of Henry Miller in *Colossus of Marousi*, or the highly personalised recollections of the late Dilys Powell. Others have done so without travelling much in Greece itself - such as Robert Graves, who never lost the poet's touch, even when ostensibly engaged in sober commentary.

I list below some of the books that those who wish to acquaint themselves better with Greece's terrain and people as well as its rich ancient history would do well to pick up. To select a short list of books is no easy matter. I have started from the broad, working through to narrower interests, and hope that it will serve your purposes. Many books of course cannot be placed precisely in categories and will overlap. The most recent known date of publication is given, except for the titles in the Personal Section, whose first dates are important for the impression they give of Greece at the time of their writing.

The Mediterranean

Durrell, Lawrence *Spirit of Place: Mediterranean Writings.* London: Faber and Faber Ltd., 1969. The title is indicative of the book and brilliantly successful at evoking it, though the author never quite manages to forget himself.

Fox, Robert. *The Inner Sea: the Mediterranean and its People.* Sinclair Stevenson Ltd., 1991.

Theroux, Paul. *The Pillars of Hercules: A Grand Tour of the Mediterranean.* Hamish Hamilton Ltd., 1995. An entertaining travelogue; chapter 16 deals with Greece.

Geography, Topography and Culture

Gage, Nicholas. *Hellas: A Portrait of Greece.* American Heritage Press, 1971 and Athens: Efstathiadis Group, SA,1995. Highly personalised, entertaining. Also, *Eleni.* New York: Random House, 1983. A soul-wrenching book.

Facaros, Dana. *Greek Islands.* London: Cadogan Books Ltd., 1986. Excellent and informative, though now a little dated.

Ellingham, M., M. Dubin, N. Jansz and J. Fisher, eds. *Greece: The Rough Guide.* Rough Guides Ltd., 1995. The best current guide to Greece.

Constantinidiou-Partheniadou, Sofia. *A Travelogue in Greece and a Folklore Calendar.* Translated by Michael Papetrou. Athens: privately printed, 1992. Essential reading, but some factual flaws.

Pettifer, James. *The Greeks: the Land and the People Since the War.* London: Viking, 1993. A sober, cultivated assessment.

Sowerby, Robin. *The Greeks: An Introduction to their Culture.* London: Routledge, 1995. An excellent account of the historico-classical aspects.

Dicks, T. R. B. *The Greeks: How they Live and Work*. David and Charles, 1972. An out of print book, but well worth reading by those who wish to see the enormous changes that have taken place since the end-1960s.

Powell, Dilys. *Affair of the Heart*. London, 1959.

Nikos Kazantzakis (1883-1957). His various novels give an authentic flavour of modern-day Greece.

Language and Literature

Divry, G.C. and C.G. Divry. *Divry's New English-Greek and Greek-English Handy Dictionary*. New York: D. C. Divry Inc., 1964. For modern Greek.

Liddell and Scott. *Greek-English Lexicon*. Oxford University Press, revised edition. For ancient Greek and essential for serious work.

Anon. *Teach Yourself Greek: A Simplified Course for Beginners*. London: Teach Yourself Books. Still useful, though largely replaced by Linguaphone.

Delicostopoulos, A. J. *Greek Idioms*. Athens: Efstathiadis Group SA, 1993. Oddly miscellaneous but useful.

Dover, K. J. *Ancient Greek Literature*. Oxford: Oxford University Press, 1990. An essential handbook.

Levi, Peter. *The Pelican History of Greek Literature*. Harmondsworth: Pelican Books, 1985. A personalised approach, full of interest and insight.

Graves, Robert. *The Greek Myths*. 2 vols. Harmondsworth: Penguin Books, 1960. Also personal, somewhat erratic and factually flawed.

Harvey, P., comp. *The Oxford Companion to Classical Literature*. Oxford: Oxford University Press, 1986.

Grimal, P. *The Penguin Dictionary of Classical Mythology*. Harmondsworth: Penguin Books, 1991.

Hammond, N. G. L. and H. H. Scullard. *The Oxford Classical Dictionary*. Oxford: Oxford University Press, 1979.

History

Morkot, Robert. *The Penguin Historical Atlas of Ancient Greece*. Harmondsworth:Penguin Books, 1996.

Boardman, J. *The Oxford History of Greece and the Hellenistic World*. Oxford: Oxford University Press, 1991.

Boardman, J. *The Greeks Overseas: Their Early Colonies and Trade*. London: Thames and Hudson Ltd., 1988.

Cotterell, Leonard. *The Bull of Minos*. London: Evans Bros., 1953 (rev. edn.1955)

Drews, Robert. *The Coming of the Greeks: Indo-European Conquests in the Aegean and the Near East*. New Jersey: Princeton University Press, 1989.

Finley, M. I. *The Ancient Greeks*. Harmondsworth: Penguin Books, 1991.

Boatswain, T. and C. Nicolson. *A Travellers' History of Greece*. Athens: Efstathiadis Group SA, 1991. One of the best single-volume histories.

Woodhouse, C. M. *Modern Greece: A Short History*. London: Faber and Faber Ltd., 1991.

Close, David H. *The Origins of the Greek Civil War [1945–1950]*. London: Longman Group Ltd., 1995. This is a terrible book in terms of subject matter, but essential for anyone wishing to understand in depth recent Greek history and politics – and the destructive power of the great and interfering nations around it.

Payne, Robert. *The Gold of Troy: The Story of Heinrich Schliemann and the Buried Cities of Ancient Greece*. London: Robert Hale, 1958, 1991.

Writings of the Ancients

Levi, Peter. *Pausanias: Guide to Greece.* 2 volumes. Harmondsworth: Penguin Books, 1971. These volumes, representing Levi's translation of the original, carry a mass of notes: linguisitic, archaeological and historical. A must for every serious reader.

West, M. L. *Theogony.* A translation and commentary on this work by Hesiod. Oxford: Oxford University Press, 1966. A much more technical work than Levi's.

Wender, Dorothea. *Hesiod: Theogony, Works and Days.* Harmondsworth: Penguin Books, 1973. Also by Wender, *Theogonis: Elegies,* Harmondsworth: Penguin Books, 1973. Both are translations by Wender with an introduction and useful glossary.

Jowett, B. *The Dialogues of Plato.* 5 volumes. Oxford: Clarendon Press.

McKeon, Richard. *Aristotle: The Basic Works.* University of Chicago Press, 1935.

Flora

Huxley, Anthony and William Taylor. *Flowers of Greece and the Aegean.* London: Chatto and Windus, 1977. Illus.

Polunin, Oleg and Anthony Huxley. *Flowers of the Mediterranean.* London: Chatto and Windus, 1965. Illus.

Sfikas, George. *Trees and Shrubs of Greece.* Athens: Efstathiadis Group SA, 1993. Richly illustrated.

Sfikas, George. *Medicinal Plants of Greece.* Athens: Efstathiadis Group SA, 1979. Richly illustrated.

Graves, Robert. *The White Goddess.* London: Faber and Faber, 1948. Somewhat *outré*, containing much tree lore – which should be handled with a pinch or two of salt.

Food and Drink

Barron, Rosemary. *Flavours of Greece*. Harmondsworth: Penguin Books, 1994.

Anon. *Traditional Greek Cooking*. Athens: Adam Editions, no date.

Paradissis, Chrissa. *The Best of Greek Cookery*. Athens: Efstathiadis Group SA, 1983. Factually flawed, disorganised.

Lambert-Gócs, Miles. *The Wines of Greece*. London: Faber and Faber, Ltd., 1990. A delightful book, deserving of everyone's shelf space.

Religion and Art

Zaidman, L. B. and P. S. Pantel. *Religion in the Ancient Greek City*. Edited by Armand Colin, Paris and translated by P. Cartledge. Cambridge: Cambridge University Press, 1994.

Ware, Timothy (Bishop Kallistos of Diokleia). *The Orthodox Church*. Harmondsworth: Penguin Books, 1991. By far the most illuminating book on the subject.

Elias, Nicolas. *The Divine Liturgy Explained*. Athens: Astir Publications, 1974.

Higgins, Reynold. *Minoan and Mycenean Art*. London: Thames and Hudson Ltd., 1992.

Richter, Gisela M. A. *Greek Art: A Survey of the Visual Arts of Ancient Greece*. London: Phaidon Press Ltd., 1992.

Sparkes, Brian A. *Greek Pottery: An Introduction*. Manchester University Press, 1991. Especially useful for showing construction techniques.

St. Clair, William. *Lord Elgin and the Marbles*. Oxford: Oxford University Press, 1983. The best book on Elgin's theft of the Parthenon frieze, which probably celebrates the vital Greek victory over the Persians at Marathon; now at the British Museum.

Talbot Rice, David. *Art and the Byzantine Era*. Penguin, 1963.

The Law

Kerameus K. and Kozrys P. *Introduction to Greek Law*. Athens: Kluwer-Sakkoulas, 1988.

Anon. *The Greek Civil Code*. Translated by Constantine Taliadorus. Privately printed, Athens, 1982. A most important piece of work but vitiated by clumsy translation and editing, and dated. See note below.

Anon. *Supplement to the Greek Civil Code*. Translated by Constantine Taliadorus. Privately printed, Athens, 1983. This details changes to the laws governing Family Relationships, as amended in Law 1329 of 18/2/83.; it is immensely important, but dated.

Note: Greek law is presently being transformed both by its own cognisance of present society and its changing demands – but especially by EU law. It is essential to have up-to-date information either from a lawyer or from the EU Information Centre or EU Library.

Personal

Durrell, Gerald. *My Family and Other Animals*. London: Rupert Hart–Davis, 1956.Whether this reflects more the eccentricity of the Greeks or that of an ex-patriate Englishman is debatable, but it has been enormously influential and entertaining.

——. *Birds, Beasts and Relatives*. Collins, 1969. A sequel to the above. It has not been quite as successful, but is still very humorous and quietly insightful.

Durrell, Lawrence. *Reflections of a Marine Venus: a Companion to the Landscape of Rhodes*. London: Faber and Faber Ltd., 1953. It concludes with a Short Calendar of Flowers and Saints for Rhodes; and Peasant Remedies – though the latter is not recommended!

Hillaby, John. *Journey to the Gods*. London: Flamingo, 1993.

Leigh Fermor, Patrick. *Mani: Travels in the southern Peloponnese.* London: John Murray Ltd., 1958. Also by him, *Roumeli: travels in northern Greece.* London: John Murray Ltd., 1966.

Levi, Peter. *The Hill of Kronos.* London: Harvill, 1981.

Miller, Henry. *The Colossus of Marousi.* USA, 1941.

Renault, Mary. *The Bull from the Sea,* Penguin, 1962; *Funeral Games,* Random House, 1981; *The King Must Die,* Reprint Society; *The Last of the Wine,* Longman, 1958; *The Persian Boy,* John Murray, 1978; *The Praise Singer,* John Murray, 1978. All are superb historical novels. She also wrote a brilliant interpretation of Alexander the Great's life and work in *The Nature of Alexander,* Penguin, 1975.

Stoneman, Richard, ed. *A Literary Companion to Travel in Greece.* Harmondsworth: Penguin, 1984. Excerpts from the poets and travellers – from Byron to Walpole. Its bibliography could well supplement this.

THE AUTHOR

Clive Leonard Rawlins was born in Birmingham, England, and was educated privately. He was destined for a military career – until the UK stopped conscription, whence he turned to accountancy, thence the ministry, thence publishing and writing.

Turning from commerce, he gained distinctions in theological studies in 1958, 1964 and 1968 (the latter at Manchester University, England) plus a medical qualification and a foreign-language certificate. He taught English for two years at Nevers in France, was ordained, married, and spent nearly four years in the ministry, from which he went into publishing, taking a variety of appointments up to Managing Director level. He has two married sons: Stephen and Philip.

He published his first book in 1978, since when he has written or edited another ten or so (e.g. *Index to the Daily Study Bible*; *William Barclay: the Authorised Biography*; *The Diaries of William Paterson Paterson*; *Leonard Cohen: Prophet of the Heart*, etc.) He lived in Greece from 1988 to 1994, concentrating mainly on Greek culture and history. In 1993 *Aegean Jewel: Poros and Tizinia* was published in Athens, which is presently being re-fashioned as *Crescent and Cross: the Saronic Gulf and its Story*. He is also engaged on a major dictionary of the Mediterranean, and a book on *Food and Faith* in the world religions.

Greece claimed his heart in 1958, to which he became 'adopted' in 1988. He lives between Greece and Scotland, as research, writing, and free-lance editing needs determine.

INDEX

293